Spiritual Science

By

Eric Dubay

Quantum Physics

For centuries the prevailing western worldview has been built upon the materialistic, mechanical model of Isaac Newton - a clockwork Universe composed of separate particles of matter interacting according to precise physical laws and existing within objective dimensions of space and time.

This model has long succeeded in describing many facets of our multi-faceted reality, but increasingly since the revelations of Einstein and the paradigm-crushing implications of quantum physics, Newton's world is quietly fading from view and being replaced by a more spiritual science.

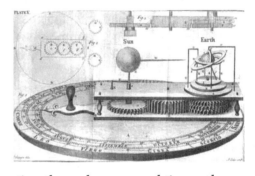

"Up until the present, biology and physics have been handmaidens of views espoused by Isaac Newton, the father of modern physics ... These, at their essence, created a world view of separateness. Newton described a material world in which individual particles of matter followed certain laws of motion through space and time – the universe as a machine ... The Newtonian world might have been law-abiding, but ultimately it was a lonely, desolate place. The world carried on, one vast gearbox, whether we were present or not ... Our self-image grew even bleaker with the work of Charles Darwin. His theory of evolution is of a life that is random, predatory, purposeless and solitary. Be the best or don't survive. You are no more than an evolutionary accident ... These paradigms – the world as a machine, man as survival machine – have led to a technological mastery of the universe, but little real knowledge of any central importance to us. On a spiritual and metaphysical level, they have led to the most desperate and brutal sense

of isolation. They also have got us no closer to understanding the most fundamental mysteries of our own being: how we think, how life begins, why we get ill, how a single cell turns into a fully formed person, and even what happens to human consciousness when we die." -Lynne McTaggart, "The Field: The Quest for the Secret Force of the Universe," (XXIV-XXV)

Newton's mechanistic, mathematical model is attractive with its law-abiding, predictable structure, but it repeatedly falls short in describing a wide array of phenomena which "classical physics" is thus forced to deny or ignore. These include things such as consciousness, the observer effect, the measurement problem, Heisenberg's uncertainty principle, nonlocality and quantum entanglement, particle/wave duality, bilocation, telepathy, psychokinesis, clairvoyance, precognition, out-of-body experiences, near-death experiences, ghosts, shamanic/spiritual healing, acupuncture, prayer, the placebo effect, psychoneuroimmunology and many more anomalies, all of which are at odds with classical physics and will be examined in the coming chapters.

"The world view which was changed by the discoveries of modern physics had been based on Newton's mechanical model of the universe. This model constituted the solid framework of classical physics. It was indeed a most formidable foundation supporting, like a mighty rock, all of science and providing a firm basis for natural philosophy for almost three centuries. The stage of the Newtonian universe, on which all physical phenomena took place, was the three-dimensional space of classical

Euclidean geometry. It was an absolute space, always at rest and unchangeable. In Newton's own words, 'Absolute space, in its own

nature, without regard to anything external, remains always similar and immovable.' All changes in the physical world were described in terms of a separate dimension, called time, which again was absolute, having no connection with the material world and flowing smoothly from the past through the present to the future. 'Absolute, true, and mathematical time,' said Newton, 'of itself and by its own nature, flows uniformly, without regard to anything external." -Fritjof Capra, "The Tao of Physics" (55)

The first steps away from Newtonian physics came with Einstein's theory (and subsequent experimental proofs) of relativity showing Newton to be incorrect in his view of absolute space and absolute time. Instead, both space and time have proven to be relativistic, interrelated concepts which are now more appropriately referred to as "space-time." As written by physicist Mendel Sachs, *"The real revolution that came with Einstein's theory . . . was the abandonment of the idea that the space-time coordinate system has objective significance as a separate physical entity. Instead of this idea, relativity theory implies that the space and time coordinates are only the elements of a language that is used by an observer to describe his environment."* Einstein showed that space and time are not absolute structures with independent a priori existence as classical physics espouses. In fact, space and time are relativistic and subjective, a notion which metaphysically places them subordinate to the mind/consciousness perceiving them! The mystical implications of this discovery are vast and will be covered in detail later, but first let's examine whether or not we even live in a "material" universe at all. What has modern physics discovered about atoms, the so-called building blocks of matter?

"For two thousand years it was believed that atoms were tiny solid balls – a model clearly drawn from everyday experience. Then, as physicists discovered that atoms were composed of more elementary, sub-atomic particles (electrons, protons, neutrons and suchlike) the model shifted to one of a central nucleus

surrounded by orbiting electrons – again a model based on experience.
An atom may be small, a mere billionth of an inch across, but these sub-
atomic particles are a hundred thousand times smaller still. Imagine the
nucleus of an atom magnified to the size of a grain of rice. The whole
atom would then be the size of a football stadium, and the electrons
would be other grains of rice flying round the stands. As the early
twentieth-century British physicist Sir Arthur Eddington put it, 'matter is
mostly ghostly empty space' – 99.9999999% empty space, to be a little
more precise." -Peter Russell, "From Science to God"

How can something which is
99.9999999% empty space be
considered the building block of
matter? And what is the fundamental
"stuff" of the universe if not matter?
If there is almost no substance to our
seemingly solid, tangible world, what
causes the illusion? German physicist
Hans-Peter Dürr keenly noted,
"Matter is not made of matter." So what is it made of?

"For a start, what we perceive to be
'physical' and 'solid' is anything but.
Science says that what we see as 'form'
- people, buildings, landscape etc. - are
made of atoms. Okay, but the trouble
with the 'solid world' theory is that
atoms are not solid. More than that,
they are basically empty. How can
something that is not solid create a
solid environment? It can't. Atoms

consist of electrons orbiting a nucleus (protons and neutrons), but it is the
proportions that tell the story. Atoms are more than 99% empty space to
our human reality, yet they are described as the fundamental building-
blocks of matter - yes, 'solid' matter." –David Icke, "The David Icke
Guide to the Global Conspiracy" (34)

"Examine each part of the cabin. The walls are made of wood. What
makes wood what it is? A configuration of wood cells exists as a log, and
each of these cells cannot exist without a configuration of molecules.

6

Likewise, each molecule is composed of atoms. Each atom contains electrons, protons, and neutrons. Each atomic particle is composed of quarks, etc., etc., etc. Everything can be broken down into parts. Even if somehow a 'thing' was found that could not be broken down, it would still have parts because if it did not, it could not be used to make more complex things. Anything that has spatial extent requires that it has a front, a back, a shape – different parts. At the level of atoms, the distance from one atom to another in relationship to the diameter of the nucleus of the atom is 'astronomical.' There is more emptiness in the atoms composing the wall of a cabin than there is matter! And this goes for all matter. All matter is mostly emptiness ... What prevents your hand, for example, from passing through a wall is not that there is some 'thing' or 'things' (atoms) in the way, but more so because there is an atomic energy field that prevents the atoms from one's hand to pass by the atoms of the wall." –Aaron G. L. Adoni, "The Gnosis of Kali Yuga" (137)

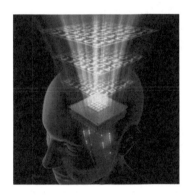

When touching a wall with your hand, both the wall and your hand are composed of 99.9999999% empty space, so your sensation of touching some "thing" comes not from physically colliding hand-atoms with wall-atoms, but rather from an energetic charge between them. That energetic charge is then electro-chemically interpreted by your brain into your felt experience of "wall."

"How can something that is not solid be the building blocks that construct this 'solid' wall I am looking at now? It can't - our brains do it. With the emergence of quantum physics, science has had to concede that atoms are not solid ... The atoms that comprise 'physical' matter are overwhelmingly 'empty' and even illustrations of this are misleading because there is not enough room in a book or science paper to accurately depict the proportions of particles to 'empty space'. As one writer put it: 'If an atom was the size of a cathedral, the nucleus would be about the size of a ten cent piece.' The rest is 'empty' to the perception of the five senses because it consists of energy vibrating on wavelengths higher than the 'physical', and even the particles are found to be empty as you go deeper into the subatomic realm. If you magnify anything powerfully enough and go deeper than the atom, you will find that nothing has solidity - No, not even buildings, cars, mountains or the

bones in your body. It's Illusion! If you find this hard to accept, think of your dreams. You dream in three-dimensional images and yet no one claims they are solid do they?" –David Icke, "Infinite Love is the Only Truth, Everything Else is Illusion" (40)

"Quantum theory thus reveals an essential interconnectedness of the universe. It shows that we cannot decompose the world into independently existing smallest units. As we penetrate into matter, we find that it is made of particles, but these are not the 'basic building blocks' in the sense of Democritus and Newton. They are merely idealizations which are useful from a practical point of view, but have no fundamental significance." -Fritjof Capra, "The Tao of Physics" (137)

Nobel Prize winning physicist Niels Bohr was the inventor of the Bohr Atom Model seen in every high-school physics/chemistry textbook depicting the atom as a mini solar system with a central nucleus orbited by bands of electrons. He created this model of the atom with which we are all so familiar, yet he himself knew the model was incorrect at a fundamental level. He wrote that, *"Isolated material particles are abstractions, their properties being definable and observable only through their interaction with other systems."* In other words, no
atom or sub-atomic particle has an isolated, separate existence. No material particle has independent properties or location as distinct from any other. At the atomic and subatomic levels, no "thing" is separate from every "thing" else – there is just One field of pulsating energy that composes the entire physical universe. It has been called The Ether, The Field, The Quantum Field, The Zero-Point Field, and many other names, all referring to this essential, energetic Oneness. So, not only was Newton's classical physics incorrect about absolute space and time, it was incorrect about the universe being composed of separate particles of matter.

"This world of separate should have been laid waste once and for all by the discovery of quantum physics in the early part of the twentieth century. As the pioneers of quantum physics peered into the very heart of

matter, they were astounded by what they saw. The tiniest bits of matter aren't even matter, as we know it, not even a set something, but sometimes one thing, sometimes something quite different. And even stranger, they are often many possible things all at the same time. But most significantly, these subatomic particles have no meaning in isolation, but only in relationship with everything else. At its most elemental, matter cannot be chopped up into self-contained little units, but is completely indivisible. You can only understand the universe as a dynamic web of interconnection. Things once in contact remain always in contact through all space and all time. Indeed, time and space themselves appear to be arbitrary constructs, no longer applicable at this level of the world. Time and space as we know them do not, in fact, exist. All that appears, as far as the eye can see, is one long landscape of the here and now." -Lynne McTaggart, "The Field: The Quest for the Secret Force of the Universe," (XXV)

Everyone knows Einstein's famous formula $E=MC^2$ meaning Energy = Mass x Light Speed squared. What we're seldom taught, however, are the implications of this equation. $E=MC^2$ shows that matter and energy are really just two different forms of the same thing. Einstein's formula and quantum physics have both verified that all matter is really just energy vibrating at a low frequency. This means that energy, the One undifferentiated field of quantum zero-point energy, is the primary reality; So-called "empty" space, "solid" matter, and "separate" forms, are just subjective interpretations of the One underlying energy. As Albert Einstein himself said, *"We may therefore regard matter as being constituted by the regions of space in which the field is extremely intense ... There is no place in this new kind of physics both for the field and matter, for the field is the only reality."*

"The discovery that mass is nothing but a form of energy has forced us to modify our concept of a particle in an essential way. In modern physics, mass is no longer associated with a material substance, and hence particles are not seen as consisting of any basic 'stuff', but as bundles of energy." -Fritjof Capra, "The Tao of Physics" (202)

Experiments in quantum physics have shown that atoms and all subatomic particles are more like verbs than nouns. They are more like energy bundles or patterns of quantum potential than they are like solid billiard balls or mini solar systems. The underlying primary reality is the energy field, and "energy" itself is more a verb, an action, a potential, than a noun – it's not some set "thing." When we peer deeply into the subatomic levels of matter, we see only this energy, this constantly flowing, interacting field. To make sense of it we create nouns/models like atoms, electrons, and quarks, but the most appropriate "model" would be a verb, like "universal energizing."

"These dynamic patterns, or 'energy bundles', form the stable nuclear, atomic and molecular structures which build up matter and give it its macroscopic solid aspect, thus making us believe that it is made of some material substance. At the macroscopic level, this notion of substance is a useful approximation, but at the atomic level it no longer makes sense. Atoms consist of particles and these particles are not made of any material stuff. When we observe them, we never see any substance; what we observe are dynamic patterns continually changing into one another - a continuous dance of energy." - Fritjof Capra, "The Tao of Physics" (203)

"Prior to Einstein's theory of relativity and quantum physics we held a firm conviction that the universe was composed of solid matter. We believed that the basic building blocks of this material universe were atoms, which we perceived as compact and indestructible. The atoms

existed in three-dimensional space and their movements followed certain fixed laws. Accordingly, matter evolved in an orderly way, moving from the past, through the present, into the future. Within this secure, deterministic viewpoint we saw the universe as a gigantic machine ... Within this image of the universe developed by Newtonian science, life, consciousness, human beings, and creative intelligence were seen as accidental by-products that evolved from a dazzling array of matter. As complex and fascinating as we might be, we humans were nevertheless seen as being essentially material objects – little more than highly developed animals or biological thinking machines. Our boundaries were defined by the surface of our skin, and consciousness was seen as nothing more than the product of that thinking organ known as the brain." -Stanislav Grof, "The Holotropic Mind," Harper, (4)

On a metaphysical level, the Newtonian worldview has instilled a common belief that all life, consciousness, and the diversity of nature are merely serendipitous accidents evolving out of complex interactions between particles of physical matter. The idea that life, consciousness, and the complexity of nature arose by accident, for holistic thinkers, seems like a ludicrous improbability. But for so-called logical, scientific thinkers, this worldview  has long-standing merit. Many are happy to accept that space, time, and matter all spontaneously came from nowhere for no reason; that a sneezing singularity expanded and evolved through trial and error and survival of the fittest over billions of years. At some point, somehow, life and consciousness arose from non-living, unconscious matter, then continued gaining complexity through time until humanity, the pinnacle of billions of years of mechanical evolution, emerged with all these perceptions, sensations, emotions, and internal experiences just by accident.

"Traditional science holds the belief that organic matter and life grew from the chemical ooze of the primeval ocean solely through the random interactions of atoms and molecules. Similarly, it is argued that matter was organized into living cells, and cells into complex multicellular organisms with central nervous systems, solely by accident and 'natural selection.' And somehow, along with these explanations, the assumption that consciousness is a by-product of material processes occurring in the brain has become one of the most important metaphysical tenets of the Western worldview. As modern science discovered the profound interactions between creative intelligence and all levels of reality, this simplistic image of the universe becomes increasingly untenable. The probability that human consciousness and our infinitely complex universe could have come into existence through the random interactions of inert matter has aptly been compared to that of a tornado blowing through a junkyard and accidentally assembling a 747 jumbo jet." -Stanislav Grof, "The Holotropic Mind" (5)

"Many processes certainly appear to be explainable in approximately mechanistic, reductionistic terms. But as physicists have delved progressively deeper into the nature of reality, they find that it cannot be understood in mechanistic terms. Mechanism assumes that there are separate objects that interact in determined, causal ways. But that's

not the reality we live in. Quantum reality is holistic, and as such any attempt to study its individual pieces will give an incomplete picture. It's like studying atoms inside an acorn in an attempt to understand the emergence of leaves on an oak tree – a futile exercise." -Dean Radin, "Entangled Minds" (222)

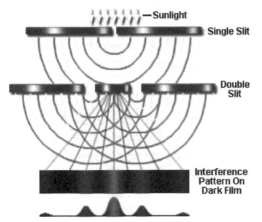

One of the most important and mind-bending findings in quantum physics which has helped us to better understand the nature of matter was first demonstrated in what is known as the "double-slit" experiment. This experiment involves projecting photons, electrons, or other quanta through a barrier with two small holes and measuring the way they are detected before, during, and after their travels. Common sense suggests that if they begin as particles, they will travel as particles and end up as particles, but the evidence shows something quite different.

"Scientists have found that when an electron, for example, passes through the barrier with only one opening available, it behaves in just the way we'd expect it to: It begins and ends its journey as a particle. In doing so, there are no surprises. In contrast, when two slits are used, the same electron does something that sounds impossible. Although it definitely begins its journey as a particle, a mysterious event happens along the way: The electron passes through both slits at the same time, as only a wave of energy can do, forming the kind of pattern on the target that only an energy wave can make." -Gregg Braden, "The Divine Matrix" (71-2)

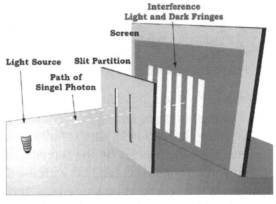

"In the classic double-slit experiment, a stream of photons (or electrons or any atomic-sized object) are shot at a screen with two tiny slits in it. On the other side of the screen, a photographic plate or sensitive video camera records where each photon lands. If one of the slits is closed, then the camera will see a smooth distribution of photons with the peak intensity directly opposite the open slit. This is what common sense would predict if the photons were individual particles. But if you open both slits, the camera sees a different pattern: an interference pattern with varying bands of high and low intensity. That is consistent with the photons being a wave." -Dean Radin, "Entangled Minds" (215-6)

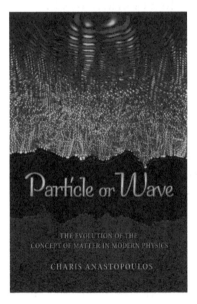

Furthermore, when physicists lower the light intensity to shoot only one photon at a time, somehow, they get the same results. With one slit open, each photon shoots through and lands on the screen evenly distributed, peak intensity perfectly aligned. So with two slits open, firing one photon at a time, you might likewise assume to see two even distributions perfectly aligned behind each slit. However, just like when firing a flood of photons through, somehow the photons "know" the second slit is open, pass through both slits simultaneously, and end up on the screen as a wave-like interference pattern. This experiment and many similar replications have produced the same results every single time: The quanta begin as single particles, shoot through the apparatus, register going through both slits simultaneously, and then show up interfered with themselves on the screen. Each individual particle is somehow interfering or entangled with itself as a wave. This phenomenon has come to be known as "particle-wave duality."

"The electron, like some shape-shifter out of folklore, can manifest as either a particle or a wave. This chameleon-like ability is common to all subatomic particles. It is also common to all things once thought to manifest exclusively as waves. Light, gamma rays, radio waves, X rays – all can change from waves to particles and back again. Today physicists believe that subatomic phenomena should not be classified solely as

either waves or particles, but as a single category of somethings that are always somehow both. These somethings are called quanta, and physicists believe they are the basic stuff from which the entire universe is made." -Michael Talbot, "The Holographic Universe" (33-4)

This particle-wave duality is a significant discovery because it shows that the basic "building blocks" of our physical reality, not only are they 99% empty space, but they constantly fluctuate between being precise, definable particles and unlimited probability waves. Thus the philosophical questions arise: What determines whether they are particles or waves? How can something be in two states at one time? How can the building blocks of matter be so immaterial?

"With the development of quantum theory, physicists have found that even subatomic particles are far from solid. In fact, they are not much like matter at all – at least nothing like matter as we know it. They can't be pinned down and measured precisely. Much of the time they seem more like waves than particles. They are like fuzzy clouds of potential existence, with no definite location. Whatever matter is, it has little, if any, substance." -Peter Russell, "From Science to God"

"Matter at its most fundamental level can not be divided into independently existing units or even be fully described. Subatomic particles aren't solid little objects like billiard balls, but vibrating and indeterminate packets of energy that can not be precisely quantified or understood in themselves. Instead they are schizophrenic, sometimes behaving as particles – a set thing confined to a small space – and sometimes like a wave – a vibrating and more diffuse thing spread out over a large region of space and time – and sometimes like both a wave and a particle at the same time." -Lynne McTaggart, "The Field: The Quest for the Secret Force of the Universe," (10)

15

Using the example of water, we see an illustration of how something can be both a particle and wave simultaneously. If you separate a drop of water from the ocean then it is an independent, distinct particle with definite location. However, put that same drop

of water back in the ocean and it becomes part of an integral, undifferentiated wave with no definite location. From the perspective of the individual H_2O molecules, nothing changes regardless of whether they are a drop or an ocean wave. The wave/particle distinction comes from us, the conscious observers, which brings us to another question: In the double-slit experiment, how does the particle "know" whether or not the second slit is open? Why does it act like a particle when one slit is open, but act like a wave when two slits are open?

"The only explanation here is that the second opening has somehow forced the electron to travel as if it were a wave ... To do so, the electron has to somehow perceive that the second opening exists and has become available. And this is where the role of consciousness comes in. Because it's assumed that the electron cannot really 'know' anything in the truest sense of the word, the only other source of awareness is the person watching the experiment. The conclusion here is that somehow the knowledge that the electron has two possible paths to move through is in the mind of the observer, and that the onlooker's consciousness is what determines how the electron travels." –Gregg Braden, "The Divine Matrix" (72-3)

It seems the particles themselves are somehow conscious of the slits, or the scientists' consciousness is informing the particles. Either way, two amazing things are happening here which rock the foundations of classical physics. Firstly, photons, electrons, and all quanta are simultaneously expressing the properties of both particles and waves simultaneously. Secondly, the quanta are essentially conscious and/or reading our minds!

"This rather simple experiment raises a central question about the role of the observer in quantum reality. This is known as the quantum measurement problem: We infer that the photon acts like a wave when we're not looking, but we never actually see those waves. So what causes the photon to 'collapse' into a particle when we do decide to look at it? In classical physics, objects are regarded as objectively real and independent of the observer. In the quantum world, this is no longer the case." -Dean Radin, "Entangled Minds" (218)

"The quantum pioneers discovered that our involvement with matter was crucial. Subatomic particles exist in all possible states until disturbed by us – by observing or measuring – at which point, they settle down, at long last, into something real. Our observation – our human consciousness – is utterly central to this process 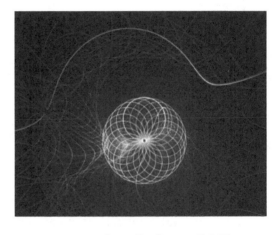 *of subatomic flux actually becoming some set thing."* -Lynne McTaggart, "The Field: The Quest for the Secret Force of the Universe," (XXVI)

The peculiar discovery known as "The Quantum Measurement Problem" ultimately shows the inseparability of the observer from the observed. All quantum experiments have confirmed that there is no measurable, solid reality "out there" independent of the measurer. What is "out there" when we're not looking is an infinite wavy cloud of criss-crossing possibilities. Then when we focus our attention on something, the wave function collapses into a defined particle in a definite location for us to observe.

"If you want to see fear in a quantum physicist's eyes, just mention the words, 'the measurement problem.' The measurement problem is this: an

atom only appears in a particular place if you measure it. In other words, an atom is spread out all over the place until a conscious observer decides to look at it. So the act of measurement or observation creates the entire universe." -Jim Al-Khalili, Nuclear Physicist

"An electron is not a precise entity, but exists as a potential, a superposition, or sum, of all probabilities until we observe or measure it, at which point the electron freezes into a particular state. Once we are through looking or measuring, the electron dissolves back into the ether of all possibilities." -Lynne McTaggart, "The Field: The Quest for the Secret Force of the Universe," (102)

Physicist Fred Alan Wolf uses the term "popping the quiff" (QWF for Quantum Wave Function) to describe the role of the observer in creating reality. Before being consciously observed, quanta (the "building blocks" of all matter) exist only as a boundary-less wave of undifferentiated quantum energy. In this state there is no matter as such, no particles or "things" with attributes and definite locations - just an infinite expanse of energy, Zero-Point, The Field. However, when a conscious observer focuses attention, they "pop the quiff," collapse the quantum wave function into a solid particle of experience with definable attributes and location.

"One of the fundamental laws of quantum physics says that an event in the subatomic world exists in all possible states until the act of observing or measuring it 'freezes' it, or pins it down, to a single state. This process is technically known as the collapse of the wave function, where 'wave function' means the state of all possibilities ... Although nothing exists in a single state independently of an observer, you can describe what the observer sees, but not the observer himself. You include the moment of observation in the mathematics, but not the consciousness doing the observing. There is no equation for an observer ... According to the mathematics, the quantum world is a perfect hermetic world of pure potential, only made real ...when interrupted by an intruder." -

Lynne McTaggart, "The Field: The Quest for the Secret Force of the Universe," (103)

These findings are so significant because they prove that the classical Newtonian model of physics (now being termed "the old physics") is fundamentally flawed. The old physics described a mechanistic material universe "out there" existing regardless of whether or not there was a conscious being alive to perceive it. The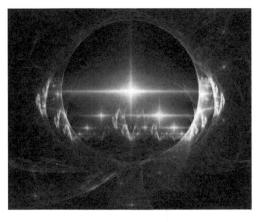
new physics shows that matter doesn't even exist without consciousness. Without a conscious observer to "pop the quiff," there is no substance, no "materiality" to that which is – just an unlimited, undifferentiated field of energy. As stated in the excellent quantum physics documentary, What the Bleep Do We Know, *"When you are not looking, there are waves of possibility. When you are looking, there are particles of experience."*

"What is real depends on whether I look and the way I look. This is not just a philosophical question. We can see this in experiments." - Anton Zeilinger, Quantum Physicist

"Cause-and-effect relationships no longer hold at the subatomic level. Stable-looking atoms might suddenly, without apparent cause, experience some internal disruption; electrons, for no reason, elect to transit from one energy state to another. Once you peer closer and closer at matter, it isn't even matter, not a single solid thing you can touch or describe, but a host of tentative selves, all being paraded around at the same time. Rather than a universe of static certainty, at the most fundamental level of matter, the world and its relationships are uncertain and unpredictable, a state of pure potential, of infinite possibility." -Lynne McTaggart, "The Field: The Quest for the Secret Force of the Universe," (10-11)

Another interesting anomaly of the quantum world is known as "The Uncertainty Principle" discovered by German physicist Werner Heisenberg. Heisenberg's uncertainty principle states that a particle's position and its momentum can never be precisely measured simultaneously. We can obtain precise information about a particle's position as long as we ignore its momentum, or we can obtain precise information about its

momentum as long as we ignore its exact position, but in no way can we obtain precise knowledge about both quantities, and this limitation has nothing to do with our measuring techniques; it is a fundamental limitation inherent in atomic reality.

"The crucial feature of atomic physics is that the human observer is not only necessary to observe the properties of an object, but is necessary even to define these properties. In atomic physics, we cannot talk about the properties of an object as such. They are only meaningful in the context of the object's interaction with the observer. In the words of Heisenberg, 'What we observe is not nature itself, but nature exposed to our method of questioning.' The observer decides how he is going to set up the measurement and this arrangement will determine, to some extent, the properties of the observed object. If the experimental arrangement is modified, the properties of the observed object will change in turn." - Fritjof Capra, "The Tao of Physics" (140)

Again, the uncertainty principle, as in the double-slit studies, shows the importance of the observer in determining the outcome of quantum experiments. Another such example of this is often termed the "Watched Quantum Pot" experiment. Just as the old proverb states, "a watched pot never boils," likewise in the quantum world this strangely proves true as verified by physicists Wayne Itano, Yakir Aharonov and M. Vardi. They state that, *"If one checks by continuous observations, if a given quantum system evolves from some initial state to some other final state along a specific trajectory ... the result is always positive, whether or not the system would have done so on its own accord."*

"If a quantum system is monitored continuously, we could say vigilantly, it will do practically anything. For example, suppose you are watching a quantum system in an attempt to determine just when it undergoes a transition from one state to another. To make this concrete, think of an imaginary subatomic 'quantum pot of water' being heated on a similarly sized stove. The transition occurs when the water goes from the calm state to the boiling state. We all know pots of water boil, given a few minutes or so. You would certainly think the watched quantum pot would also boil.

It turns out, because of the vigilant observations, the transition never occurs; the watched quantum pot never boils. Another example is the decay of an unstable system. On its own the system would decay in a few microseconds. But if it is watched continuously, it will never decay. All vigilantly watched 'quantum pots' never boil, even if they are heated forever." -Fred Alan Wolf, Ph.D., "The Spiritual Universe" (217-8)

So a watched quantum "pot" (particle) will "boil" (transition states) if you intently observe it to do so, and a watched quantum pot will never boil if you intently observe it not to do so. Even the radioactive decay of subatomic particles which normally have the lifespan of microseconds can be prolonged indefinitely as long as we are watching.

"This implies there is a deep connection between the observer and the observed. So deep, in fact, that we really cannot separate them. All we can do is alter the way we experience reality. This is where intent comes in. If the system were unobserved, it would certainly undergo the physical transition. The pot would boil. The observer effect causes the anomaly to occur. Let me explain. When the system is first observed, it is seen to be in its initial state. When it is observed just a smidgen of time

later, well before the time in which it should change, the system is observed with more than 99.99 percent chance to be in its initial state. In other words, the system is found to be exactly where it was initially. Now repeat this measurement again and again, each time just a tiny bit of time later, and with a very high probability, the same observation occurs: The system is found in its initial state. But time marches on, and eventually we pass all reasonable time limits for the transition to occur, yet it still doesn't happen. The system 'freezes' in its initial state. The only requirement to freeze the motion is that the observer must have the intent to see the object in its initial state when he looks. This intent is determined by the frequency of his observations." -Fred Alan Wolf, Ph.D., "The Spiritual Universe" (218-9)

We, the observers, cannot be ignored. Our consciousness and our bodies are integral parts of the universe and thus exhibit measurable effects on whatever aspects of the universe we turn our attention to. Scientists try to observe the world "objectively" but they, subjectively performing the experiment, are already an integral part of any "objective" measurement being taken. Specifically, it is their consciousness, their attention and intention which affect the results.

"It's important to remember that the equations of quantum physics don't describe the actual existence of particles. In other words, the laws can't tell us where the particles are and how they act once they get there. They describe only the potential for the particles' existence – that is, where they <u>may</u> be, how they <u>might</u> behave, and what their properties <u>could</u> be like. And all of these characteristics evolve and change over time. These things are significant because we're made of the same particles that the rules are describing. If we can gain insight into the way they function, then maybe we can become aware of greater possibilities for how we work. Herein lies the key to understanding what quantum physics is really saying to us about our power in the universe. Our world, our lives, and our bodies exist as they do because they were chosen (imagined) from the world of quantum possibilities ... Which of

the many possibilities becomes real appears to be determined by consciousness and the act of observation. In other words, the object of our attention becomes the reality of our world." -Gregg Braden, "The Divine Matrix" (70-71)

"*Quantum physics calculates only possibilities, but if we accept this, then the question immediately comes, who/what chooses among these possibilities to bring the actual event of experience? So we directly, immediately see that consciousness must be involved.*" -Amit Goswami Ph.D, "What the Bleep Do We Know?"

If the underlying unity of energy in the universe exists as an "infinite anything of possibilities," and it is consciousness which chooses and experiences all manifestations of the infinite anything, then it would seem that consciousness is much more fundamental and primary than classical physics espouses. If consciousness is what changes waves of possibility into particles of experience, then how could consciousness be some emergent property of the material universe? The "material universe" doesn't even exist yet without immaterial consciousness existing to have that experience!

"*The doctrine that the world is made up of objects whose existence is independent of human consciousness turns out to be in conflict with quantum mechanics and with facts established by experiment.*" -Physicist Bernard d'Espagnat, Scientific American, 1979

"*Leading physicist Lee Smolin has estimated that from its inception, had the primary forces and physical attributes of our universe varied by more than an unimaginably precise one part in 10^{27} – that's one part in a thousand trillion trillion! – our complex universe of chemistry, galaxies, and biological life could not have evolved.*" -Ervin Laszlo and Jude Currivan, "Cosmos" (20)

The odds of our universe containing these precise forces and physical attributes are 1 in 1,000,000,000,000,000,000,000,000,000 without which matter and life could not have emerged. If that's not a strong case for intelligent design, I don't know what is. The old physics claims that life, consciousness, the incredible beauty and diversity of nature is all the result of chance – even though the odds against chance are a thousand trillion trillion to one. Personally, for me, the idea that our universe exists due to non-intelligent, random, mechanical forces is utterly laughable. Just by sitting in meditation, smelling a flower, watching an eclipse, hearing children's laughter, tasting ice-cream, or feeling an orgasm, it is quite clear to me that the universe was intelligently and purposefully designed.

In his 2005 Nature Magazine article, The Mental Universe, Johns Hopkins physics professor Dr. R.C. Henry bluntly recommends we *"get over it"* and accept the logical conclusion that *"the universe is immaterial - mental and spiritual."* In the same article, Cambridge physicist Sir James Jeans is quoted as saying, *"The stream of knowledge is heading toward a non-mechanical reality; the universe begins to look more like a great thought than like a great machine. Mind no longer appears to be an accidental intruder into the realm of matter . . . we ought rather hail it as the creator and governor of the realm of matter."*

"Matter is not what we have long thought it to be. To the scientist,

matter has always been thought of as sort of the ultimate in that which is static and predictable ... We like to think of space as empty and matter as solid but in fact, there is essentially nothing to matter whatsoever. It's completely insubstantial ...The most solid thing you can say about all this insubstantial matter is that it's more like a thought - it's like a concentrated bit of information." -Physicist/Psychologist Dr. Jeffrey Satinover, "What the Bleep Do We Know?"

British astrophysicist Sir Arthur Eddington said that *"physics is the study of the structure of consciousness. The 'stuff' of the world is mindstuff."* Even Nobel Prize winning physicist Max Planck, the "father" of quantum physics, before his passing in 1947 conceded that, *"As a man who has devoted his whole life to the most clear-headed science, to the study of matter, I can tell you as the result of my research about the atoms, this much: There is no matter as such! All matter originates and exists only by virtue of a force which brings the particles of an atom to vibration and holds this most minute solar system of the atom together ... We must assume behind this force the existence of a conscious and intelligent Mind. This Mind is the matrix of all matter."*

"With these words, Max Planck, the father of quantum theory, described a universal field of energy that connects everything in creation: the Divine Matrix. The Divine Matrix is our world. It is also everything in our world. It is us and all that we love, hate, create, and experience. Living in the Divine Matrix, we are as artists expressing our innermost passions, fears, dreams, and desires through the essence of a mysterious quantum canvas. But we are the canvas, as well as the images upon the canvas. We are the paints, as well as the brushes. In the Divine Matrix, we are the container within which all things exist, the bridge between the creations of our inner and outer worlds, and the mirror that shows us

what we have created." -Gregg Braden, "The Divine Matrix" (Introduction)

Another two mind-bending, paradigm-shattering findings in the new physics are known as "Non-Locality" and "Quantum Entanglement." In classical physics, objects were seen as localized and isolated from one another within space; through dozens of replicated and verified experiments we now know, however, that the universe at the quantum level is entangled, non-local, One integrated whole.

"Quantum physicists discovered a strange property in the subatomic world called 'nonlocality'. This refers to the ability of a quantum entity such as an individual electron to influence another quantum particle instantaneously over any distance despite there being no exchange of force or energy. It suggests that quantum particles once in contact retain a connection even when separated, so that the actions of one will always influence the other, no matter how far they get separated." -Lynne McTaggart, "The Field: The Quest for the Secret Force of the Universe," (11)

Before the advent of quantum physics, Albert Einstein, still thinking in the classical paradigm, thought that nothing in the universe could travel faster than light. In the past two decades, however, it has been experimentally proven that one thing can indeed move faster than the speed of light: information. Information can be sent between two objects at any distance instantaneously.

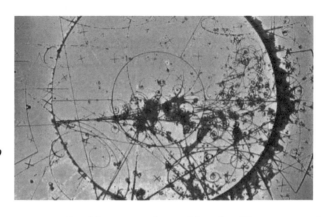

"In 1997, scientific journals throughout the world published the results of something that traditional physicists say shouldn't have happened. Reported to over 3,400 journalists, educators, scientists, and engineers in more than 40 countries, an experiment had been performed by the University of Geneva in Switzerland on the stuff that our world is made of – particles of light called photons – with results that continue to shake the foundation of conventional wisdom." -Gregg Braden, "The Divine Matrix" (30)

This ground-breaking experiment conclusively proved the existence of "Quantum Entanglement" which is basically a fancy name for "instantaneous information travel." First scientists took single photons and split them into separate "twin" particles with identical properties. Then they fired both particles away from each other in opposite directions through specially designed fiber-optic chambers. At the end of these long pathways, the twin particles were forced to choose between two random but exactly identical routes. Curiously, without fail, in every trial the particles made precisely the same choices and traveled the same paths. Classical physics has always assumed that separate particles have no communication with one another, but quantum physics has now proven that assumption erroneous.

The first entanglement experiments were designed and tested in 1982 by French physicist Alain Aspect at Orsay's Institut d'Optique. These crude but conclusive studies later inspired Nicholas Gisin's University of

Geneva group of physicists to replicate them at greater distances. In 1997 Gisin built a 14 mile fiber-optic chamber and repeated Aspect's experiment with exactly the same results. Later in 2004 Gisin extended the chamber to 25 miles and once again, as usual, no matter how far apart, the particles always chose and traveled the same random pathways.

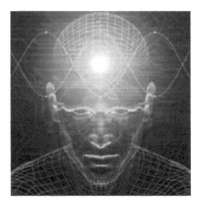

"Quantum mechanics has shown through experimentation that particles, being after all but moving points on some infinite wave, are in communication with one another at all times. That is to say, if our quantum mechanic does something to particle A over in Cincinnati, Ohio, planet Earth, the experience of this event will be instantly communicated to particle Z, at speeds faster than light, over in Zeta Reticuli. What this suggests is that anything one given particle experiences can be experienced by another particle simultaneously, and perhaps even by all particles everywhere. The reason for this is that they are all part of the same wave, the same energy flow." –Jake Horsley, "Matrix Warrior" (90-91)

"For a message to travel between them, it would have to be moving faster than the speed of light. But according to Einstein's theory of relativity, nothing can travel that quickly. So is it possible that these particles are violating the laws of physics ... or are they demonstrating something else to us? Could they be showing us something so foreign to the way we think about our world that we're still trying to force the mystery of what we see into the comfortable familiarity of how we believe energy gets from one place to another? What if the signal from one photon never traveled to reach the other? Is it possible that we live in a universe where the information between photons, the prayer for our loved ones, or the desire for peace in a place halfway around the world never needs to be transported anywhere to be received? The answer is yes!

28

This appears to be precisely the kind of universe we live in." -Gregg Braden, "The Divine Matrix" (105-6)

Robert Nadeau, historian of science, and Menas Kafatos, a physicist from George Mason University wrote an entire book together on the results and implications of quantum entanglement and non-locality entitled, The Nonlocal Universe. In it they state, *"All particles in the history of the cosmos have interacted with other particles in the manner revealed by the Aspect experiments ... Also consider ... that quantum entanglement grows exponentially with the number of particles involved in the original quantum state and that there is no theoretical limit on the number of these entangled particles. If this is the case, the universe on a very basic level could be a vast web of particles, which remain in contact with one another over any distance in 'no time' in the absence of the transfer of energy or information. This suggests, however strange or bizarre it might seem, that all of physical reality is a single quantum system that responds together to further interactions."*

Nadeau and Kafatos argue that we live in a non-local universe which is the obvious conclusion from the quantum entanglement experiments. The fact is quanta can exchange information over any distance in the universe instantaneously. These entanglement experiments prove that Eintstein was incorrect in stating that nothing travels faster than light (186,000 miles per second). Quantum information "travels" at infinite speed "arriving" at its destination without any time elapsing. Here we see how the Newtonian/Einsteinian language of a local universe fails to describe our actual reality. It's not that information is "traveling" at infinite "speed" to "arrive" at another location, but rather that the universe with all its so-called parts and particles is actually One non-local quantum system. Information from one particle to another doesn't need to "travel" there because the space between them is illusory, as is the language of calling them "separate" particles. As we have seen, before observation quanta are not particles with definite attributes and location; they are merely waves in the One universal quantum ocean until our conscious observation individualizes the wave into droplets of experience.

"Nonlocality shatters the very foundations of physics. Matter can no longer be considered separate. Actions do not have to have an observable cause over an observable space. Einstein's most fundamental axiom isn't correct: at a certain level of matter, things can travel faster than the speed of light. Subatomic particles have no meaning in isolation but can only be understood in their relationships. The world, at its most basic, exists as a complex web of interdependent relationships, forever indivisible." -Lynne McTaggart, "The Field: The Quest for the Secret Force of the Universe," (11)

"As an aside, it's interesting to note that Nadeau and Kafatos mention early in their book that readers accidentally encountering their book in the 'new age' section of a bookstore would likely be disappointed. That's because the book is about physics and not new age ideas. But the fact that Nadeau and Kafatos felt it important to mention this at all illustrates the rising tension between the leading edge of interpretations in physics and the tail end of metaphysics. Physicists interested in quantum ontology are painfully aware that some interpretations of quantum reality are uncomfortably close to mystical concepts. In the eyes of mainstream

science, to express sympathy for mysticism destroys one's credibility as a scientist. Thus the taboo persists." -Dean Radin, "Entangled Minds" (262)

The old view was a material universe separated by objective space and time, a clockwork machine operating under fixed laws which evolved in complexity until consciousness (the ability to experience) mysteriously manifested into the first ever self-aware unit of (now "living") matter. No scientist, however, could explain how something as complex as life and consciousness, our complex immaterial internal worlds of thought, emotion, sensation, and perception could ever arise from something as simple as random interactions of physical matter. No biological, chemical, electrical, magnetic, or other quantitative, qualitative such formula, can ever explain how consciousness could emerge from mere physical interactions of non-experiencing, non-living, unconscious particles of matter.

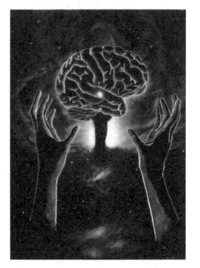

"*In the old thinking I cannot change anything because I don't have any role at all in reality. Reality is already there. It is material objects moving in their own way from deterministic laws and mathematics determines what they will do in a given situation. I, the experiencer, have no role at all. In the new view, yes, mathematics can give us something. It gives us the possibilities that all these movements can assume, but it cannot give us the actual experience that I'll be having in my consciousness. I choose that experience, and therefore, literally, I create my own reality. It may sound like a tremendous, bombastic claim by some New Agey without any understanding of physics whatsoever, but really quantum physics is telling us that.*" -Amit Goswami Ph.D, "What the Bleep Do We Know?"

"Quantum theory has thus demolished the classical concepts of solid objects and of strictly deterministic laws of nature. At the subatomic level, the solid material objects of classical physics dissolve into wave-like patterns of probabilities, and these patterns, ultimately, do not represent probabilities of things, but rather probabilities of interconnections. A careful analysis of the process of observation in atomic physics has shown that the subatomic particles have no meaning as isolated entities, but can only be understood as interconnections between the preparation of an experiment and the subsequent measurement. Quantum theory thus reveals a basic oneness of the universe. It shows that we cannot decompose the world into independently existing smallest units. As we penetrate into matter, nature does not show us any isolated 'basic building blocks', but rather appears as a complicated web of relations between the various parts of the whole. These relations always include the observer in an essential way. The human observer constitutes the final link in the chain of observational processes, and the properties of any atomic object can only be understood in terms of the object's interaction with the observer." -Fritjof Capra, "The Tao of Physics" (68)

Princeton physicist and colleague of Albert Einstein, Dr. John Wheeler, often remarked that nothing is more important in quantum physics than the observer effect and the measurement problem because they destroy the materialist concept of the world "sitting out there" with the observer "safely separated from it by a 20 centimeter slab of plate glass." Even to observe something as miniscule as an electron that slab of plate glass must be shattered. The scientist must reach in, install his devices, and decide whether to measure position or momentum. It is up to him which he decides, but installing the equipment to measure one prevents and excludes the possibility of measuring the other, because his act of measuring actually changes the state of the electron. Due to the free-willed decision of the observer, the universe afterwards will never again be the same. Thus to accurately describe what has happened, Wheeler insisted that the old word "observer" must be replaced with the new word "participator" because in some strange and fantastic way, our universe is a participatory universe.

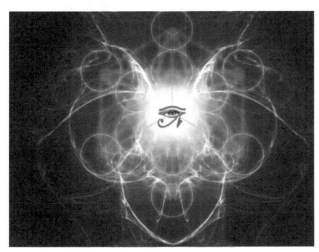

"What a shift! In a radically different interpretation of our relationship to the world we live in, Wheeler states that it's impossible for us to simply watch the universe happen around us. Experiments in quantum physics, in fact, do show that simply looking at something as tiny as an electron – just focusing our awareness upon what it's doing for even an instant in time – changes its properties while we're watching it. The experiments suggest that the very act of observation is an act of creation, and that consciousness is doing the creating. These findings seem to support Wheeler's proposition that we can no longer consider ourselves merely onlookers who have no effect on the world that we're observing." -Gregg Braden, "The Divine Matrix" (xi)

"The idea of 'participation instead of observation' has been formulated in modern physics only recently, but it is an idea which is well known to any student of mysticism. Mystical knowledge can never be obtained just by observation, but only by full participation with one's whole being. The notion of the participator is thus crucial to the Eastern world view, and the Eastern mystics have pushed this notion to the extreme, to a point where observer and observed, subject and object, are not only inseparable but also become indistinguishable. The mystics are not satisfied with a situation analogous to atomic physics, where the observer

and the observed cannot be separated, but can still be distinguished. They go much further, and in deep meditation they arrive at a point where the distinction between observer and observed breaks down completely, where subject and object fuse into a unified undifferentiated whole." - Fritjof Capra, "The Tao of Physics" (141-2)

Mystics, yogis, shamans, Eastern philosophers and the like have no trouble whatsoever understanding quantum physics. These amazing discoveries causing such a stir among the "scientific" community are really just experimental proofs of ancient wisdom long understood by such "simple" folk. The ideas of cosmic mind and the participatory universe are already fundamental tenets of their worldview. It is only modern Westerners raised on the materialist paradigm that find these facts puzzling.

Fermi award-winning American physicist, successor to Albert Einstein at Princeton's IAS, and director of the Manhattan Project, Dr. Robert Oppenheimer, was well aware of quantum physics' uncanny resemblance to Eastern philosophy. He once stated that, *"the general notions about human understanding . . . which are illustrated by discoveries in atomic physics are not in the nature of things wholly unfamiliar, wholly unheard of, or new. Even in our own culture they have a history, and in Buddhist and Hindu thought a more considerable and central place. What we shall find is an exemplification, an encouragement, and a refinement of old wisdom."*

Nobel Prize-winning German physicist, successor to Max Plank, and pioneer of the Uncertainty Principle, Dr. Werner Heisenberg, was also well aware of the parallels between quantum physics and Eastern thought. He stated that, *"the great scientific contribution in theoretical physics that has*

come from Japan since the last war may be an indication of a certain relationship between philosophical ideas in the tradition of the Far East and the philosophical substance of quantum theory."

"We are poised on the brink of a revolution – a revolution as daring and profound as Einstein's discovery of relativity. At the very frontier of science new ideas are emerging that challenge everything we believe about how our world works and how we define ourselves. Discoveries are being made that prove what religion has always espoused: that human beings are far more extraordinary than an assemblage of flesh and bones ... Human beings and all living things are a coalescence of energy in a field of energy connected to every other thing in the world. This pulsating energy field is the central engine of our being and our consciousness ... There is no 'me' and 'not-me' duality to our bodies in relation to the universe, but one underlying energy field." - Lynne McTaggart, "The Field: The Quest for the Secret Force of the Universe," (XXIII)

"Quantum physics illustrates how everything in the Universe, in all dimensions of life and reality ultimately consists of 'Quanta' of Energy, vibration. This Energy not only pervades and is integral to everything in

existence, it is also 'living' Mind, living Consciousness. Everything in the Universe therefore has its being within this infinite intelligent Energy. Everything is an aspect of this infinite intelligence, every person, every animal, every tree, every star and every planet, and every micro-organism, however small, is ultimately an equal aspect of the very same Energy; there is no separatedness except as an illusion created by the ego and five physical senses; we and everything in the Universe without exception are one." -Adrian Cooper, "Our Ultimate Reality" (89-90)

In Hinduism "Mahamaya" is a goddess personifying the power to create the material universe. In Buddhism, Buddha's supernatural mother is known as "Maya." In ancient Egypt Ma'at or Mayet was the female Goddess responsible for setting order and balance at the moment of creation. The Indian word "Maya" has the same meaning as the Mesoamerican "Mayan" civilization half a world away. In both cultures, Maya, loosely translates to "illusion" or "delusion" as both peoples believed the entire physical universe to be an illusion, a delusion of our

consciousness separating our fundamental Oneness (the Father) into individualized subjective perspectives throughout time/space (the Mother, Matter, Ma'at, Mayan illusion).

"So it is conceivable that all of this really is just a great illusion, that we have no way of really getting outside of to see what is really out there. Your brain doesn't know the difference between what's taking place out there and what's taking place in here. There is no 'out there'' out there independent of what's going on in here." -Fred Alan Wolf Ph.D, "What the Bleep Do We Know?"

"One of the discoveries that proved to be most astonishing to physicists was the observation that the only time Quanta ever manifest as particles is when people are actually looking at them. The significance of this

realization alone is extremely profound in terms of the understanding of the material world and of all creation. The wisdom of the ages has always maintained and taught the physical world of matter is nothing but an illusion, only perceived by most as 'reality' due to observation and experience by the mediation of the five physical senses." -Adrian Cooper, "Our Ultimate Reality" (75)

Everything, the entire material universe, at the most fundamental level is simply one undifferentiated interconnected energy resonating at various frequencies. Solid matter, for instance, is energy of a very slow, dense vibration, such as H_2O in ice form. In a block of ice, the collective vibration of H_2O molecules slows and freezes into a rigid, highly-structured alignment. The vibration of that block of ice is so slow that your hand cannot pass through the dense mass of H_2O molecules. However, if you take that same mass of molecules and raise the temperature so they vibrate at a faster rate, then that rigid impenetrable solidity gives way to more flowing/fluid, chaotic, lower-density, liquid state – water - which your hand can pass right through. If you continue heating the same mass of molecules, causing them to vibrate even faster, then that flowing, liquid state gives way to an even more chaotic, lower-density, free-form, gaseous state – steam - which your hand passes through with even less resistance than water. This example illustrates how "materiality" is simply an illusion created by interfering energy patterns of varying vibrations decoded by mind/consciousness.

"Quantum physicist David Bohm was absolutely correct when he made the observation that the physical Universe is actually 'frozen light.' This can be likened to the process of water freezing. As water gets progressively colder the molecules comprising that water progressively slow down as they vibrate at lower rates of Energy of which they ultimately comprise, until eventually the Energy vibration of the molecules becomes too low to sustain the water as a liquid at which point the water freezes and becomes ice. The physical composition of the ice

and the atoms and molecules that comprise it are exactly the same as when it existed as water, the only difference being that as ice the Energy that ultimately comprises that water or ice is now vibrating at a much lower level. Exactly the same principle applies to the existence of the physical Universe within the greater Universe as a whole. As Energy vibrates at a progressively lower rate and density increases as a result, there came a point during the initial creation of the Universe where the vibrations of Energy became too low to be sustainable in its usual fine free Energy form, and therefore differentiated into particles of various increasing sizes, ultimately manifesting as matter, the physical Universe as observed by science and people on Earth generally." -Adrian Cooper, "Our Ultimate Reality" (209)

Classical physics and the old science taught us that human beings were mere survival machines powered by chemicals and genes. They taught us that the brain was the originator of consciousness, and that our internal worlds of thought, emotion, sensation, and morality were mere by-products of material evolution. They taught us that we humans were separate, isolated entities in a desolate, mechanical, clockwork universe. They taught us that time and space were finite and that nothing traveled faster than light.

Quantum physics and the new science, however, teach us that human beings are spiritual entities having this physical experience. They teach us that consciousness is the primary mind-stuff of the universe, and that time, space, and matter exist only within and by virtue of consciousness. They teach us that we humans are indivisible from our environment and each other, that our bodies, the stars and space are composed of One undifferentiated expanse of vibrating energy.

In short, the old material science brought us a disempowering message of division and haphazard coincidence; the new spiritual science brings us the empowering message of absolute unity and divine cosmic mind.

"Western science is approaching a paradigm shift of unprecedented proportions, one that will change our concepts of reality and of human nature, bridge the gap between ancient wisdom and modern science, and reconcile the differences between Eastern spirituality and Western pragmatism." -Dr. Stanislav Grof, "Beyond the Brain"

"The exploration of the atomic and subatomic world in the twentieth century has revealed an unsuspected limitation of classical ideas, and has necessitated a radical revision of many of our basic concepts. The concept of matter in subatomic physics, for example, is totally different from the traditional idea of a material substance in classical physics. The same is true for concepts like space, time, or cause and effect. These concepts, however, are fundamental to our outlook on the world around us and with their radical transformation our whole world view has begun to change. These changes, brought about by modern physics, have been widely discussed by physicists and by philosophers over the past decades, but very seldom has it been realized that they all seem to lead in the same direction, towards a view of the world which is very similar to the views held in Eastern mysticism ... [and] if physics leads us today to a world view which is essentially mystical, it returns, in a way, to its beginning, 2,500 years ago. It is interesting to follow the evolution of Western science along its spiral path, starting from the mystical philosophies of the early Greeks, rising and unfolding in an impressive development of intellectual thought that increasingly turned away from its mystical origins to develop a world view which is in sharp contrast to that of the Far East. In its most recent stages, Western science is finally overcoming this view and coming back to those of the early Greek and the Eastern philosophies. This time, however, it is not only based on intuition, but also on experiments of great precision and sophistication, and on a rigorous and consistent mathematical formalism." -Fritjof Capra, "The Tao of Physics" (17-19)

"Quantum physics, which explores reality beyond the 'physical' world of the atom, is saying basically the same as the mystics, and people like me, who talk of different dimensions and frequencies of existence interpenetrating our own. Spirituality and true science - in its open-minded, open-hearted form – are essentially at one. It is mainstream science and mainstream religion that has caused the apparent rift because they are slaves to arrogance, ignorance and dogma. One is not science and the other is not spiritual. They are two polarities of the same falsehood. The open-minded quantum physicist would  *have no problem with most of what I am going to say in this book, while the cap-touching, protecting-my-funding, mainstream 'scientist' would roll his eyes in bewilderment. Such is the chasm of view that exists in the so-called scientific community."* –David Icke, "Infinite Love is the Only Truth, Everything Else is Illusion" (21-22)

Consciousness

In the Eskimo/Inuit language of cold, wintry Alaska there are dozens of words for "snow" - Dozens of words with intricacies and connotations well-known and understood by them, but typically unnoticed and misunderstood by others. Similarly, in the Sanskrit language of ancient, spiritual India there are approximately a dozen different words for "consciousness" – a dozen clearly delineated words with subtle nuances which in English we can only loosely, clumsily call "consciousness."

"*For every psychological term in English there are four in Greek and forty in Sanskrit.*" -A. K. Coomaraswamy

So what exactly is consciousness? When western doctors say someone is conscious or unconscious they really just mean "awake" or "asleep." The patient is called unconscious under anesthetics and conscious when awakened. However this particular meaning is clearly a misnomer because even when supposedly "unconscious" during sleep, coma, or under anesthetics we still dream and are "conscious" of that experience, so our consciousness hasn't disappeared as implied, it has merely altered/shifted to another state.

"*In medicine, the presumption that consciousness is nothing more than a function of the brain is reflected in such statements as, 'The patient regained consciousness' – this routine, narrow depiction has assumed that consciousness is a mundane physical phenomenon, a self-evident priority for experience about which nothing more needs to be said.*" -David R. Hawkins, M.D., Ph.D., "Power Vs. Force" (249)

Other common (mis)uses of the word consciousness are "awareness" as in "being conscious of something," and "spirituality" as in "attaining higher consciousness," but again these are not the denotations understood by modern scientists or ancient mystics. As best expressed by Theoretical Physicist/Experimental Psychologist Peter Russell, the true,

41

simple meaning of consciousness is "the capacity for experience." Consciousness is the ability to have an inner experience. It is our internal world of thoughts, emotions, sensations, perceptions, and choices, the "I," the little me in our minds, the sense of self inside us that has never changed since childhood – that is consciousness.

"The identification and experience of self could be limited to a description of one's physical body. Then, of course, we might well ask, how does one know that one has a physical body? Through observation, we note that the presence of the physical body is registered by the senses. The question then follows, what is it that's aware of the senses? How do we experience what the senses are reporting? Something greater, something more encompassing than the physical body, has to exist in order to experience that which is lesser – and that something is the mind ... The question then arises: How does one know what's being experienced by the mind? By observation and introspection, one can witness that thoughts have no capacity to experience themselves, but that something both beyond and more basic than thought experiences the sequence of thoughts, and that that something's sense of identity is unaltered by the content of thoughts." -David R. Hawkins, M.D., Ph.D., "Power Vs. Force"(252)

That something is consciousness, the capacity for experience, the inner witness of our outer lives. As written by philosopher Malcolm Hollick, *"Events are experienced by an experiencer, thoughts are thought by a thinker, pain is felt by a feeler, imaginings are created by an imaginer, and choices are made by a chooser."*

"What is it that observes and is aware of all of the subjective and objective phenomena of life? It's consciousness itself that resonates as both awareness and experiencing, and both are purely subjective. Consciousness isn't determined by content; thoughts flowing through consciousness are like fish swimming in the ocean. The ocean's existence is independent of the fish; the content of the sea doesn't define the nature of the water itself." -David R. Hawkins, M.D., Ph.D., "Power Vs. Force" (252-3)

Given the definition, "the capacity for inner experience," we can easily observe that consciousness is not a phenomenon limited only to human beings. In fact, as we trace the trait of consciousness back through the animal kingdom, it becomes increasingly difficult to say there exists any animal which doesn't have its own inner experience of the outer world. In his excellent book "From Science to God," Peter Russell examines this issue in detail starting with the example of a dog:

CONSCIOUSNESS:
That annoying time between naps.

"A dog may not be aware of all the things of which we are aware. It does not think or reason as humans do, and it probably does not have the same degree of self-awareness, but this does not mean that a dog does not have its own inner world of experience. When I am with a dog, I assume that it has its own mental picture of the world, full of sounds, colors, smells and sensations. It appears to recognize people and places, much as we might. A dog may at times show

43

fear, and at other times excitement. Asleep, it can appear to dream, feet and toes twitching as if on the scent of some fantasy rabbit. And when a dog yelps or whines we assume it is feeling pain –indeed, if we didn't believe that dogs felt pain, we wouldn't bother giving them anesthetics before an operation." -Peter Russell, "From Science to God"

My dog, Buddy, always recognizes me and shows excitement when I come through the door. He also recognizes the veterinarian's office and shows fear when we pull into the parking lot. If I ignore Buddy and give more attention to his sister, Harley, then Buddy will exhibit signs of feeling slighted and jealous, he will sulk by himself in the corner of the room, his tail no longer wagging when I go to pet him. If I raise my voice at him, he will cower, lower his  head, and scamper off. From facial recognition to dreams to complex emotions, dogs exhibit a multitude of expressions associated with consciousness. To assume they exhibit all these external characteristics of consciousness without having their own internal experience is quite implausible. And as Peter Russell points out, if we actually believed that dogs didn't "feel" pain, we wouldn't give them anesthetics before an operation.

"If dogs possess consciousness then so do cats, horses, deer, dolphins, whales, and other mammals. They may not be self-conscious as we are, but they are not devoid of inner experience. The same is true of birds; some parrots, for example, seem as aware as dogs. And if birds are sentient beings, then so, I assume, are other vertebrates – alligators, snakes, frogs, salmon, and sharks. However different their experiences may be, they all share the faculty of consciousness. The same argument applies to creatures further down the evolutionary tree. The nervous systems of insects are not nearly as complex as ours, and insects probably do not have as rich an experience of the world as we do, but I see no

44

reason to doubt that they have some kind of inner experience. Where do we draw the line?" -Peter Russell, "From Science to God"

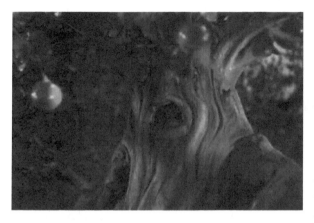

Carefully considering where to draw the line between conscious and non-conscious entities, the closer one examines the issue, the more difficult it becomes to argue that any animal is insentient. Regardless of whether they have a brain or nervous system, no matter how small or simple, all animals seem to have their own inner experience and exhibit common characteristics of consciousness.

So what about the plant kingdom? While most would agree that animals are conscious, most would probably agree that plants are not. Is this where we can draw the line? Apparently not - Thanks to the work of Cleve Backster, Dr. Ken Hashimoto and others, it is clear that even plants are remarkably conscious.

In 1966, polygraph-expert Cleve Backster conducted a series of experiments which conclusively demonstrated that plants are capable of intelligent thought processes. First he took a Dracaena plant (dragon tree) in his office and connected lie detection equipment to its leaves. Next he watered the plant and found that its polygraph output was similar to the undulation of human happiness. In order to test

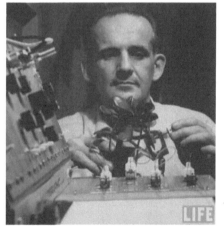

his developing theory and elicit a stronger reaction, Backster thought to threaten the plant by burning one of its leaves. With this thought in mind, even before retrieving a match, he noticed a strong positive curve appear on the polygraph paper. He then left the room to find some matches, and as soon as he arrived back, another high peak appeared on the paper. As he lit a match, the plant's fear reaction spiked and remained high as he proceeded to burn one of its leaves. In further trials Backster found that if he showed less inclination to burn the plant, its reaction was weaker, and if he merely pretended to burn it, there was no reaction. So not only was the plant appearing to show genuine happiness and fear, but it seemed to be discerning true intentions from false ones.

"[In] 1966 Cleve Backster, a pioneer of lie-detection methods, decided to threaten a dragon plant in his office. A few minutes before, and having on a whim connected the plant to the electrodes of one of his lie detectors, he had noticed that when he watered its roots, the plant gave what in a human being would be interpreted as an emotional reaction. To arouse the strongest reaction he could, Backster first placed a leaf of the plant in hot coffee, with no apparent response. He then decided on a worse threat: to burn the leaf. But as soon as he thought about the flame, there was an instant response from the plant – without Backster moving but just thinking about the threat, the plant had reacted! When he left the room and returned with some matches, there was a second surge of anticipation from the plant. And as he reluctantly burned the leaf, there was a subdued but still noticeable reaction from the dragon plant. Over the next 40 years, Backster ran a large series of experiments, building up a huge archive of data showing that all organisms are in continual communication in a vast matrix of dynamic and nonlocal awareness." -Ervin Laszlo and Jude Currivan, "Cosmos" (91)

In further trials Backster tried burning the leaves of other nearby plants not connected to the polygraph, and the original dragon plant, still connected, registered the same wild response to its friend's pain as when its own leaves were burned. In another experiment Backster placed two plants in an empty room, blindfolded 6 students, and had them draw straws. The receiver of the short straw was then secretly instructed to uproot and destroy one of the two plants. Since they were all blindfolded, only the short straw student and the remaining plant knew the identity of the murderer. Two hours later Backster connected the remaining plant to the polygraph machine

and instructed each student to walk past it. The murder-witness plant registered absolutely no reaction as the 5 innocent students walked by, but then went crazy almost off the charts as the murderer came close. Somehow it correctly identified and emotionally reacted to the guilty student.

Backster's experiments suggest that plants are not only conscious,

intelligent, and emotional, but also telepathic! Plants will indeed register a typical human "fear" reaction on the polygraph precisely when someone directs a malevolent thought towards them. These experiments have been replicated many times with the same results. Somehow plants are able to intuit and react to certain human thought patterns.

"The 'Backster effect' had also been seen between plants and animals. When brine shrimp in one location died suddenly, this fact seemed to instantly register with plants in another location, as recorded on a standard psychogalvanic response (PGR)

instrument. Backster had carried out this type of experiment over several hundred miles and among paramecium, mold cultures and blood samples, and in each instance, some mysterious communication occurred between living things and plants. As in Star Wars, each death was registered as a disturbance in The Field." -Lynne McTaggart, "The Field: The Quest for the Secret Force of the Universe," (145)

Other experiments have been performed testing the effect of prayer, positive and negative directed intention and emotion on plants. Dr. Bernard Grad of McGill University had a team of psychic healers habitually direct positive or negative feelings onto a variety of plants. The positively-infused plants survived and thrived, while negatively-infused plants withered and many of them died. Reverend Franklin Loehr, a Northampton pastor, performed similar studies with his parishioners testing the power of prayer to affect plants and seeds. In one

experiment he planted 46 corn kernels evenly spaced in a round pan with 23 on each side. He then gave daily "positive-growth" prayer to half the kernels and "anti-growth" prayer to the other half. Eight days later, the

positive side had 16 sturdy, budding, seedlings growing and the negative side had only 1 barely left alive. In another test, one of his parishioners, Erwin Prust, subjected 6 Ivy plants to daily "anti-growth" prayer while watering them and within 5 weeks, 5 of them were dead.

In the incredible documentary, "The Secret Life of Plants" Fuji electronics managing director and chief of research Dr. Ken Hashimoto created special instruments which translate the electrical output of plants into modulated sounds effectively giving them a voice. His wife has since been teaching the Japanese alphabet to her favorite plants. In the documentary Mrs. Hashimoto recites Japanese letters/phonemes/words and the plants repeat them back to her! Reminiscent of a small child trying to sound-out new words, the plants are unable to properly imitate the language at first, but then actually struggle and practice, slowly improving until they are able to perfectly imitate the human sounds via their electrical output. She says she looks forward to the day when she can have a conversation with her plants.

So if plants can learn languages, show emotional output, react to emotional / intellectual stimulus, communicate with other plants, and read the minds and intentions of humans, it is quite rational to assume that the plant kingdom, just like the animal kingdom, is conscious.

"This demonstrates extremely well that plant life, like all life and indeed everything in the Universe are an inseparable aspect of the same infinite Mind, Consciousness, and intelligence of The Source, The First Cause, of God. Human beings, still totally steeped in the material world and

personal ego assume that just because a plant does not appear to have a physical brain, or a mouth, or any other animal characteristics that they are 'unintelligent' or simply 'inanimate.' Nothing in fact can be further from the truth. The human brain is not the real Mind any more than physical parts of a plant or a mineral are real Mind." - Adrian Cooper, "Our Ultimate Reality" (217)

So how far down the evolutionary line does consciousness exist? The work of Dr. Masaru Emoto suggests that even water is in some sense conscious. His research began by exposing H_2O to nonphysical stimulus and photographing the resulting water crystals with a dark field microscope.

Water Molecule, Before Offering a Prayer Water Molecule, After Offering a Prayer

Thank You You Make Me Sick, I Will Kill You Love and Appreciation

"*Japanese researcher, Masaru Emoto, of the I.H.M.-Institute in Tokyo, has revealed how water is fundamentally affected by words, thoughts and emotions - all of which are waveforms. He and his team exposed water to various music and different words and expressions, and then froze it to produce water crystals. When these were examined under a microscope the response of the water was amazing. Look at the way it reacted to the words and thoughts (vibrations) of 'Love and appreciation', and, 'You make me sick - I will kill you'. Imagine the effect on the body of our words and deeds when it is some 70 per cent water. This is how thoughts and words affect us energetically. I should stress that it is not the words that have the effect, but the intent behind them. If you said 'I will kill you' in a light-hearted fashion, as a bit of fun, it would not have the same effect as it would if you meant it, or said it with malevolence.*" –David Icke, "The David Icke Guide to the Global Conspiracy" (47)*

  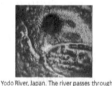

Sanbu-ichi Yusui Spring water Japan Shimanto River, referred to as the last clean stream in Japan Antarctic Ice

Fountain in Lourdes, France Biwako Lake, the largest lake at the center of Japan. Pollution is getting worse. Yodo River, Japan. The river passes through most of the major cities in Kasai.

Untreated Distilled Water Fujiwara Dam, before offering a prayer Fujiwara Dam, after offering a prayer

Thus even water has the ability to distinguish between real human emotions and fake platitudes. When infused with positive intent the H_2O molecules align themselves into beautiful, symmetric, sacred geometrical forms, and when infused with negative intent they align themselves into chaotic, non-symmetrical blobs. Obviously the level and type of consciousness operating in water molecules is far different from human consciousness, but the fact that something in the molecules is identifying and reacting to human emotional/intellectual content suggests that even water is indeed in some sense conscious.

"We usually assume that some kind of brain or nervous system is necessary before consciousness can come into being. From the perspective of the materialist metaparadigm, this is a reasonable assumption. If consciousness arises from processes in the material world, then those processes need to occur somewhere, and the obvious candidate is the nervous system. But then we come up against the inherent problem of the materialist metaparadigm. Whether we are considering a human brain with its tens of billions of cells, or a nematode worm with a hundred or so neurons, the problem is the same: How can any purely material process ever give rise to consciousness?" -Peter Russell, "From Science to God"

Can we truly draw a definitive line between conscious and non-conscious entities in the universe? At what level of simplicity do we assume matter to be insentient? Even single-cell organisms react to external stimulus, reproduce, communicate, respire, hunt and consume food – is this all an unconscious, insentient "program" of Newton's mechanical universe or are even single cells imbued with a slight degree of consciousness, a miniscule internal experience of their own? When sperm and egg unite, each human begins their life as a single-cell organism which then rapidly divides and multiplies into the conscious community of 50 trillion cells we generally know as human. In classical science, consciousness is a mysterious emergent property of this process; in spiritual science, consciousness is the known primary property and the physical world is the emergent mystery.

"The capacity for inner experience could not evolve or emerge out of entirely insentient, non-experiencing matter. Experience can only come from that which already has experience. Therefore the faculty of consciousness must be present all the way down the evolutionary tree…There is nowhere we can draw a line between conscious and non-conscious entities; there is a trace of sentience, however slight, in viruses, molecules, atoms, and even elementary particles. Some argue this implies that rocks perceive the world around them, perhaps have thoughts and feelings, and enjoy an inner mental life similar to human beings. This is clearly an absurd suggestion, and not one that was ever intended. If a

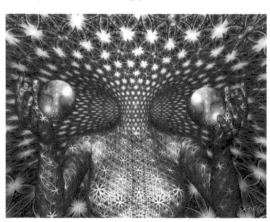

bacterium's experience is a billionth of the richness and intensity of human being's, the degree of experience in the minerals of a rock might be a billion times dimmer still. They would possess none of the qualities of human consciousness – just the faintest possible glimmer of sentience." -Peter Russell, "From Science to God"

The ancient Sufi teaching states that *"God sleeps in the rock, dreams in the plant, stirs in the animal, and awakens in the man."* What if we replaced the word "God" with "The One Infinite Consciousness?" If God is defined as - an omniscient, omnipotent, omnipresent intelligence – then

God must exist inside all things, yet outside of all space, time, and matter. What has quantum physics (and honest introspection) shown exists inside all things, yet outside space, time, and matter? Consciousness.

"Without consciousness, there would be nothing to experience form. It could also be said that form itself, as a product of perception with no independent existence, is thus transitory and limited, whereas consciousness is all-encompassing and unlimited. How could that which is transitory (with a clear beginning and ending), create that which is formless (all encompassing and omnipotent)?" -David R. Hawkins, M.D., Ph.D., "Power Vs. Force"(250-1)

How can non-experiencing, unintelligent, insentient matter randomly coalesce into a form that magically creates conscious intelligent life? What mechanical process could possibly bring consciousness, intelligence, and life into being? How could any material process create something as immaterial as consciousness? Why would the material universe even exist without a consciousness to perceive it? Quantum physics and Eastern Mysticism are both quite clear that matter does <u>not</u> exist without a consciousness to  perceive it. Albert Einstein himself said, *"A human being is a part of the whole, called by us 'Universe' – a part limited in time and space. He experiences himself, his thoughts and feelings as something separated from the rest – a kind of optical delusion of consciousness."*

"Whatever our beliefs – irrespective of how far we expand our perception and regardless of how profound the ability of science may be to understand processes of emergence – sooner or later we arrive at the requirement for an originating creative act. We arrive ultimately at the concept of a cosmic mind. Although science has so far chosen to ignore this inescapable logic, the deeper we delve into the fundamental mysteries of Nature – as did Einstein – we see order, harmony, and cosmic mind

manifest in our universe. What is revealed doesn't require us to choose between intelligent design and evolution, but to recognize a co-creative design for evolution. What we see, literally hidden in full view, is Einstein's concept of a cosmic mind at work." -Ervin Laszlo and Jude Currivan, "Cosmos" (22)

Unless you actually think "God" is a bearded white man living in the clouds, perhaps replacing that word, as Einstein did, with something like "Cosmic Mind," "Universal Being," or "Infinite Consciousness" will help bridge the mental gap most Westerners seem to have between science and spirituality.

"After I shook the dust of organized religion from my sandals, I learned that the link between big 'ol God and little 'ol me was no more and no less than consciousness. And each of us, at and as the very center of us, have this same feeling of I Am, for the not-so-obvious reason that each one of us is really God pretending to be each one of us. There is only one I Am, there is only one God, one Brahma, one Tao, one beingness ... we both see the same world, because we both are the same world. But we have so cleverly and convincingly hidden ourselves from ourselves that we really believe that we are separate entities." -Roger Stephens, "A Dangerous Book" (56)

"The coming scientific revolution heralds the end of dualism in every sense. Far from destroying God, science for the first time is proving His existence – by demonstrating that a higher, collective consciousness is out there." - Lynne McTaggart, "The Field: The Quest for the Secret Force of the Universe," (226)

As shown previously, the plenum of physical forms in the universe is fundamentally an energetic Oneness with consciousness playing the role of creator and experiencer. This means the multitude of transitory material forms and bodies about us, don't exist without us, and come from within us.

"A growing body of research suggests that we're more than cosmic latecomers simply passing through a universe that was completed long ago. Experimental evidence is leading to a conclusion that we're actually creating the universe as we go and adding to what already exists! In other words, we appear to be the very energy that's forming the

cosmos, as well as the beings who experience what we're creating. That's because we are consciousness, and consciousness appears to be the same 'stuff' from which the universe is made." -Gregg Braden, "The Divine Matrix" (39)

"The universe holds its breath as we choose, instant by instant, which pathway to follow; for the universe, the very essence of life itself, is highly conscious. Every act, thought, and choice adds to a permanent mosaic; our decisions ripple through the universe of consciousness to affect the lives of all. Lest this idea be considered either merely mystical or fanciful, let's remember that fundamental tenet of the new theoretical physics: Everything in the universe is connected with everything else." -David R. Hawkins, M.D., Ph.D., "Power Vs. Force" (148)

"Matter is derived from mind, not mind from matter." -Tibetan Book of the Great Liberation

More and more, scientists are catching up with ancient mystics regarding the primacy of consciousness, the fact that consciousness is an a priori facet of reality, and not some emergent property of materiality. One of the fathers of modern brain research, Wilder Penfield wrote *The Mystery of Mind* in which he argues his opinion as a neurosurgeon that consciousness does not have its source in the brain. The prestigious VISION 97 award-winning psychiatrist Dr. Stanislav Grof M.D., Ph.D. also agrees that consciousness is a primary, non-local phenomenon that precedes and transcends time and space:

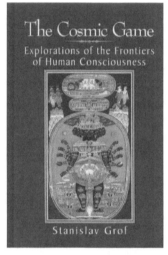

"Over three decades of systematic studies of the human consciousness have led me to conclusions that many traditional psychiatrists and psychologists might find implausible if not downright incredible. I now firmly believe that consciousness is more than an accidental by-product of the neurophysiological and biochemical processes taking place in the human brain. I see consciousness and the human psyche as expressions and reflections of a cosmic intelligence that permeates the entire universe and all of existence. We are not just highly evolved animals with biological computers embedded inside our skulls; we are also fields of consciousness without limits,

transcending time, space, matter, and linear causality." -Stanislav Grof, "The Holotropic Mind" (17-18)

The idea that consciousness mysteriously arises from the nervous system or brain functioning is proven erroneous by the plethora of organisms which exhibit clear signs of consciousness without having a brain or nervous system. Plants, bacteria, single-cell and many multi-cellular organisms all seem quite conscious without these. Are we to believe these life-forms are insentient just because they don't have a brain or nerves?

"While new technologies are enabling scientists to understand more and more of the mechanics of how mind is expressed through the brain, after many years of research this still sheds no light on their central quest – one that we believe is fruitless because the premise on which it is based is

wrong. We agree with transpersonal psychologist Stanislav Grof, who, for more than 50 years, has studied human consciousness. Grof has compared the effort of trying to discover how mind arises from the brain to an engineer trying to understand the content of a television program solely by watching what components light up in the interior of the TV set. If someone sought to do such a thing, we'd laugh, yet this is the approach that mainstream science has taken and insisted is correct, despite no evidence to support it and a great deal that contradicts it." -Ervin Laszlo and Jude Currivan, "Cosmos" (76-77)

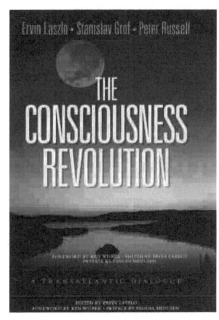

"New scientific findings are beginning to support beliefs of cultures thousands of years old, showing that our individual psyches are, in the last analysis, a manifestation of cosmic consciousness and intelligence that flows through all of existence. We never completely lose contact with this cosmic consciousness because we are never fully separated from it." - Stanislav Grof, "The Holotropic Mind" (195-6)

There are documented cases of hydrocephalus, otherwise known as "water in the brain," where people have lived perfectly normal lives with almost no cerebral cortex or neocortex whatsoever. This is quite significant considering that classical science has always assumed the neocortex to be the supposed "center of consciousness." British neurologist John Lorber recorded one case in which a young man's hydrocephalus was so extreme that his brain was virtually nonexistent. Inside his skull was just a thin layer of brain cells surrounding a mass of cerebrospinal fluid. Amazingly, everything else about the young man was normal; he was even an honor student. If consciousness arises from brain functioning, how is this possible?

"The underlying assumption of the current meta-paradigm is that matter is insentient. The alternative is that the faculty of consciousness is a fundamental quality of nature. Consciousness does not arise from some particular arrangement of nerve cells or processes going on between

them, or from any other physical features; it is always present. If the faculty of consciousness is always present, then the relationship between consciousness and nervous systems needs to be rethought. Rather than creating consciousness, nervous systems may be amplifiers of consciousness, increasing the richness and quality of experience." -Peter Russell, "From Science to God"

Peter Russell asks us to consider a couple simple thought experiments to prove to ourselves the non-locality of consciousness beyond space and time. When asked to locate their consciousness most people sense it to be somewhere in their heads. Since our brains are in our heads, and the brain is often associated with consciousness, many people assume their consciousness is located in the middle of their heads, but actually the apparent location of ones consciousness has nothing to do with the placement of ones brain, and rather depends on the placement of sense organs. Since your primary senses (eyes and ears) are in your head, the central point of your perception, the place from which you seem to be experiencing the world is somewhere behind your eyes and between your ears (in your head). However, the fact that your brain is also in your head is merely coincidence as shown by the following thought experiment: Imagine that your eyes and ears were somehow transplanted to your knees so you now observed the world from this new vantage point. Now if asked to locate your consciousness where would you point? If your eyes and ears were on your knees, would you still experience your "self" to be in your head?

"I don't think consciousness is in the brain. The brain receives consciousness. Consciousness is probably a non-local function of the space-time continuum and every individual brain is an individual receiver. Just like the world is full of television signals and each television set is a receiver. The delusion that you are in your body is a

primitive, savage kind of logic, taking the data of perception at face value, similar to the delusion that Johnny Carson is inside your television set. Johnny Carson is not in your television set. Johnny Carson is in Hollywood. Your television set just receives Johnny Carson's signals. And consciousness is not in the brain, the brain just receives signals from the vast undifferentiated ocean of consciousness that makes up the space-time continuum." -Robert Anton Wilson

"The faculty of consciousness can be likened to the light from a video projector. The projector shines light on to a screen, modifying the light so as to produce any one of an infinity of images. These images are like the perceptions, sensations, dreams, memories, thoughts, and feelings that we experience – what I call the 'contents of consciousness.' The light itself, without which no images would be possible, corresponds to the faculty of consciousness. We know all the images on the screen are composed of this light, but we are not usually aware of the light itself; our attention is caught up in the images that appear and the stories they tell. In much the same way, we know we are conscious, but we are usually aware only of the many different perceptions, thoughts and feelings that appear in the mind. We are seldom aware of consciousness itself." -Peter Russell, "From Science to God"

In deep meditation, during spontaneous OBE, or under the effects of entheogens many people temporarily transcend their contents of consciousness completely and achieve a lucid state of awareness that is purely the faculty of consciousness. In this state there is no space and time, just the infinite here and now, no "me" and "not me" division, just one universal awareness. Such experiences are referred to as "mystical" and deemed "unscientific" because they are subjective and unrepeatable under laboratory conditions, but for those who experience such transcendental states, this first-hand gnosis provides them with an intuitive knowingness of the primacy of consciousness beyond all space, time, and matter.

"The Eastern mystics link the notions of both space and time to particular states of consciousness. Being able to go beyond the ordinary state through meditation, they have realized that the conventional notions of space and time are not the ultimate truth. The refined notions of space and time resulting from their mystical experiences appear to be in many ways similar to the notions of modern physics, as exemplified by the theory of relativity." - Fritjof Capra, "The Tao of Physics" (164)

"In short, the impression that your consciousness is located in space is an illusion. Everything you experience is a construct within consciousness. Your sense of being a unique self is merely another construct of the mind. Quite naturally, you place this image of your self at the center of your picture of the world, giving you the sense of being in the world. But the truth is just the opposite. It is all within you. You have no location in space. Space is in

you." -Peter Russell, "From Science to God"

If a tree falls in the forest and no one is around to hear it, does it still make a sound? At first you might think, "of course it still makes a sound!" until further defining what "sound" actually means: *the sensation produced by stimulation of the organs of hearing by vibrations transmitted through the air or other medium* (dictionary.com). When a tree falls there are certainly pressure waves vibrating through the air, but since "sound" is a quality of consciousness, if no ears are around to "hear" those waves, then the tree literally does not make a sound.

"To the surprise of many, the world 'out there' has turned out to be quite unlike our experience of it. Consider our experience of the color green. In the physical world there is light of a certain frequency, but the light itself is not green. Nor are the electrical impulses that are transmitted from the eye to the brain. No color exists there. The green we see is a quality appearing in the mind in response to this frequency of light. It exists only as a subjective experience in the mind. The same is true of sound. I hear the music of a violin, but the sound I hear is a quality appearing in the mind. There is no sound as such in the external world, just vibrating air molecules. The smell of a rose does not exist without an experiencing mind, just molecules of a certain shape." -Peter Russell, "The Primacy of Consciousness"

What we call "colors" or "sounds" or "smells" are all qualities created in consciousness which have no independent existence without a sentient observer. Colors are just electromagnetic energy of a specific frequency, sounds are just vibrations of specific patterns, and smells are just various

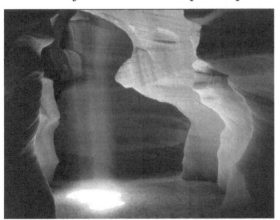

combinations of air molecules - all of which require the key element of consciousness to mystically transform these energetic emanations into our intricate and amazing everyday sensations.

"All our perceptions, sensations, dreams, thoughts and feelings are forms appearing in consciousness. It doesn't always seem that way. When I see a tree it seems as if I am seeing the tree directly. But science tells us

something completely different is happening. Light entering the eye triggers chemical reactions in the retina; these produce electro-chemical impulses which travel along nerve fibers to the brain. The brain analyses the data it receives, and then creates its own picture of what is out there. I then have the experience of seeing a tree. But what I am actually experiencing is not the tree itself, only the image that appears in the mind. This is true of everything I experience. Everything we know, perceive, and imagine, every color, sound, sensation, every thought and every feeling, is a form appearing in the mind. It is all an in-forming of consciousness." -Peter Russell, "The Primacy of Consciousness"

Electromagnetic radiation with a wavelength between 380 and 760 nanometers (frequency of 790–400 terahertz) is detected by the human eye and perceived as

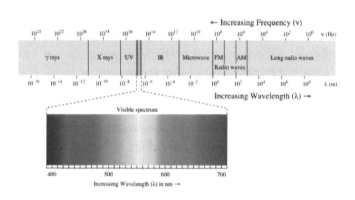

visible light; everything beyond that is invisible to us. All the colors of the rainbow and absolutely everything we see comes from just a narrow frequency on an infinite electromagnetic spectrum. Our highest perceivable frequency, at 790 terahertz, is the color violet. However with the use of tools/technology we know that above violet are ultra violet light, X-rays, and gamma rays. Our lowest perceivable frequency, at 400 terahertz, is the color red. However, with the use of tools/technology we know that below red are infrared, microwaves, and radio waves. The spectrum is infinite, yet we base our entire experience on the minute sliver perceivable to us and assume that is "reality."

"Our eyes detect none of these other frequencies, and our image of reality represents but a tiny fraction of what is there. The same holds true of the other senses. What we hear, smell and taste is but a limited sample of the physical reality. Furthermore, there are aspects of the physical world, such as magnetic fields and electric charge that have very little, if any, impact on our experience." -Peter Russell, "From Science to God"

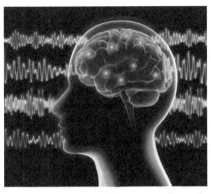

"In the space that you are occupying now are all the radio and television frequencies broadcasting to your area. You can't see them and they are not aware of each other because you and they are on different frequencies, or wavelengths. Only when the frequencies are really close do they experience 'interference'. It is the same with our reality. Our 'physical world' is just one of countless wavelengths, frequencies or dimensions, and to experience and interact with this realm we need an outer shell that is vibrating within this frequency range. Our consciousness is vibrating too fast to interact efficiently with this frequency ... The body is the means through which our Infinite Awareness can directly experience this range of frequencies that I will call, to keep it simple, the five-sense realm, world or dimension. This is why the five senses of sight, touch, smell, hearing and taste are so limited. They are confined to perceiving only this range of frequencies - this dimension." –David Icke, "The David Icke Guide to the Global Conspiracy" (13-14)

So in the universe there exists an infinite array of electromagnetic radiation, but only the tiniest glimpse of that array is available for sensory experience. Our physical bodies act like electromagnetic transistors for our awareness by switching on/off, amplifying or muting the multitude of signals around us and funneling what we focus on. All visual, auditory, kinesthetic, olfactory, and gustatory sensations are brought to our consciousness through this frequency decoding process, just like tuning a radio, and in the grand scheme of things, we are barely receiving a signal.

"There is no 'solid' world 'outside' of you. All those people, streets, cars and buildings only exist, in that 'solid' 3D state, in your mind. Everywhere else, they are frequency fields, thought fields, energy matrices, call them what you will. Television and the Internet are perfect

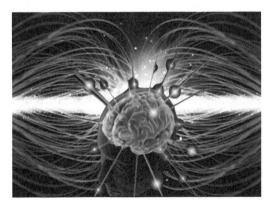

illustrations of what I am talking about here. When we think of television we think of pictures and programs, but the only place television exists in that form is on the TV screen. Everywhere else television consists of frequency broadcasts and electrical circuitry. When we think of the Internet we think of websites, pictures and graphics, but the only place the Internet exists in that form is on your computer screen. Everywhere else it consists of mathematical codes and electrical circuitry ... To summarize: the 'physical' world is a tiny frequency range or dimension within Infinite Awareness - the 'ocean'. The body-computer tunes us into this strictly limited sense of perception, this television channel, and acts as our vehicle to interact with this 'world'. We have been manipulated into believing that 'we' are the computer and its mental, emotional and physical software programs. This dimension, like all the others, is a mass of frequency fields that the body-computer decodes into apparently 3D

scenes, but in that form they only exist in the brain or, more accurately, the energy matrix we call the brain. There is no 'physical' world unless it is observed into form - decoded into form." –David Icke, "The David Icke Guide to the Global Conspiracy" (35-7)

The "outside" world around us has a convincing appearance of being "out there" somewhere, when in actuality the 3D world is no more "out there" than a dream. In dreams we perceive sights, sounds, and sensations, we have all our emotional and rational faculties, we encounter people, places and situations all seeming to be happening in a world "out there" around us. Not until we awaken do we realize that all those sights, sounds, sensations, people, places, and situations were simply creations of our minds, appearing around us, but coming from within us.

"Since the Greeks, philosophers have been thinking about 'the ghost in the machine', 'the small man within the small man' etc. Where is 'I', the person who uses his brain? Who is it that realizes the act of knowing?

As Saint Francis of Assisi said: 'What we search for is the one that sees.'" -Ken Wilber, "Holographic Paradigm" (37)

"Today, after thirty years of investigation into the nature of consciousness, I have come to appreciate how big a problem consciousness is for the contemporary science. Science has had remarkable success in explaining the structure and functioning of the material world, but when it comes to the inner world of the mind – to our thoughts, feelings, sensations, intuitions, and dreams – science has very little to say. And when it comes to consciousness itself, science falls curiously silent. There is nothing in physics, chemistry, biology, or any other science that can account for our having an interior world." -Peter Russell, "From Science to God"

How and why do we have an inner life at all? Professor of Philosophy at University of Arizona, Dr. David Chalmers has coined this issue, "the hard problem" of consciousness. How could any complex material process in the brain create our rich immaterial internal worlds of thought, emotion, sensation, and perception? Why is there a subjective aspect to reality at all?

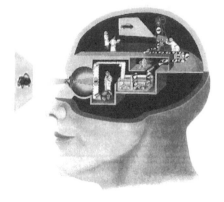

"Nothing in Western science predicts that any living creature should be conscious. It is easier to explain how hydrogen evolved into other elements, how they combined to form molecules, and then simple living cells, and how these evolved into complex beings such as ourselves than it is to explain why we should ever have a single inner experience." -Peter Russell, "From Science to God"

Let's put the "hard problem" of consciousness through the process of elimination. We now know from multiple experiments in quantum physics that quanta, the building blocks of matter, the fundamental units of "stuff" in the universe, do not become a set "something" with definite properties, location, and materiality without the key element of consciousness to collapse the wave function; In other words, no consciousness, no matter. So if consciousness is supposedly an emergent property of a Newtonian/Darwinian mechanistic universe, what used to collapse the wave function in the days before the "evolution of consciousness?"

"[Since] a key component in the quantum measurement process includes an observer and his or her knowledge, this means the mind is inextricably wound into quantum reality ... Based on the classical assumptions of local realism and mechanism, the brain – like any other physical object – is a clockwork object. Since clockworks are not conscious, then what we call 'I' can only be an emergent property of a complicated piece of machinery. And thus our sense of conscious awareness, or the feeling one has when smelling a rose, are illusions – though illusions to whom is not quite clear. From a classical physics point of view, the 'you' that is currently reading this sentence is an illusion. This seems to be a rather important limitation, as most people reading these sentences probably believe that they (their conscious minds) do exist." -Dean Radin, "Entangled Minds" (256-7)

We often falsely assume that we <u>are</u> our physical bodies because our consciousness seems trapped inside. We feel pain and pleasure, all emotions, perceptions and sensations through the body and so we identify with it, but is the body who/what we really are? If your leg gets cut off, is the leg still you? Or was the leg just a tool, a vehicle you used to experience the physical realm?

"We are energy beings residing in bodies so that we can experience this physical dimension. The relationship between our energy being and our physical body is kind of like a person driving a car, except imagine that the person driving believes the car is their true being. It might strike you as funny to imagine a person who believes that they are the car, but that

is the way most of us think of ourselves. We do not separate our physical bodies from the pure energy being that controls the body. When people drive cars, they do not become car-beings. We are the energy beings within our bodies." -Eric Pepin, "Handbook of the Navigator" (111-112)

Anyone who has experienced an OBE, NDE, or taken DMT will tell you emphatically that we are <u>not</u> our physical bodies. Indigenous peoples and shamanic cultures regularly practiced meditation, "dreamtime," trance-inducing chants, dances, fasts and ingested psychedelic entheogens all of which put them directly in touch with non-physical aspects of their consciousness. Even the staunchest materialists are compelled beyond their will every night to relax their bodies to sleep while their consciousness travels to various dream worlds/dimensions beyond the physical. The signs are all around us but the point is easy to miss: the physical world is simply a recurring dream that we awaken from when our bodies die.

"So the first revelation on the road to freedom: your body is not 'you' - it is a fantastic biological computer that 'you' are using to experience this reality. It is a vehicle, a means, not a 'you' or an 'I'. The spacesuit is the means by which an astronaut can experience other 'worlds'. So is your 'body'. We are not our bodies; we are Infinite Consciousness, the All That Is, a seamless energy field within which all 'worlds' and no 'worlds' exist. The only difference between everything is the level of awareness that we are All

That Is. The deeper this awareness, the more you will access that level of 'knowing' and perception; the more you think you are an 'individual' and apart from everything else, the more you will disconnect from the Infinite One that you really are." –David Icke, "The David Icke Guide to the Global Conspiracy" David Icke Books (2)

Still unconvinced that you are not your body? Did you know that every 5 to 7 years, every single cell in your body dies and is replaced? Your entire body, every cell in your brain, every cell in your eye, absolutely everything that composes your physical body has died and been replaced multiple times. Meanwhile, your unique essence, your feeling of "I am-ness," your consciousness, has remained exactly the same as when you were a child.

"This feeling of being lonely and very temporary visitors in the universe is in flat contradiction to everything known about man (and all other living organisms) in the sciences. We do not 'come into' this world; we come out of it, as leaves from a tree. As the ocean 'waves,' the universe 'peoples.' Every individual is an expression of the whole realm of nature, a unique action of the total universe. This fact is rarely, if ever, experienced by most individuals. Even those who know it to be true in theory do not sense or feel it, but continue to be aware of themselves as isolated 'egos' inside bags of skin [but] the cat has already been let out of the bag. The inside information is that yourself as 'just little me' who 'came into this world' and lives temporarily in a bag of skin is a hoax and a fake. The fact is that because no one thing or feature of this universe is separable from the whole, the only real You, or Self, is the whole. The rest of this book will attempt to make this so clear that you will not only understand the words but feel the fact." -Alan Watts, "The Book on the Taboo Against Knowing Who You Are" (8)

Synchronicity is a term coined by Swiss psychologist Carl Jung which he defined as the "temporally coincident occurrence of acausal events." In other words, synchronicities are meaningful coincidences – highly improbable, highly significant, serendipitous happenings. When it is clear that there is no cause-and-effect connection between two events, yet a meaningful relationship nevertheless exists, this is synchronicity. Jung believed synchronicity is an acausal connecting principle of our collective unconscious through which we are shown mystical glimpses of meaningful connections between our subjective and objective worlds, divine bridges between our inner and outer experiences.

"Synchronicities are revelations of the absence of any division between the physical world and inner, psychological reality. Synchronistic events are 'lucidity stimulators,' neon-signs from the dreamlike nature of the universe to help us wake up to its, and our, dreamlike nature. Just like a dream, mind and matter are not separate, distinct realities, but rather, are seemingly different fundamental components of the same deeper, underlying reality that has both an external-matter aspect and an internal-mind aspect." –Paul Levy, "God the Imagination"

"The blurring of boundaries between consciousness and matter challenges everything we are taught in traditional Western thinking. From a very early age we are urged by our parents, teachers, and religious leaders to draw clear lines between the 'subjective' and the 'objective,' the 'real' and the 'unreal,' the existent and the non-existent, or the tangible and the intangible. However, a reality that is very similar to Jung's acausal universe is becoming recognized in modern science, notably in quantum-relativistic physics ... It was Jung's recognition of phenomena that exist outside cause and effect that led him to define synchronicity as an 'acausal connecting principle.' Meaningful coincidences between the inner world - the world of visions and dreams - and the outer world of 'objective reality' suggested to Jung that the two worlds were not as

clearly separated as we might think." -Stanislav Grof, "The Holotropic Mind" (169)

Have you ever experienced visions or emotional pangs related to some person or incident outside your sensory experience? Have you ever had déjà vu or coincidences so meaningful yet improbable that it boggled your mind? Have you ever had a friend or relative pop into your head and then seconds later the phone rings and it is them? Myself and many others have experienced such synchronicities, all of which can only be seen as chance/coincidence in a Newtonian world, but have special meaning in a Jungian, consciousness-based world.

"How many times have you gone to call someone on the phone, and found that he or she was already on the line when you picked up the receiver ... or when you dialed the number, you discovered that the line was busy because your pal was calling you? On how many occasions have you found yourself enjoying time with friends in a busy street, mall, or airport, only to have the eerie feeling that you've already been in that place or with those people before, doing exactly what you're doing at that moment? While these simple examples are fun to talk about, they're more than random coincidences. Although we may not be able to prove scientifically why these things happen, we all know that they do. In such moments of connectedness and déjà vu, we find ourselves spontaneously transcending the limits imposed by physical laws. In those brief instances, we're reminded that there's probably more to the universe and us than we may consciously acknowledge." -Gregg Braden, "The Divine Matrix" (57-58)

I have personally experienced many synchronicities, déjà vu's, and prophetic dreams which have convinced me that something like Jung's acausal connecting principle truly does exist within consciousness outside of space and time. For instance, one night in college I actually dreamed of a conversation that I would be having the next day and experienced paradigm-shattering déjà vu as I found myself enacting my dream in reality. Stunned in revelatory paralysis, the dream came flooding back to me and I realized that I was standing in the exact place, wearing the exact clothes, and having the exact discussion that I had dreamt. Suddenly it occurred to me that I knew exactly the entire next sentence my friend was about to speak, so I quickly snapped out of the reverie and said the whole sentence along with her verbatim simultaneously. My friend then stared at me dumbfounded as I laughed and tried to explain.

Another time, a few years ago I was meditating and started to feel a tight clenching at my solar plexus so I tried to relax, took a deep breath and exhaled with an Om. The very second I finished my Om breath, the electricity in my 3rd floor apartment room, all the lights and my digital clock, went dark for 2 seconds then came back on. Shocked, I phoned my friends on the 2nd and 5th floors to see if their power had gone out and it hadn't. This meant at most the power went out only on my floor and perhaps only in my room! Perplexed and curious I then said a little prayer to "God," my "higher self," or whatever aspect of the one consciousness was listening, and said, "it seems like that was more than just a coincidence, if that was some kind of sign, could I please have another one?" And so the next day I was downstairs in my girlfriends's room watching the cartoon South Park on DVD, the episode where Cesar Millan comes to deal with Cartman. Just as Cesar finished saying the words "you must express the dominant energy," the lights, the television, everything went dark once again, then came back on 2 seconds later and the DVD somehow skipped back and said once again "express the dominant energy." "Express the dominant energy" coinciding with 2 power outages, my meditation, and my asking for a sign was quite an odd, memorable and mysterious synchronicity for me.

"Most of us have encountered strange coincidences that defy ordinary explanation. The Austrian biologist Paul Kammerer, one of the first to be interested in the scientific implications of this phenomenon, reported a situation where his tram ticket bore the same number as the theater ticket that he bought immediately afterward; later that evening the same sequence of digits was given to him as a telephone number. The astronomer Flammarion cited an amusing story of a triple coincidence involving a certain Mr. Deschamps and a special kind of plum pudding. As a boy, Deschamps was given a piece of this pudding by a Mr. de Fortgibu. Ten years later, he saw the same pudding on the menu of a Paris restaurant and asked the waiter for a serving. However, it turned out that the last piece of the pudding was already ordered—by Mr. de Fortgibu, who just happened to be in the restaurant at that moment. Many years later, Mr. Deschamps was invited to a party where this pudding was to be served as a special rarity. While he was eating it, he remarked that the only thing lacking was Mr. de Fortgibu. At that moment the door opened and an old man walked in. It was Mr. de Fortgibu who burst in on the party by mistake because he had been given a wrong address for the place he was supposed to go." -Stanislav Grof, "The Holotropic Mind" (171)

"Jung was treating a woman whose staunchly rational approach to life made it difficult for her to benefit from therapy. After a number of frustrating sessions the woman told Jung about a dream involving a scarab beetle. Jung knew that in Egyptian mythology the scarab represented rebirth and wondered if the

72

woman's unconscious mind was symbolically announcing that she was about to undergo some kind of psychological rebirth. He was just about to tell her this when something tapped on the window, and he looked up to see a gold-green scarab on the other side of the glass (it was the only time a scarab beetle had ever appeared at Jung's window). He opened the window and allowed the scarab to fly into the room as he presented his interpretation of the dream. The woman was so stunned that she tempered her excessive rationality, and from that point on her response to therapy improved." -Michael Talbot, "The Holographic Universe" (78)

These kinds of anecdotes are not exactly "scientific" but due to the very nature of synchronicities, science and the scientific method are unfortunately ill-equipped to offer any insight into such intangible, immeasurable, and subjective phenomena. However, for many people who have personally experienced such highly improbable, unbelievable synchronicities, confirmation from science is unnecessary because like a glimpse behind the veil, they are given a kind of gnosis, an intuitive recognition of the subtle interplays between consciousness, space, time and matter.

"In a mechanical universe where everything is linked by cause and effect, there is no place for 'meaningful coincidences' in the Jungian sense. In the practice of traditional psychiatry, when a person perceives meaningful coincidences, he or she is, at best, diagnosed as projecting special meaning into purely accidental events; at worst he or she is diagnosed as suffering from hallucinations or delusions. Traditional psychiatrists either do not know about the existence of true synchronicities or they prefer to ignore the concept. As a result they may

wrongly diagnose 'meaningful coincidences' as the result of serious pathology (delusions of reference). In many cases of spiritual emergencies, where valid synchronicities were reported, people have all too often been hospitalized unnecessarily. Had those experiences been correctly understood and treated as manifestations of psycho-spiritual crisis those same people might have been quickly helped through approaches supporting spiritual emergence, rather than undergoing all the problems that unnecessary hospitalization entails." -Stanislav Grof, "The Holotropic Mind" (173)

Physicist F. David Peat believes synchronicities are very real phenomena which provide circumstantial evidence for an absence of division between the outer physical world and our inner psychological worlds. He states that *"the self lives on but as one aspect of*

the more subtle movement that involves the order of the whole of consciousness." It has been an arduous process, but as explored in the first chapter, quantum physics is slowly dragging the world of "rational science" kicking and screaming to the realization that staunch materialism is untenable, and concepts like Jung's collective unconscious are not so fantastic or fanciful after all.

"Jung himself was fully aware of the fact that the concept of synchronicity was incompatible with traditional science and he followed with great interest the revolutionary new worldview that was emerging from developments in modern physics. He maintained a friendship with Wolfgang Pauli, one of the founders of quantum physics, and the two of them had a very fruitful exchange of ideas. Similarly, in personal communications between Jung and Albert Einstein, the latter explicitly encouraged him to pursue the concept of synchronicity because it was

fully compatible with the new thinking in physics. Sadly, however, mainstream psychologists and psychiatrists have still not caught up with the revolutionary developments in modern physics and Jungian psychology." -Stanislav Grof, "The Holotropic Mind" (173-4)

The Holographic Universe

In the 1950s and 60s inventor Dennis Gabor discovered that when you photograph objects with a split light beam and store the information as wave interference patterns, you get a better image than with ordinary point-to-point intensity photographs. Not only is the captured image clearer, but it is completely three dimensional.

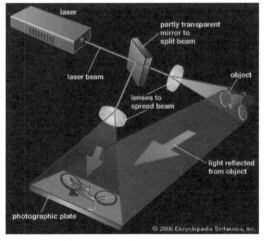

"*In a classic laser hologram, a laser beam is split. One portion is reflected off an object – a china teacup, say – the other is reflected by several mirrors. They are then reunited and captured on a piece of photographic film. The result on the plate – which represents the interference pattern of these waves – resembles nothing more than a set of squiggles or concentric circles. However, when you shine a light beam from the same kind of laser through the film, what you see is a fully realized, incredibly detailed, three-dimensional virtual image of the china teacup floating in space (an example of this is the image of Princess Leia which gets generated by R2D2 in the first movie of the Star Wars series).*" -Lynne McTaggart, "The Field: The Quest for the Secret Force of the Universe," (83)

"A hologram is produced when a single laser light is split into two separate beams. The first beam is bounced off the object to be photographed. Then the second beam is allowed to collide with the reflected light of the first. When this happens they create an interference pattern which is then recorded on a piece of film ... as soon as another laser beam is shined through the film, a three-dimensional image of the original object reappears. The three-dimensionality of such images is often eerily convincing. You can actually walk around a holographic projection and view it from different angles as you would a real object. However, if you

reach out and try to touch it, your hand will waft right through it and you will discover there is really nothing there." -Michael Talbot, "The Holographic Universe" (14-15)

The three-dimensionality of holographic images is not their only amazing attribute. In holograms, all parts are reflected in the whole and the whole is reflected in all parts, so if you chop a piece of holographic film into tiny bits then shine a laser onto any of them, no matter how small, you will still get a complete image.

"Back in the 1980s, a series of bookmarks appeared on the market using holographic technology. Each one was made of a shiny strip of silver

paper that looked like glossy aluminum foil at first glance. When the paper was held directly under a bright light and tilted back and forth, however ... Suddenly, the images in the foil looked as though they'd come to life and were hovering in the air just above the paper itself ... If you have one of these bookmarks, you can do an experiment to demonstrate for yourself just how a hologram works ... use a sharp pair of scissors to cut your beautiful, shiny

bookmark into hundreds of pieces of any shape. Then, take the smallest
of the fragments and cut it again into an even tinier piece. If the
bookmark is truly a hologram, you'll be able to look at your tiny speck of
a bookmark under a magnifying glass and still see the entire image, only
on a smaller scale. The reason why is that it exists everywhere
throughout the bookmark." -Gregg Braden, "The Divine Matrix" (104-5)

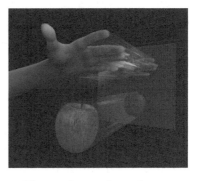

The "physical" world around us behaves
much like a hologram. Just like a piece of
holographic film, all quanta exist as
interfering wave patterns. In and of
themselves, these interference waves have
no "solidity" – no definite properties or
location – just like the squiggles/circles on
holographic film. The image is distributed
throughout the entire film, just as quanta
are distributed throughout the entire universe. Then when a laser beam
(the light of consciousness) is directed at those interference waves,
seemingly solid particles (three dimensional images) appear before our
eyes. One of the first physicists to consider this "cosmic hologram"
metaphor was David Bohm who defined the universe as an "undivided
wholeness in flowing motion" which he termed the "holomovement."

*"Einstein's
protégé, American
physicist David
Bohm, felt that
quantum theory
suggested the
existence of a
deeper reality than
the one presented
by our senses. He
dubbed the
implicate order an
undivided holistic realm that is beyond concepts like spacetime, matter,
or energy. In the implicate order everything is fully enfolded or
entangled with everything else. By contrast, the explicate order world of
ordinary observations and common sense emerge, or unfold, out of the
implicate order. Bohm used a hologram as a metaphor to illustrate how*

information about a whole system can be enfolded into an implicit structure, any part of which reflects the whole." -Dean Radin, "Entangled Minds" (254)

Bohm's implicate order is analogous to the two dimensional piece of holographic film and the explicate order is analogous to the three dimensional holographic image. The implicate order is the underlying undivided wholeness of the universe and the explicate order is the multitude of seemingly separate forms. To illustrate this duality, consider the following passages from my book Asbestos Head:

"If you blur your vision enough, forms disappear and you are left with nothing but a mass of color in motion. There is no word that describes the blur, but perhaps you make one up. Then you make a habit of making up words for blurs and start recognizing similarities - you label *tree* blurs, *rock* blurs, other *animal* blurs and maybe even *atom* blurs. This allows you to compare and categorize, make judgments, and express artistic concerns about the blurs, but the fact remains that the boundaries between blurs are perceptual, not actual. We know no two trees, rocks, animals, or atoms are exactly alike, but if no two things are exactly alike, we have no way to measure what constitutes one thing or it's other. If no two things are exactly alike then there must be only one true form that is everything (i.e. the universal hologram)

We know that sub-atomic particles are constantly in motion, but on a smaller scale than we can perceive. We know that the planet beneath us is constantly in motion, but on a larger scale than we can perceive. We know the Universe is perpetually changing and in motion, but we perceive most things as unchanging and still. Then we use language to label this fallacious stillness. We recognize similarities in the stillness and create categories and definitions. We forget all about our faulty premise and attribute a priori importance to these forms we perceive; though in fact knowing no two things are truly separate and everything's constantly moving (a.k.a. the holomovement)."

"Bohm cautions that this does not mean the universe is a giant undifferentiated mass. Things can be part of an undivided whole and still possess their own unique qualities. To illustrate what he means he points to the little eddies and whirlpools that often form in a river. At a glance such eddies appear to be separate things and possess many individual characteristics such as size, rate, and direction of rotation, et cetera. But careful scrutiny reveals that it is impossible to determine where any given whirlpool ends and the river begins. Thus, Bohm is not suggesting that the differences between 'things' is meaningless. He merely wants us to be aware constantly that dividing various aspects of the holomovement into 'things' is always an abstraction, a way of making those aspects stand out in our perception by our way of thinking. In attempts to correct this, instead of calling different aspects of the holomovement 'things,' he prefers to call them 'relatively independent subtotalities.'" -Michael Talbot, "The Holographic Universe" (48-9)

For Bohm, atoms are not the "building blocks of matter" but rather just a term given to one aspect of the holomovement. The various forms we name, words and categories we create, are all ultimately arbitrary because at the implicate level of reality, everything is one. No two atoms, two rocks, two trees, or two people are any more separate from one another than whirlpools are separate from the river. The universe is a holographic oneness in perpetual motion, both created and navigated by consciousness. Matter is not separated by space and time; rather, matter, space, and time are always already ever-present and one. To illustrate this, think of a DVD. At the explicate level of the DVD, you see a movie with people, places and events happening in space and time. For the actors on your television screen, they experienced everything happening in "real" time in the "real" world during filming. But for

you the viewer, holding the DVD in your hand, you can see the implicate level of the movie where all the people, places, and events on it are mere projections of a single totality. You can rewind, fast-forward, slow-mo, or freeze-frame the entire realistic three-dimensional explicate world of the DVD because you are operating from the implicate world of remote control. The One, God, infinite consciousness, cosmic mind, or whatever you want to call it, operates at the objective, omnipresent, omniscient, omnipotent level of the implicate DVD, and meanwhile us humans, animals, plants, insects, and every other subjective entity in the physical universe are method actors in the explicate movie. Bohm himself said, *"It will be ultimately misleading and indeed wrong to suppose, for example, that each human being is an independent actuality who interacts with other human beings and with nature. Rather, all these are projections of a single totality."*

"While it may look as though we're disconnected from one another and the rest of the world, that detachment doesn't exist on the plane where the hologram originates ... On this level of unity, there really can be no such things as 'here' and 'there.'" -Gregg Braden, "The Divine Matrix" (107)

"Matter does not exist independently from so-called empty space. It is a part of space ... Space is not empty. It is full, a plenum as opposed to a vacuum, and is the ground for the existence of everything, including ourselves."* - Michael Talbot, "The Holographic Universe" (51)

"David Bohm's work into quantum physics and quantum mechanics also realized and affirmed a single ultimate reality; the true nature of the Universe. Time will inevitably show the Universal explicate, implicate and super implicate orders of David Bohm and the holomovement, will eventually have most profound implications for humanity which all science will quite simply have to accept sooner or later, thus proving conclusively the Universe rather than being a vast and disparate multitude of separately interacting particles of matter, is in reality a

magnificent unbroken completeness, a continuum, an infinite flowing movement of Energy, vibration, the holomovement." -Adrian Cooper, "Our Ultimate Reality" (88)

Independently of David Bohm's research, Stanford neuroscientist Karl Pribram proposed a holographic model for explaining the structure and function of the human brain.   His work strongly suggests that the brain stores information, not locally in so-called "engrams," but holographically throughout its entirety.

"*Interestingly, while Pribram and David Bohm began their work independently, both were using the same explanation to describe the results of their experiments. They were each applying the holographic model to make sense of life. Bohm, as a quantum physicist, was looking at the universe as a hologram. Pribram, as a neuroscientist, was studying the brain as a holographic processor ... When the two theories are combined, what results is nothing less than a paradigm-shattering possibility.*" -Gregg Braden, "The Divine Matrix" (113)

Individual memories were long thought to exist locally in specific areas of the brain; however, thanks to the work of Dr. Karl Pribram, Dr. Karl Lashley, Dr. Paul Pietsch and others, we now know this is not the case. Dr. Karl Lashley and other scientists have trained rats to navigate mazes, then removed their brains piece by piece, attempting to find where "engrams" (individual memories) exist. Strangely, however, in the experiments the rats always remember the training no matter which piece or how much of the brain is removed.

"*Even after removing as much as 90 percent of a rat's visual cortex (the part of the brain that receives and interprets what the eye sees), he found it could still perform tasks requiring complex visual skills. Similarly, research conducted by Pribram revealed that as much as 98 percent of a cat's optic nerves can be severed without seriously impairing its ability to perform complex visual tasks. Such a situation was tantamount to believing that a movie audience could still enjoy a motion picture after 90 percent of the movie screen was missing, and his experiments presented once again a serious challenge to the standard understanding of how vision works.* -Michael Talbot, "The Holographic Universe" (18-9)

The orthodox explanation of vision is that the eye sees by taking a photographic image and reproducing it onto the cortical surface of the brain where we interpret it like an internal movie screen. Dr. Lashley's experiments showed, however, that even when 90-98% of that internal projector screen is missing, the brain still receives and registers the whole movie!

"Experiments demonstrated that animals retained memories and continued their lives even though the parts of their brains that were believed to hold these functions were removed. In other words, it appeared that there wasn't a direct correspondence between the memories and a physical place in the brain. It was obvious that the mechanical view of brains and memory wasn't the answer – something else strange and wonderful must be happening." -Gregg Braden, "The Divine Matrix" (112)

These and other experiments have shown that Dr. Lashley's engram theory of individual memories existing in certain areas of the brain is provably incorrect. Memories and images are distributed all throughout the brain, just like a picture is stored all throughout a piece of holographic film.

"Paul Pietsch began as an ardent disbeliever in Pribram's theory. He was especially skeptical of Pribram's claim that memories do not possess any specific location in the brain. To prove Pribram wrong, Pietsch devised a series of experiments … Pietsch reasoned that if a salamander's feeding behavior is not confined to any specific location in the brain, then it should not matter how its brain is positioned in its head. If it did matter, Pribram's theory would be disproven. He then flip-flopped the left and right hemispheres of a salamander's brain, but to his dismay, as soon as it recovered, the salamander quickly resumed normal

feeding. He took another salamander and turned its brain upside down. When it recovered, it too fed normally. Growing increasingly frustrated, he decided to resort to more drastic measures. In a series of over 700 operations he sliced, flipped, shuffled, subtracted, and even minced the brains of his hapless subjects, but always when he replaced what was left of their brains, their behavior returned to normal. These findings and others turned Pietsch into a believer." -Michael Talbot, "The Holographic Universe" (26)

Salamanders were good subjects for this experiment because they simply go comatose when their brains are removed and then quickly regain normal functioning once it's replaced. In Dr. Pietsch's 700 trials he subtracted, sliced, diced, mashed, and even sausage-ground salamander brains but no matter what, after putting back whatever was left of their brains, they always regained normal functioning.

 "*Mainstream science has been unable to locate the area of the brain that contains all the memory because what we call memory exists throughout the brain and body. This must be the case because it's a hologram. People with tumours, who have large parts of their brains removed, do not lose specific memories. They might not remember, in general, quite as well because they have moved to a smaller level of the holographic memory where there is less clarity than in the whole. But they don't lose one memory completely and retain another in crystal clarity as they would if memory was located in one area. The body hologram stores information from all the senses and so when we smell something it can trigger a memory just as powerfully as sight or hearing. Even this is another level of the illusion because if the brain is a hologram it must also be illusory. It is, like everything in this reality, the 'physical' expression of a frequency field or resonance. Incidentally, the holographic nature of the body means the whole brain/body is involved in decoding the five senses and not just the 'visual cortex' and other areas of the brain associated with these specific duties.*" –David Icke, "Infinite Love is the Only Truth, Everything Else is Illusion" (51)

So you can obliterate a salamander's brain in any number of ways, and it will still have a normal life as long as you put a tiny piece of brain back in its head. You can teach a rat to run a maze, then remove any part of its brain, and it will still remember the run. You can remove 90% of a rat's visual cortex and it will still perform complex visual tasks. You can sever 98% of a cat's optic nerves and it will still see normally. These, along with many other experiments, strongly suggest that the brain processes images and stores information holographically (all parts in the whole and the whole in all parts) because the brain, like a hologram, no matter how small the piece, can still reconstruct the whole.

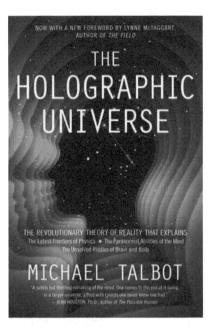

"Our brains mathematically construct objective reality by interpreting frequencies that are ultimately projections from another dimension, a deeper order of existence that is beyond both space and time: The brain is a hologram enfolded in a holographic universe ... What is 'out there' is a vast ocean of waves and frequencies, and reality looks concrete to us only because our brains are able to take this holographic blur and convert it into the sticks and stones and other familiar objects that make up our world." - Michael Talbot, "The Holographic Universe" (54)

In Michael Talbot's "The Holographic Universe," he suggests our experience of the smoothness of fine china or the feel of beach sand beneath our feet is like an elaborate version of the so-called "phantom limb syndrome" – when amputees can still "feel" their missing limb(s) long after having been removed. In other words, there are two realities, like Bohm's implicate and explicate orders. In the implicate order, a "china cup" is just an energetic interference pattern vibrating at a certain frequency, but in the explicate order, after being filtered through the lens of our brains, eyes, and nervous systems, those interference patterns manifest to us as the look and feel of fine china. When asked, *"so which is real and which is an illusion?"* Dr. Pribram replied that, *"both are real to me, or if you want to say, neither of them are real."*

"Although the metaphor of the holograph was important to Pribram, the real significance of his discovery was not holography per se, which conjures up a mental image of the three-dimensional ghostly projection, or a universe which is only our projection of it. It was the unique ability of quantum waves to store vast quantities of information in a totality and in three dimensions, and for our brains to be able to read this information and from this to create the world. Here was finally a mechanical device that seemed to replicate the way that the brain actually worked: how images were formed, how they were stored and how they could be recalled or associated with something else. Most important, it gave a clue to the biggest mystery of all for Pribram: how you could have localized tasks in the brain but process or store them throughout the larger whole. In a sense, holography is just convenient shorthand for wave interference – the language of The Field." -Lynne McTaggart, "The Field: The Quest for the Secret Force of the Universe," (84)

"So here we are – all part of this great hologram called Creation, which is everybody else's Self ... It's all a cosmic play, and there is nothing but you!" -Itzhak Bentov

In the 18th century a Frenchman named Jean Fourier discovered a mathematical method of converting patterns into simple wave forms called the Fourier transform, a process which later led to the discoveries of both television and holography. When a video camera captures

85

scenes on film it converts pictures into electromagnetic frequencies which are then converted back again by your television set. Scientists are now finding that this Fourier transform process is how the brain works, as an electromagnetic frequency decoder. We have long known that through our 120 billion miles of DNA/RNA our entire bodies are involved in a frequency decoding process. We know our ears are audio frequency decoders, Nobel Prize winner Georg von Bekesy has proven that our skin responds to frequencies, and thanks to neurophysiologists Russell and Karen DeValois, we now know that brain cells in the visual cortex react and activate based on frequency patterns.

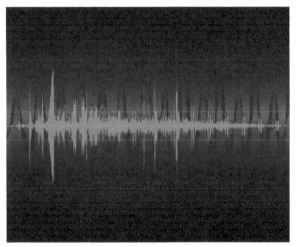

"University of California at Berkeley Neurophysiologists Russell and Karen DeValois converted simple plaid and checkerboard patterns into Fourier waves and discovered that the brain cells of cats and monkeys responded not to the patterns themselves but to the interference patterns of their component waves. Countless studies, elaborated on by the DeValois team in their book Spatial Vision, show that numerous cells in the visual system are tuned into certain frequencies. Other studies have showed that the human cerebral cortex may be tuned to specific frequencies … Pribram conjectured that these wave collisions must create the pictorial images in our brain. When we perceive something, it's not due to the activity of neurons themselves but to certain patches of dendrites distributed around the brain, which, like a radio station, are set to resonate only at certain frequencies. It is like having a vast number of piano strings all over your head, only some of which would vibrate as a particular note is played." -Lynne McTaggart, "The Field: The Quest for the Secret Force of the Universe," (86-88)

Dr. Pribram has conjectured that wave-interference patterns are likely not created or received by any particular brain cells, but in the spaces between them. Dendrites, the tiny nerve endings of neurons where synapses are fired, communicate with other neurons by sending and receiving electrical/chemical wave impulses. It is plausible that this is where wave frequencies are received and transformed into holographic images, because there are constantly millions of wave-interference patterns criss-crossing here anyway.

"The fact that movement could somehow be represented formally in terms of Fourier equations made Pribram realize that the brain's conversations with the body might also be occurring in the form of waves and patterns, rather than as images. The brain somehow had the capacity to analyze movement, break it down into wave frequencies and transmit this wave-pattern shorthand to the rest of the body. This information, transmitted nonlocally, to many parts at once, would explain how we can fairy easily manage complicated global tasks involving multiple body parts, such as riding a bicycle or roller skating. It also accounts for how we can easily imitate some task. Pribram also came across evidence that our other senses – smell, taste and hearing – operate by analyzing frequencies. In Pribram's own studies with cats, in which he recorded frequencies from the motor cortex of cats while their right forepaw was being moved up and down, he discovered that, like the visual cortex, individual cells in the cat's motor cortex responded to only a limited number of frequencies of movement, just as individual strings in a piano respond to a limited range of frequencies." -Lynne McTaggart, "The Field: The Quest for the Secret Force of the Universe," (87)

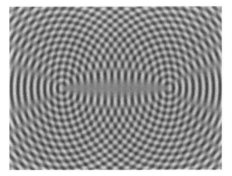

The color "red" in our explicate experience is really just an implicate wave-interference pattern vibrating at a frequency of 400 THz. The color "violet" in our experience is really just a wave-interference pattern vibrating at a frequency of 790 THz. Above the spectrum visible to humans are ultra-violet rays, x-rays,

87

and gamma rays. Below the spectrum visible to us are infra-red, microwaves, and radio waves. Our brains decode this small sliver of electromagnetic frequencies and create the perceptions and sensations we experience in our consciousness. Using the piano analogy, think of the color red as a low note and the color violet as a high note, a rainbow is a major chord, and a lakeside sunset is a concerto.

"Our brain is not a storage medium but a receiving mechanism in every sense, and memory is simply a distant cousin of ordinary perception. The brain retrieves 'old' information the same way it processes 'new' information – through holographic transformation of wave interference

patterns. Lashley's rats with the fried brains were able to conjure up their run in its entirety because the memory of it was never burned away in the first place. Whatever reception mechanism was left in the brain – and as Pribram had demonstrated, it was distributed all over the brain – was tuning back into the memory through The Field. Some scientists went as far as to suggest that all of our higher cognitive processes result from an interaction with the Zero Point Field. This kind of constant interaction might account for intuition or creativity – and how ideas come to us in bursts of insight, sometimes in fragments but often as a miraculous whole. An intuitive leap might simply be a sudden coalescence of coherence in The Field." -Lynne McTaggart, "The Field: The Quest for the Secret Force of the Universe," (95)

If you take a piece of regular film and cut it up, your image is destroyed forever. However, when you cut up a piece of holographic film, the image is never destroyed - a smaller scale version of the image always exists. If memories were stored locally, like regular film, and you cut out that part of the brain, the memory would be lost. But in reality, like holographic film, when you cut out parts of the brain, a smaller scale version of the memory always exists. So just as a piece of holographic film stores complete images as interference patterns throughout its entirety, the human brain stores complete memories as interference patterns throughout its entirety. And just like a laser light focused on a piece of holographic film creates a seemingly physical three-dimensional image, the light of our consciousness focusing on quanta creates a seeming physical three-dimensional world.

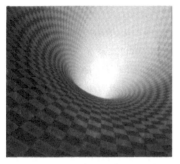

"The holographic model offers revolutionary possibilities for a new understanding of the relationships between the parts and the whole. No longer confined to the limited logic of traditional thought, the part ceases to be just a fragment of the whole but, under certain circumstances, reflects and contains the whole. As individual human beings we are not isolated and insignificant Newtonian entities; rather, as integral fields of the holomovement each of us is also a microcosm that reflects and contains the macrocosm. If this is true, then we each hold the potential for having direct and immediate experiential access to virtually every aspect of the universe, extending our capacities well beyond the reach of our senses." -Stanislav Grof, "The Holotropic Mind" (10)

Another markedly holographic processor present in our bodies and the universe is DNA. Watch any movie or TV series about crime-scene investigation and notice that the identity of the culprit can be determined from tiny traces of their DNA. A drop of blood, a fingernail, or a single strand of hair is enough to positively identify the perpetrator. The reason for this is that DNA, like our brains, holographically mirrors each part in the whole and the whole in each part.

"DNA (like RNA) emits light-energy in the form of photons to such an extent that it has been compared by some to an 'ultra weak laser'. They generate coherent light in the same way that our technological lasers do - the lasers that create holograms. The [universe] broadcasts its signals in wave, or interference, patterns and it may be that the laser light emitted

by the DNA/RNA is part of the process of turning them into holographic representations of that waveform ...One mystery of quantum physics is how particles can either express themselves as a 'wave' form (nonphysical) or as a particle (apparently 'physical') and the waveforms only become particles when they are being observed - when we are looking at them. What is actually happening is that the DNA/RNA/brain is causing the waveform or interference pattern to project an illusory hologram. The act of 'observation' - focus - projects the holograms from the waveforms and when this happens the quantum physicists see the waveform 'becoming' a particle. Both the waveform and the particle exist at the same time and they don't move from one state to another. When a laser is shone onto a photographic interference pattern to manifest a hologram, one does not replace the other. Both waveform and hologram coexist. It is just that the observer sees the hologram as the prime reality. The waveform is possibility; the particle is 'physical' experience." –David Icke, "Infinite Love is the Only Truth, Everything Else is Illusion" (62-3)

 Ever-increasing evidence overwhelmingly suggests that our brains, bodies, DNA, and the entire universe are non-local holographic transducers incessantly interacting with a deeper quantum reality. This "holomovement" is an "undivided wholeness in flowing motion" where all perceived separation is ultimately illusory like whirlpools in a river. Even the seeming separation of forms and consciousness into "relatively independent subtotalities" only exists at the explicate level. As David Bohm put it simply, *"deep down, the consciousness of mankind is one."*

"Scientists can't understand why subatomic particles can communicate instantly with each other over staggering distances because they are thinking in terms of space. But there is no space involved. It is like the droplet of water and the ocean. There are no particles, plural, except in the way we perceive them in the illusion. All particles are the same One. They don't have to communicate between each other because there is no 'each other' and they don't move from one place to another because there is no space and so there can be no places. Appropriately the word 'Utopia' means 'no place' - beyond the illusion of time and space. The

90

superhologram appears to occupy space and we talk of the vastness of space. But it's a hologram and so that cannot be. If there is no space how come we seem to travel through it? Once again because that is the illusion our DNA/RNA decodes for us and we travel through space only as electrical signals interpreted by the brain." –David Icke, "Infinite Love is the Only Truth, Everything Else is Illusion" (93)

"Every particle in the universe is a carrier of knowledge. In other words, in some form or another, every particle can be said to be conscious. As humatons, we tend to assume that only we are conscious, because only we seem to be self-conscious ... Not only that, we have attributed our consciousness to a single organ only, the brain (And it is possible we only use ten percent of that organ with which to deduce all of this). It would seem to be equally possible, however - and a lot more logical - to assume that the brain is merely a receiver of information - a tuning dial that picks up data and translates it into sense impressions and rational thought, images, and so forth - and that knowledge as such, memory, is stored in every single atom of our bodies. For organic beings, the 'filing system' provided for every living molecule is DNA. As such, if we were to tune in with the remaining ninety percent of our brains, we would be capable of receiving vastly greater amounts of data than we are presently accustomed to ... Just as knowledge / memory / experience is passed through generations of a given species, presumably via DNA, in order for the species to evolve as a whole, so information would appear to be shared freely amongst all the billions upon billions of particles that make up the physical universe. This is cooperation on a grand scale. Every particle is conscious. Every particle is potentially conscious of what every other particle is conscious of. And all particles

are connected together into a single tapestry of consciousness / information / energy which is, it therefore follows, conscious of what every particle is conscious of, and conscious of itself as a unified whole; a living, conscious organism. Ergo, the universe is a superconscious being within which all beings exist and have life and consciousness. It is God, and every one of its parts and components - as in a hologram in which each fragment contains the whole - is also God, the totality, in and of itself. –Jake Horsley, "Matrix Warrior" (90-91)

The Morphic Field

Another short-coming of traditional Western science is its inability to explain the existence of forms in nature. No matter how we magnify or manipulate the material world, no mechanical model explains the emergence of the variety of unique and semi-unique forms in nature. Every type of rock, plant, animal, organism, bacteria, all aggregate themselves into distinct and definite types with traits/characteristics semi-unique to their form and completely unique to them individually. For example each oak tree has many semi-unique features that characterize it clearly as an oak and not a pine, like the shape of its leaves, being non-coniferous, etc. These features are semi-unique as all oak trees share them, however on another level, no two oak trees are exactly alike either. Exact size, shape, dimensions, growth patterns, ring patterns etc. are completely unique to each tree. So what is the mechanism in nature which constantly creates these unique and semi-unique forms? Newton's model, nor the 300+ subsequent years of material science since have been able to explain this. British biologist Rupert Sheldrake's concept of morphogenic resonance, however, seems to be our best current theory.

"British biologist Rupert Sheldrake has offered an incisive critique of traditional science ... He pointed out that in its single-minded pursuit of 'energetic causation,' Western science neglected the problem of form in nature. He pointed out that our study of substance alone cannot explain why there is order, pattern, and meaning in nature any more than the examination of the building materials in a cathedral, castle, or tenement house can explain the particular forms those architectural structures

have taken. No matter how sophisticated our study of the materials, we will not be able to explain the creative forces that guided the designs of these structures. Sheldrake suggests that forms in nature are governed by what he calls 'morphogenic fields,' which cannot be detected or measured by contemporary science. This would mean that all scientific efforts of the past have totally neglected a dimension that is absolutely critical for understanding the nature of reality." -Stanislav Grof, "The Holotropic Mind" (11)

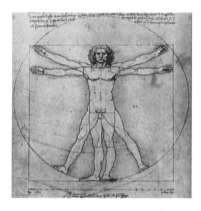

As an example Sheldrake asks us to consider the complexity of the human body. For instance, take notice of your arms, how they twist, bend, and rotate, notice how your fingers separate and clasp with opposable thumbs, giving your upper-limbs unique function and purpose. Now take notice of your legs, how they are designed, how they bend and move, notice your feet/toes, and how your lower-limbs perfectly serve their unique function and purpose. Arms and legs look different; have different functions and locations, but the DNA, chemicals, nerves, cells and molecules composing them are exactly the same. So how did they become different and why? What property within leg cells determined them to become a leg, and what property within arm cells determined them to become an arm?

"Sheldrake proposes a theory he calls Morphic Resonance. This theory basically states that there is a field of energy surrounding and permeating an organism which contains, among other things, the form of the organism. He writes that each species has its own field, that there are fields within fields, and that these fields have built-in memory, based upon what has happened in the past derived from previous organisms or forms of a similar kind. In other words, each organism on

the planet shares fields of similar energy or we could say a specific frequency." -Eric Pepin, "Handbook of the Navigator" (78)

What biological mechanism recognizes, stores, and develops the evolution and various adaptations of a species? If a species of insect develops camouflage coloration like nearby foliage to hide from predators, where is that information stored? If a species of bird develops curvature in its beak to assist in gathering low-laying food/materials, what mechanism informs new beak cells to curve? The typical answer is that this information is stored and transmitted by genes/DNA, however, no biologist can explain how this occurs. Sheldrake compares it to studying building materials at a construction site and attempting to determine the structure of the house to be built.

"British biologist Rupert Sheldrake has mounted one of the most constant and vociferous challenges to this approach ...Current genetic theory also doesn't explain, he says, how a developing system can self-regulate, or grow normally in the course of development if a part of the system is added or removed, and doesn't explain how an organism regenerates – replacing missing or damaged structures. In a rush of fevered inspiration while at an ashram in India, Sheldrake worked out his hypothesis of formative causation, which states that the forms of self-organizing living things – everything from molecules and organisms to societies and even entire galaxies – are shaped by morphic fields. These

fields have a morphic resonance – a cumulative memory – of similar systems through cultures and time, so that species of animals and plants 'remember' not only how to look but also how to act ... 'Morphic resonance,' is, in his view, 'the influence of like upon like through space and time.' He believes these fields are different from electro-magnetic fields because they reverberate across generations with an inherent memory of the correct shape and form." -Lynne McTaggart, "The Field: The Quest for the Secret Force of the Universe," (46-7)

The question of form and process in nature is still a complete mystery, no matter how many fancy explanations or Latin terms scientists create. How do embryos develop from fertilized eggs? How does a tiny seed grow into a huge tree? Inside every apple seed there is the potential to grow an entire apple tree with deep roots, winding branches, colorful leaves, and hundreds of apples with thousands more seeds inside! Where is this amazing blueprint in those tiny seeds? How does part of the seed become a root, another part become a branch, another part become a leaf, and another part become an apple?

"Imagine a little acorn planted in the ground. The form and shape of that little acorn, hidden in the earth, is vastly different from the giant tree it will become, with branches sticking out in every direction, leaves and bark, roots reaching far into the earth. We could say that the acorn contains some kind of genetic program that tells it how to grow and how to form. But, where is this program? If we said this genetic program was within the DNA, science and biologists such as Rupert Sheldrake, tell us we would be wrong. DNA codes for proteins and the micro components which make up proteins. Coding the structure of single, solitary parts that make up organisms, such as proteins, is very different than coding the shape and structure of an entire organism." -Eric Pepin, "Handbook of the Navigator" (77)

In 1921 an interesting phenomenon relevant to morphic fields was first observed in Southampton, England. In the morning when people came out to get the milk from their doorsteps, they found the cardboard lids torn to shreds and the cream disappeared from their bottles. It turns out blue tit birds in the area had learned to perch atop the bottles, pull off the cardboard lids with their beaks and drink the cream. Several months later this phenomenon began occurring elsewhere in Britain about 50 miles away, then later about 100 miles away, then again and again in many diverse locations throughout Europe:

"Whenever the bluetit phenomenon turned up, it started spreading locally, presumably by imitation. However, bluetits are very home-loving creatures, and they don't normally travel more than four or five miles. Therefore, the dissemination of the behavior over large distances could only be accounted for in terms of an independent discovery of the habit ... The people who did the study came to the conclusion that it must have been 'invented' independently at least 50 times. Moreover, the rate of spread of the habit accelerated as time went on ... Here is an example of a pattern of behavior which was spread in a way which seemed to speed up with time, and which might provide an example of morphic resonance." -Eric Pepin, "Handbook of the Navigator" (79-80)

Decades later, further evidence for morphic resonance was provided by Dutch blue tits. Due to the German occupation of Holland during World War II, their milk delivery ceased in 1939, not to resume again until 1948 (9 years later). Since the average lifespan of a blue tit is only 2-3 years, it is safe to assume that none of them alive in 1939 were still around in 1948, yet mysteriously when milk delivery resumed, the phenomenon quickly sprang up again in diverse locations spreading rapidly throughout the country. This time, however, the behavior began right away and independently popped up in various places at a higher rate of frequency. This lends credence to the idea that the evolutionary spread of new behaviors are likely not genetic but rather due to a kind of "collective memory" phenomenon like Sheldrake's morphogenic fields or Carl Jung's collective unconscious.

"Jung thought of the collective unconscious as a collective memory, the collective memory of humanity. He thought that people would be more tuned into members of their own family and race and social and cultural group, but that nevertheless there would be a background resonance from all humanity: a pooled or averaged experience of basic things that all people experience (e.g., maternal behavior and various social patterns and structures of experience and thought). It would not be a memory from particular persons in the past so much as an average of the basic forms of memory structures; these are the archetypes. Jung's notion of the collective unconscious makes extremely good sense in the context of the general approach that I am putting forward. Morphic resonance theory would lead to a radical reaffirmation of Jung's concept of the collective unconscious." –Rupert Sheldrake, "Morphic Resonance" (11-12)

Biologist Lyall Watson in his book "Lifetide" also offers evidence in support of Sheldrake's theory with his discovery of "the hundredth monkey effect." This phenomenon was first observed during an experiment on a remote Japanese island where scientists were leaving sweet potatoes on the beach to feed  Macaque monkeys. These particular monkeys had never eaten sweet potatoes before; they enjoyed them very much but didn't like eating the beach sand covering them. Soon one intelligent monkey started taking his potatoes to the shoreline and scrubbing them underwater which both removed the sand and gave them a desirable salty taste. Shortly after this more and more monkeys began to copy the potato washing habit until the entire island's monkey population was doing it. Next, strangely, whole communities of Macaques on many other unconnected islands not part of the experiment, Macaques who already ate sweet potatoes as a staple food, spontaneously began washing their potatoes in the sea as well! There was no possible connection or communication between the islands or various communities of Macaques, so how and why did this behavior spread?

"Consider the hypothesis that if you train rats to learn a new trick in Santa Barbara, then rats all over the world should be able to learn to do the same trick more quickly, just because the rats in Santa Barbara have learned it. This new pattern of learning will be, as it were, in the rat collective memory -in the morphic fields of rats, to which other rats can tune in, just because they are rats and just because they are in similar circumstances, by morphic resonance. This may seem a bit improbable, but either this sort of thing happens or it doesn't. Among the vast number of papers in the archives of experiments on rat psychology, there are a number of examples of experiments in which people have actually monitored rates of learning over time and discovered mysterious increases. In my book, A New Science of Life, I describe one such series of experiments which extended over a 50-year period. Begun at Harvard and then carried on in Scotland and Australia, the experiment demonstrated that rats increased their rate of learning more than tenfold. This was a huge effect - not some marginal statistically significant result. This improved rate of learning in identical learning situations occurred in these three separate locations and in all rats of the breed, not just in rats descended from trained parents." –Rupert Sheldrake, "Morphic Resonance" (6-7)

Monica England of Nottingham University's Psychology Department knew about Sheldrake's theory of morphic resonance and devised an interesting experiment to test for collective consciousness in humans. She reasoned that if morphic resonance is occurring, it should be easier to do today's newspaper crossword puzzle tomorrow than it would have been yesterday. London's Evening Standard newspaper provided their crossword in advance for her experiment. First students all completed a control crossword to measure their ability, then half were tested in Nottingham

the day before and half the day after the crossword was published in London. Amazingly, the students who did the already published crossword (the puzzle that had already been completed by thousands of Evening Standard readers) improved their scores by an average of 25% What can account for this huge jump in scores?

In another similar study, two teams from Australia and Britain did an experiment with face recognition. They created a photo image with over a hundred faces in it, big ones, small ones, faces within faces etc. then asked people to point out as many faces as they could find within an allotted time. Because they were so well hidden a control group of several hundred Australians could only see about six to ten faces total. Then back in England, the other team of researchers showed a group of volunteers the picture on a closed-cable BBC TV station with a narrator pointing out one-by-one every single face. A few minutes later the Australian team repeated the experiment with several hundred more volunteers ready and waiting. Amazingly, this time most people were able to find not just a few, but the majority of faces within the allotted time limit! What could account for this other than some mechanism like Jung's collective memory or Sheldrake's morphic resonance? The typical "DNA" explanation is insufficient.

"As we will see, this model does not work very well. The genetic program is assumed to be identical with DNA, the genetic chemical. The genetic information is coded in DNA and this code forms the genetic program. But such a leap requires projecting onto DNA properties that it does not actually possess. We know what DNA does: it codes for proteins; it codes for the sequence of amino acids which form proteins. However, there is a big difference between coding for the structure of a protein - a chemical constituent of the organism - and programming the development of an entire organism. It is the difference between making bricks and building a house out of the bricks. You need the bricks to build the house. If you

99

have defective bricks, the house will be defective. But the plan of the house is not contained in the bricks, or the wires, or the beams, or cement. Analogously, DNA only codes for the materials from which the body is constructed: the enzymes, the structural proteins, and so forth. There is no evidence that it also codes for the plan, the form, the morphology of the body." -Rupert Sheldrake, "Morphic Resonance" (3-4)

More scientific verification for Sheldrake's theory came from Yale University with Dr. Harold S. Burr's studies of electromagnetic radiation fields. He discovered that there are electrical fields surrounding all organisms from molds, bacteria and plants to salamanders, frogs and humans, and that within these fields there exists an observable energetic blueprint of each organism's future. For instance plant seedlings have electrical fields which resemble the eventual adult plant. Baby salamanders possess energy fields shaped like adult salamanders and the energetic blueprint can even be seen in an unfertilized egg.

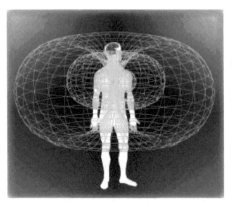

"Each species has its own fields, and within each organism there are fields within fields. Within each of us is the field of the whole body; fields for arms and legs and fields for kidneys and livers; within are fields for the different tissues inside these organs, and then fields for the cells, and fields for the sub-cellular structures, and fields for the molecules, and so on. There is a whole series of fields within fields. The essence of the hypothesis I am proposing is that these fields, which are already accepted quite widely within biology, have a kind of in-built memory derived from previous forms of a similar kind. The liver field is shaped by the forms of previous livers and the oak tree field by the forms and organization of previous oak trees. Through the fields, by a process called morphic resonance, the influence of like upon like, there is a connection among similar fields.

That means that the field's structure has a cumulative memory, based on what has happened to the species in the past." –Rupert Sheldrake, "Morphic Resonance" (5)

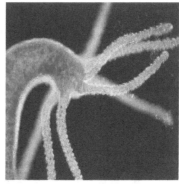

Elmer Lund at the University of Texas discovered that he could control the regeneration of limbs in hydras using electrical fields. By applying an electrical current strong enough to override the hydras' natural morphogenic field, he was able to cause heads to form where tails should be and vice versa. Similar experiments have been performed on flatworms, salamanders and other organisms all of which have had their natural "genetic" or "morphogenic" data re-programmed by electrical frequencies. This provides yet more evidence that all organisms must be involved in some type of energetic data transference that determines things like form and process in nature. It seems DNA holds the blueprint, but rather than being set in stone, it is constantly being edited and re-worked by various fields of influence both from within and outside our bodies.

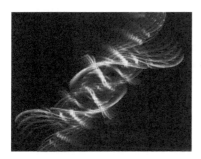

"Rather than a system of fortunate but ultimately random error, if DNA uses frequencies of all variety as an information tool, this would suggest instead a feedback system of perfect communication through waves which encode and transfer information." -Lynne McTaggart, "The Field: The Quest for the Secret Force of the Universe," (51)

"One fact which led to the development of this theory is the remarkable ability organisms have to repair damage. If you cut an oak tree into little pieces, each little piece, properly treated, can grow into a new tree. So from a tiny fragment, you can get a whole. Machines do not do that; they do not have this power of remaining whole if you remove parts of them. Chop a computer up into small pieces and all you get is a broken computer. It does not regenerate into lots of little computers. But if you chop a flatworm into small pieces, each piece can grow into a new

101

flatworm. Another analogy is a magnet. If you chop a magnet into small pieces, you do have lots of small magnets, each with a complete magnetic field. This is a holistic property that fields have that mechanical systems do not have unless they are associated with fields. Still another example is the hologram, any part of which contains the whole. A hologram is based on interference patterns within the electromagnetic field. Fields thus have a holistic property which was very attractive to the biologists who developed this concept of morphogenetic fields." –Rupert Sheldrake, "Morphic Resonance" (5)

The Human Energy Body

During the 1990s three independent scientific studies brought to light the importance of DNA and emotions in creating quantum reality. The first major study performed by Vladimir Poponin and Peter Gariaev at the Russian Academy of Science was deemed the "Phantom DNA Experiment" and yielded some fascinating results. First they created a vacuum in a specially designed test tube, and then measured the location

of light photons inside to see if they were clumped at the bottom, clung to the sides, or dispersed all throughout. As expected, the photons were scattered randomly throughout the tube. When a strand of DNA was placed in the tube, however, the particles acted as if drawn by an invisible force and spontaneously arranged themselves around the DNA strand! Even stranger, when the DNA was removed from the tube, the particles stayed in exactly the same shape. This is notable because nothing in conventional physics allows for such an effect, yet now we have observable documented proof that DNA, the substance that composes us, can have a direct and powerful effect on the quantum world around us.

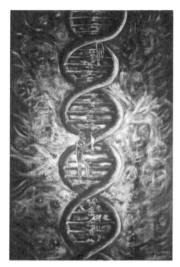

"This experiment is important for a number of reasons. Perhaps the most obvious is that it clearly shows us a direct relationship between DNA and the energy that our world is made of. Of the many conclusions that we may draw from this powerful demonstration, two are certain: 1. A type of energy exists that has previously gone unrecognized. 2. Cells/DNA influence matter through this form of energy. Produced under the rigid control of laboratory conditions, evidence arose of the powerful relationship that ancient traditions have held sacred for centuries. The DNA changed the behavior of the light particles – the essence of our world. Just as our most cherished traditions and spiritual texts have informed us for so long, the experiment validated that we have a direct effect on the world around us. Beyond wishful thinking and New Age isms, this impact is real. The DNA phantom effect shows us that under the right conditions and with proper equipment, this relationship can be documented." -Gregg Braden, "The Divine Matrix" (45-6)

Around the same time Poponin and Gariaev recorded their Phantom DNA findings, similar experiments were being conducted by the U.S. Army testing the power of emotion on DNA and living cells. They hooked volunteers up to specially designed electrometers then played series' of graphic video images designed to create genuine states of feeling (from comedy to torture to erotica) in order to collect a broad spectrum of emotional fluctuation. Just as expected, peaks and dips in volunteers' electrical responses coincided perfectly with changes in emotional stimuli. The big surprise came during the next phase in which they took tissue/DNA swabs from the volunteers, placed them in a vault several hundred feet away, and repeated the experiment. Strangely enough, the tissue/DNA samples locked hundreds of feet away still registered the same electrical peaks and dips coincident with the donor's response to emotional video clips.

"For the DNA and the donor to have any connection whatsoever, there must be something that links them together. The experiment suggests four things: A previously unrecognized form of energy exists between living tissues; Cells and DNA communicate through this field of energy; Human emotion has a direct influence on living DNA; Distance appears to be of no consequence with regard to the effect." -Gregg Braden, "The Divine Matrix" (49-50)

Dr. Cleve Backster more recently performed this experiment with a distance of 350 miles between the donor and his cells. Even at this extreme distance, in experiments gauged by an atomic clock, the donor and his cells still responded absolutely identically, simultaneously! The fact that a donor and his DNA 350 miles away have such coincident responses suggests that the energy of the donor's emotions doesn't "travel" anywhere but is already everywhere, as demonstrated by Bohm's holographic universe metaphor. This experiment also grants credence to such practices as prayer and energy healing, showing that emotion and intention can produce measurable physiological results at any distance.

"We've been conditioned to believe that the state of the DNA in our body is a given. Contemporary thinking suggests that it's a fixed quantity – we 'get what we get' when we're born – and with the exception of drugs, chemicals, and electrical fields, our DNA doesn't change in response to anything that we can do in our lives. But this experiment shows us that nothing could be further from the truth ... There's absolutely nothing in conventional wisdom that allows for the material of life in our bodies to have any effect whatsoever on our outer world. And there's also nothing to suggest that human emotion can in any way affect DNA when it's

inside the body of its owner, let alone when it's hundreds of miles away. Yet this is precisely what the results are showing us." -Gregg Braden, "The Divine Matrix" (52)

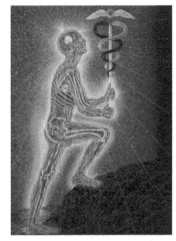

The third relevant study conducted around this time was performed at the Institute of HeartMath in Northern California. Scientists began by isolating human DNA in glass beakers then exposed them to "coherent emotion" which is an intentionally created physiological state achieved by practicing specially designed mental/emotional self-management techniques such as meditation and deep breathing. Volunteers trained in applying coherent emotion directed it towards the glass beakers and actually succeeded in changing both the physical and chemical structures of the DNA! Different directed intentions produced varying effects on the DNA molecules causing them to wind or unwind, change shape or even separate atomic/chemical components.

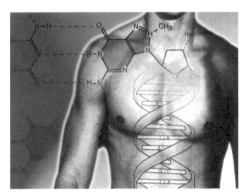

"In the first experiment, Poponin showed us that human DNA has a direct effect on the vibration of light. In the second – the military experiment – we learned that whether we're in the same room with our DNA or separated by distances of hundreds of miles, we're still connected to its molecules, and the effect is the same. In the third experiment, the HeartMath researchers showed us that human emotion has a direct effect on DNA, which in turn directly impacts the stuff our world is made of. This is the beginning of a technology – an inner technology – that does more than simply tell us we can have an effect on our bodies and our world ... it shows us that this effect exists and how it works!" -Gregg Braden, "The Divine Matrix" (53)

In further studies The HeartMath Institute found that our hearts actually have the strongest magnetic field in the body and that field has an effect well beyond our own bodies. When we feel love or joy the heart's magnetic field relaxes and unwinds DNA, but when we feel anger or frustration it tightens and winds up. Furthermore, when tested for immune response, researchers found the relaxed DNA performed far more proficiently than the control group while the tightened DNA performed far worse. This proves scientifically that positive/negative emotions alter both our DNA and our immune systems, which means our emotional states are significant contributing factors in our physical health and wellness.

"If you are someone who thinks sad, angry or negative thoughts most of the day, you are weakening your immune system. The chemicals in your body which fight off infection can be clinically shown to decrease." - Cathy Chapman, Ph.D. "Strengthening the Immune System"

"All these experiments suggest two similar conclusions, which are the crux of this book: 1) There is something 'out there': the matrix of an energy that connects any one thing with everything else in the universe. This connective field accounts for the unexpected results of the experiments. 2) The DNA in our bodies gives us access to the energy that connects our universe, and emotion is the key to tapping in to the field." -Gregg Braden, "The Divine Matrix" (53)

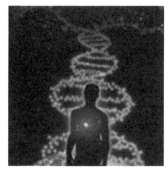

"When quantum physics was first becoming accepted as the mechanisms by which the universe operates, the physicists had trouble with this themselves. They could say, 'Well, I can see these ideas working at the level of atoms and molecules but I can't bring that kind of weirdness into my life.' So there was an arbitrary decision back in the 1920s to say, 'Let's restrict quantum mechanics to the world of atoms and molecules and use Newtonian physics to describe the rest of the world.' That is why biology went on its merry way using Newtonian physics. Yet we are today beginning to see work by very reputable scientists that says the universe is created by our observations; we create the field and the field shapes the particle. The big lesson is that what you think or ask for is what you are going to get. It is not a coincidence; we are actively involved in physically shaping the world that we experience." -Dr. Bruce Lipton, "How Your Beliefs Control Your Biology"

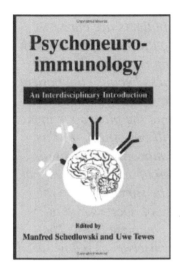

There is an entire legitimate and well-researched branch of medicine called "psychoneuroimmunology" which studies the effect of thoughts and emotions on human biochemistry. Biologist Dr. Bruce Lipton actually left his tenured University position to pursue his research in this fascinating field.

"Until recently, conventional medicine dismissed the role of the mind in the functioning of the body, except for one pesky exception - the placebo effect, which demonstrates that the mind has the power to heal the body when people hold a belief that a particular drug or procedure will effect a cure, even if the remedy is actually a sugar pill with no known pharmaceutical value. Medical students learn that one third of all illnesses heal via the magic of the placebo effect. With further education, these same students will come to dismiss the value of the mind in healing because it doesn't fit into the flow charts of the Newtonian paradigm. Unfortunately, as doctors, they will unwittingly disempower their patients by not encouraging the healing power inherent in the mind." -Dr. Bruce Lipton, "Spontaneous Evolution"

The placebo effect cures one-third of all illnesses. This is a staggering statistic - It means that a wide range of health problems can be cured by our minds! In fact many ailments are literally created, sustained, and eventually healed via completely non-physical processes involving the mind and emotions. Acne, allergies, angina pectoris, rheumatoid

and degenerative arthritis, asthma, cancer, the common cold, diabetes, fever, multiple sclerosis, Parkinson's disease, radiation sickness, seasickness, ulcers, and many more diseases have all been cured using a mere placebo. This of course strikes another blow at the root of the western medical paradigm which traditionally teaches health as a purely physical bio-chemical phenomenon. The non-physical psycho-emotional aspects of health are dismissively disregarded.

"In numerous cases patients are cured simply by taking the placebo alone and with no genuine supporting medication whatsoever. This works because the patient sincerely believes, beyond any doubt in the mind of the patient that the placebo is in fact real medicine that will cure them. In this case the patient has subconsciously used their own imagination upon themselves, but the result is exactly the same, often to the considerable surprise of doctors and all others concerned; a complete cure. The patient visualized themselves as being cured as a direct result of taking what they believe to be an effective medicine, in turn influencing the energy of the inner bodies, thereby manifesting as an observable cure within the physical body. This process works both ways of course and there are people who unwittingly become ill due to the subconscious use of creative visualization and of the imagination generally and thought processes generally. This occurs when a normally healthy person strongly believes they are, or should become ill for some reason, perhaps out of guilt, or for example as happens in the case of someone considered to be a hypochondriac. This belief coupled with the person subconsciously and very often intensively imagining and believing themselves to be ill, will in turn attract that illness." -Adrian Cooper, "Our Ultimate Reality" (563-4)

Experiments have shown that even an injection of caffeine will put caffeine-sensitive patients to sleep if they believe that they are receiving a sedative. People with multiple personalities can change eye color, turn off/on allergies, and even have multiple menstruation cycles for each personality. Under hypnosis people can control heart rate, body temperature, visual acuity, and will away scars and birthmarks. If humans are simply biochemical machines as the western medical paradigm professes, and our beliefs/subconscious plays no role in bodily

health, how can such physical effects possibly come about from non-physical causes?

"We may not think that a thought could be enough to undermine an entire system, but, in fact, misperceptions can be lethal. Consider the situation of a person with anorexia. While relatives and friends clearly perceive that this skin-and-bones individual is near death, the anorexic looks in a mirror and sees a fat person. Using this distorted view, that resembles an image in a funhouse mirror, the anorexic's brain attempts to control a misperceived runaway weight gain, by-oops!-inhibiting the system's metabolic functions."

-Dr. Bruce Lipton, "Spontaneous Evolution"

"Even surgery has been used as a placebo. In the 1950s, angina pectoris, recurrent pain in the chest and left arm due to decreased blood flow to the heart, was commonly treated with surgery. Then some resourceful doctors decided to conduct an experiment. Rather than perform the customary surgery, which involved tying off the mammary artery, they cut patients open and then simply sewed them back up again. The patients who received the sham surgery reported just as much relief as the patients who had the full surgery." -Michael Talbot, "The Holographic Universe" (90)

Psychologist Shlomo Breznitz at Hebrew University in Jerusalem performed a telling experiment with several troops of Israeli soldiers. Each troop had to march 40 kilometers but different groups were given different information. Some groups were told they would march 30 kilometers, and later informed they had another 10 to go, other groups were told they would march 60 kilometers, but were then stopped after 40. Some groups were allowed to see distance markers along the way to keep track of how far they had marched; other groups were not shown distance markers. Once the 40 kilometers were complete Breznitz performed blood tests and found that the stress hormone levels in the soldiers' blood always reflected their projections and not the actual distance they marched. This experiment shows another example of our bodies physically responding not to "reality" but to our perception of reality.

"*Just as surely as positive thoughts can heal, negative ones - including the belief we are susceptible to an illness or have been exposed to a toxic condition - can actually manifest the undesired realities of those thoughts. Japanese children allergic to a poison ivy-like plant took part in an experiment where a leaf of the poisonous plant was rubbed onto one forearm. As a control, a nonpoisonous leaf resembling the toxic plant was rubbed on the other forearm. As expected almost all of the children broke out in a rash on the arm rubbed with the toxic leaf and had no response to the imposter leaf. What the children did not know was that the leaves were purposefully mislabeled. The negative thought of being touched by the poisonous plant led to the rash produced by the nontoxic leaf! In the majority of cases, no rash resulted from contact with the toxic leaf that was thought to be the harmless control. The conclusion is simple: positive perceptions enhance health, and negative perceptions precipitate disease. This mind-bending example of the power of belief was one of the founding experiments that led to the science of psychoneuroimmunology.*" -Dr. Bruce Lipton, "Spontaneous Evolution"

"*Our ability to control the body holographic is molded by our beliefs. Our minds have the power to get rid of warts, to clear our bronchial tubes, and to mimic the painkilling ability of morphine, but because we are unaware that we possess the power, we must be fooled into using it ... No incident better illustrates this than a now famous case reported by psychologist Bruno Klopfer.*" -Michael Talbot, "The Holographic Universe" (93)

110

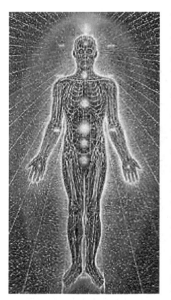

Dr. Bruno Klopfer had exhausted all standard treatments trying to cure a man named Wright of his advanced cancer of the lymph nodes. Wright's entire torso from groin to neck was covered in tomato-sized tumors. His spleen and liver were so enlarged and toxic that he had two quarts of milky fluid drained out of him every day. At his wits end, Wright heard about an exciting new experimental drug called Krebiozen and begged Dr. Klopfer to let him try it. At first Klopfer refused because Krebiozen was in the testing phase and only being tried on people with very short life expectancies. Regardless Wright was persistent and insisted that they try this remedy.

Eventually Klopfer agreed and within a week Wright's tumors "melted like snowballs on a hot stove" to half their original size, a result far surpassing even the strongest radiation therapy. Within another week, the tumors had vanished completely and Wright walked out of the hospital seemingly cancer-free. Later on, after two months of good health, Wright began reading articles on the internet claiming that Krebiozen actually had no effect on cancer of the lymph nodes. He started becoming nervous and depressed reading more and more studies until he suffered a relapse, all the tumors came back and he had to be readmitted to the hospital. Seeing that Wright's hypochondria brought back the tumors, this time Dr. Klopfer decided to try an experiment. He informed Wright that Krebiozen in fact was effective on lymph node cancer as they had seen themselves, but some of the initial supplies had deteriorated during shipping and that was to blame for the relapse. Furthermore, Klopfer said he just received a new highly concentrated version of Krebiozen and this time it would work for sure. Wright enthusiastically agreed, rolled up his sleeve, and his fibbing doctor injected him with a plain water placebo. Miraculously within days Wright's tumors once again melted away, his chest fluid emptied, and he was released from the hospital feeling healthy and symptom-free from the mere water injection. About two months after this the American Medical Association published their nationwide study of Krebiozen which flatly stated that the drug had no effect whatsoever on treating cancer. Wright read the study and was devastated. He immediately lost all faith in the treatment causing the tumors and chest fluid to come back full force, and he died two days later.

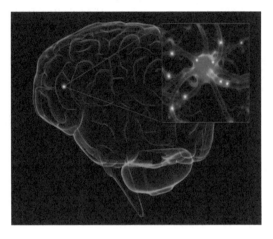

"One reason why people who are not aware of true healing cannot be cured is because they believe in their own mind that only doctors, surgeons and other members of the medical profession can 'cure' an illness. Unfortunately, that very belief will ensure that true healing will not be effective, due to the fact the true channels of healing will be blocked by the conscious and subconscious mind, and energy influenced in the same direction. It is sensible to visit a doctor with any ailment, and to respect their words and actions, but it is extremely important to know beyond any doubt the true origin of healing, and to focus accordingly. Even if you are given a course of medicine, exercises or even a surgical procedure, view these as secondary influences while always knowing that the primary and true healing influence is by virtue of the energy from which we are all made." -Adrian Cooper, "Our Ultimate Reality" (571)

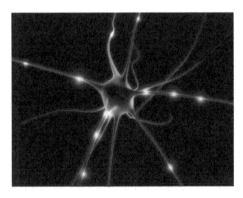

Our brains are made up of tiny nerve cells called "neurons" which branch out and connect to each other forming a neural network. At each connection point, thoughts and emotions are incubated and holographically stored by associative memory. This means that all ideas, thoughts, feelings, and memories are interconnected and have possible relationships with one another. For instance the concept of motherhood is stored in all our neural networks, but each person's concept is built from their own unique amalgamation of ideas, emotions and past experiences. Some people may have motherhood connected to unconditional love and forgiveness, so when they think about motherhood, they experience memories/feelings of happiness and acceptance. Other people may have motherhood connected to disappointment and ridicule, so when they think about motherhood, they experience memories/feelings of rejection and depression. We all build our own neural networks based on our own subjective experiences, how we perceive and what we believe.

"What we ultimately do is tell ourselves a story about what the outside world is. Any information that we process, any information that we take in from the environment is always colored by the experiences that we've had and an emotional response that we're having to what we're bringing in. Who is in the driver's seat when we control our emotions or we respond to our emotions? We know physiologically that nerve cells that fire together, wire together. If you practice something over and over, those nerve cells have a long-term relationship. If you get angry on a daily basis, if you get frustrated on a daily basis, if you suffer on a daily basis, if you give reason for the victimization in your life, you're rewiring and reintegrating that neural net on a daily basis, and that neural net now has a long-term relationship with all those other nerve cells called an 'identity.' We also know that nerve cells that don't fire together, no longer wire together. They lose their long-term relationship because every time we interrupt the thought process that produces a chemical response in the body, every time we interrupt it, those nerve cells that are connected to each other start breaking the long-term relationship." –Dr. Joe Dispenza, "What the Bleep Do We Know?"

Inside our brains, the hypothalamus acts like a tiny factory assembling various chemicals called "peptides," small chain amino acid sequences that match the different emotions we experience. There are quite literally chemical combinations for sadness, chemical combinations for anger, chemical combinations for fear, and chemical combinations for love. There are chemical combinations to match every emotional state we experience. So the moment we feel anger, the hypothalamus immediately

113

assembles a complementary neuro-peptide or neuro-hormone and releases it through the pituitary gland into the blood stream. Once in the bloodstream, the peptides/hormones work their way through the body and we begin developing long-term relationships between thoughts/emotions and our physical biochemistry.

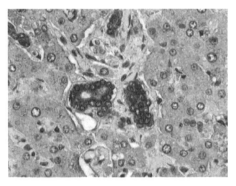

"Candace Pert, former chief of brain biochemistry at the National Institute of Mental Health, believes the separation of mind and body is also an illusion. She and her co-workers have discovered that neuropeptides previously thought to exist only in the brain are found throughout the body.
Neuropeptides are known to be important in the flow of electrical activity, resulting in transmission of electrical signals from one neuron to another when emotional activity is going on. Thus, they are believed to be messenger molecules literally carrying information around the brain. Finding them throughout the body suggests that mind is present throughout the body and that emotions are the links between matter and mind." -Fred Alan Wolf, Ph.D., "The Spiritual Universe" (193)

"Thoughts change brain chemistry. That sounds so simple but that's the way it is, with our thoughts changing neurotransmitters on a daily basis. If a man walks into a room with a gun, we think "threat", and the brain releases norepinephrine. We become tense, alert, develop sweaty palms, and our heart beats faster. If he then bites the barrel of the gun, telling us the gun is actually chocolate, the brain rapidly changes its opinion and we relax and laugh — the joke is on us... We feel what we think! Positive thinking works. As the above example suggests, what we think about a situation actually creates our mood. Passed over for a promotion, we can either think we'll never get ahead in this job (lowering serotonin and making us depressed) or assume that we are being held back for another promotion or job

transfer (makes a better mood)." -Dr. Joseph M. Carver PhD, "Emotional Memory Management: Positive Control Over Your Memory"

Every single cell in the body has thousands of peptide receptors scattered around its surface. When a peptide enters a receptor it sends a signal to the cell which actually alters its physical and chemical makeup. If we are constantly bombarding our cells with the same negative attitudes, emotions, and beliefs, our biochemistry adapts by creating more receptor sites for those particular peptides. This leaves less receptors for essentials like nutrients, vitamins, minerals, fluid exchange, detoxing and as a result we start becoming physically / chemically addicted to the peptides produced by our negative emotions.

"We bring to ourselves situations that will fulfill the biochemical craving of the cells of our body by creating situations that meet our chemical needs. And the addict will always need a little bit more in order to get a rush or a high of what they're

looking for chemically. So my definition really means that if you can't control your emotional state, you must be addicted to it ... It's biochemical. Think about this. Heroin uses the same receptor mechanisms on the cells that our emotional chemicals use. It's easy to see then that if we can be addicted to heroin then we can be addicted to any neural peptide, any emotion." -Dr. Joe Dispenza, "What the Bleep Do We Know?"

Much like drug addicts, people often become physically/chemically addicted and dependent on various negative states of being such as depression, victimization, frustration, or jealousy. Over time we crave more of the peptides we're addicted to and create repetitive dramas in our lives in order to receive our next dose. As this behavior continues and our unhealthy cells divide, they create sickly offspring with more receptors for neuropeptides, less receptors for essential nutrients, and become unable to carry on proper protein production.

"Now, all aging is the result of improper protein production. What happens when we age? Our skin loses elasticity. Well, elastin is a protein. What happens to our enzymes? We don't digest as well. What happens to our synovial fluid? Those are proteins that become brittle and stiff. What happens to our bones? They become thin. So all aging is a result of improper protein production. So then the question arises ... does nutrition really have an effect if the cell doesn't even have the receptor sites after years of emotional abuse to even receive or to let in the nutrients that are necessary for its health?" - JZ Knight, "What the Bleep Do We Know?"

Here we see once again how negative thoughts/emotions/beliefs, especially habitual patterns, lead to physical disease and degeneration. On the flip side however, living with positive, life-affirming, non-limiting thoughts/emotions/beliefs leads to physical health, wellness, and even miraculous supernormal abilities.

One such ability of mind over matter is known as "Inedia" or "Breatharianism." While normal people die after a couple months without food, or a few days without water, breatharians have lived for years without either! For example, a devout Christian named Therese Neumann did not eat or drink for 35 years. In 1923 she began to drink only liquids and by 1927 she stopped even that. Under the close eye of a medical doctor and four Franciscan nurses, she was watched 24 hours a day and confirmed not to have eaten or drank anything for 2 weeks with no ill-effects, dehydration or weight loss.

"When the local bishop in Regensburg first learned of Neumann's fast, he sent a commission into her home to investigate. From July 14, 1927, to July 29, 1927, and under the supervision of a medical doctor named Seidl, four Franciscan nursing sisters scrutinized her every move. They watched her day and night, and the water she used for washing and rinsing her mouth was carefully measured and weighed. The sisters discovered several unusual things about Neumann. She never went to the bathroom (even after a period of six weeks she only had one bowel movement, and the excrement, examined by a Dr. Reismanns, contained only a small amount of mucus and bile, but no traces of food). She also showed no signs of dehydration, even though the average human expels about four hundred grams of water daily in the air he or she exhales, and a like amount through the pores. And her weight remained constant ... At the end of the inquiry Dr. Seidl and the sisters were completely convinced that Neumann had not eaten or drunk a thing for the entire fourteen days. The test seems conclusive, for while the human body can survive two weeks without food, it can rarely survive half that time without water. Yet this was nothing for Neumann; she did not eat or drink a thing for the next thirty-five years." -Michael Talbot, "The Holographic Universe" (153)

 Jainist Hira Ratan Manek claims not to have eaten anything since 1995. He has been studied under controlled conditions by teams of scientists and doctors many times and was never observed to eat or drink at all. One time he went 211 days under careful supervision, another time 411 days. Even more impressive, 81 year-old Indian Sadhu Prahlad Jani claims not to have eaten or drunk anything for 70 years! He was also studied carefully under 24 hour CCTV surveillance for weeks at a time by medical professionals and didn't eat, drink, urinate, or deficate. Many more

examples of documented inedia can be found in Herbert Thurston's book "The Physical Phenomena of Mysticism."

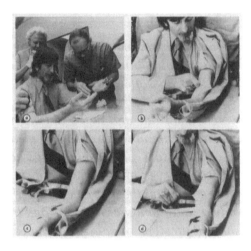

"In the 1970s, Jack Schwarz, a Dutch-born author and lecturer, astounded researchers in laboratories across the United States with his ability to willfully control his body's internal biological processes. In studies conducted at the Menninger Foundation, the University of California's Langley Porter Neuropsychiatric Institute, and other, Schwarz astonished doctors by sticking mammoth six-inch sailmaker's needles completely through his arms without bleeding, without flinching, and without producing beta brain waves (the type of brain waves normally produced when a person is in pain). Even when the needles were removed, Schwarz still did not bleed, and the puncture holes closed tightly. In addition, Schwarz altered his brain-wave rhythms at will, held burning cigarettes against his flesh without harming himself, and even carried live coals around in his hands. He claims he acquired these abilities when he was in a Nazi concentration camp and had to learn how to control pain in order to withstand the terrible beatings he endured. He believes anyone can learn voluntary control of their body and thus gain responsibility for his or her own health." -Michael Talbot, "The Holographic Universe" (102-3)

In 1947, during public performances at the Corso Theater in Zurich, Mirin Dajo stunned audiences with his extreme piercings. Dajo would have an assistant stab a fencing sword completely through his abdomen, clearly piercing vital organs, yet somehow causing him no pain or lasting injury. When the sword was removed he did not bleed and had only two small red spots at the entry and exit points. Dajo's performances were so gut-wrenching and nerve-racking that one spectator actually suffered a heart attack while watching. Having piqued the interest of one Swiss doctor named Hans Naegeli-Osjord, Dajo was invited to Switzerland to have his abilities formally studied under

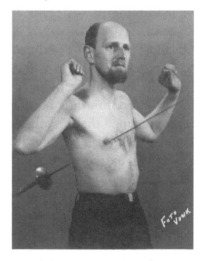

laboratory conditions. In front of a group of doctors and journalists, Dajo had his assistant stab him through with the steel rapier and as always he did not bleed or even flinch. He then calmly walked upstairs with doctors to take his X-ray which undeniably proved that no trickery was involved and he was indeed impaled. Dajo was later tested again by scientists in Basel and allowed them to personally stab him. He even insisted that they treat him roughly and jogged several blocks while impaled to show his tolerance for pain.

Mirin Dago and Jack Schwartz's stories are certainly amazing but far from unique. Hawaiian Kahunas, Indian Yogis, African Shamans and others have traditionally trained to control their pain receptors so as to perform extreme piercings, lie on beds of nails, and walk on burning hot coals.

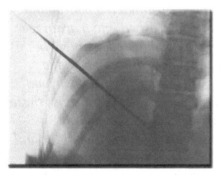

"For thousands of years, people of many different cultures and religions from all parts of the world have practiced fire walking. A recent Guinness World Record for longest fire walk was set by 23-year-old Canadian Amanda Dennison in June 2005. Amanda walked 220 feet over coals that measured 1,600 to1,800 degrees Fahrenheit. Amanda didn't jump or fly, which means her feet were in direct contact with the glowing coals for the full 30 seconds it took her to complete the walk. Many people attribute the ability to remain burn-free during such a walk to paranormal phenomena. In contrast, physicists suggest that the presumed danger is an illusion,

claiming the embers are not great conductors of heat and that the walker's feet have limited contact with the coals. Yet, very few scoffers have actually removed their shoes and socks and traversed the glowing coals, and none have matched the feat of Amanda's feet. Besides, if the coals are really as benign as the physicists suggest, how do they account for severe burns experienced by large numbers of 'accidental tourists' on their firewalks?" -Dr. Bruce Lipton, "Spontaneous Evolution"

For most people, fire walking will burn their feet, extreme piercings will cause severe pain/bleeding, and prolonged dry fasting will result in certain death, but for people who have reprogrammed their psyches with non-limiting beliefs, such feats become attainable. Another example is extreme weight lifting. The strongest record-holding bodybuilders can dead lift about 700-800 pounds (400-500 for females) but under intense psychological pressure untrained unathletic people have actually lifted several times this weight and held it for minutes at a time!

"To save her trapped son, Angela Cavallo lifted a 1964 Chevrolet and held it up for five minutes while neighbors arrived, reset a jack, and rescued her unconscious boy. Similarly, a construction worker lifted a 3,000-pound helicopter that had crashed into a drainage ditch, trapping his buddy under water. In this feat captured on video, the man held the aircraft aloft while others pulled his friend from beneath the wreckage. To dismiss these feats as the consequence of an adrenaline rush misses the point. Adrenaline or not, how can an untrained average man or woman lift and hold a half ton or more for an extended duration? These stories are remarkable because neither Ms. Cavallo nor the construction worker could have performed such acts of superhuman strength under normal circumstances. The idea of lifting a car or helicopter is unimaginable. But with the life of their child or friend hanging in the balance, these people unconsciously suspended their limiting beliefs and focused their intention

on the foremost belief at that moment: I must save this life!" -Dr. Bruce Lipton, "Spontaneous Evolution"

The movie "Star Wars" is famous for its idea of "the Force" which is described as "an energy field created by all living things that surrounds us, penetrates us, and binds the galaxy together." Though the Force is treated as fiction by Hollywood and most Westerners, in fact the concept has a rich history around the world. In traditional Chinese philosophy and medicine it is called "Chi." Japanese mystics and martial artists call it "Ki." Indian yogis and sadhus call it "Prana." The Ancient Greeks called it "Pneuma." Jewish Kabbalists call it "Nefish." Christians call it the "Holy Ghost." Muslims call it "Baraka." And the Polynesians call it "Mana."

"Qi or chi is the source of everything, the building block of all things. Human beings are made of living cells, and when we look into each cell we see a membrane, the nucleus and so on. Then if you look further into that structure you'll see atoms - electrons, protons, and neutrons. And if you look even further, scientists now tell us that they can see energy there. However, according to the 5,000-year-old Chinese Qigong theory, if you go beyond scientific measurement - this is called the chi level. We can communicate with the chi level using our minds to do different things, such as healing."
- Luke Chan, Chi Kung Master

Chi has been studied and written about for over ten thousand years in diverse places such as China, Japan, India, Tibet, Nepal, Hawaii, and South America. It is the foundation of numerous health and fitness practices around the world including Chi Kung, Falun Gong, Reiki,

Therapeutic Touch, Acupressure and Acupuncture, Reflexology, Orgone Therapy, Pranayama, Yoga, Feng Shui, and Martial Arts.

"Through scientific experiment they have demonstrated that there may be such a thing as a life force flowing through the universe – what has variously been called collective consciousness or, as theologians have termed it, the Holy Spirit. They have provided a plausible explanation of all those areas over the centuries mankind has had faith in but no solid evidence of or adequate accounting for, from the effectiveness of alternative medicine and even prayer to life after death. They have offered us, in a sense, a science of religion." - Lynne McTaggart, "The Field: The Quest for the Secret Force of the Universe," (XXVIII)

"In Chinese philosophy, the field idea is not only implicit in the notion of the Tao as being empty and formless, and yet producing all forms, but is also expressed explicitly in the concept of ch'i. This term played an important role in almost every Chinese school of natural philosophy ... The word ch'i literally means 'gas' or 'ether', and was used in ancient China to denote the vital breath or energy animating the cosmos. In the human body, the 'pathways of ch'i' are the basis of traditional Chinese medicine. The aim of acupuncture is to stimulate the flow of ch'i through these channels. The flow of ch'i is also the basis of the flowing movements of T'ai Chi Ch'uan, the Taoist dance of the warrior. Thus ch'i condenses and disperses rhythmically, bringing forth all forms which eventually dissolve into the Void. As Chang Tsai says again, The Great Void cannot but consist of ch'i; this ch'i cannot but condense to form all things; and these

things cannot but become dispersed so as to form (once more) the Great Void. As in quantum field theory, the field - or the ch'i - is not only the underlying essence of all material objects, but also carries their mutual interactions in the form of waves." -Fritjof Capra, "The Tao of Physics" (214)

Qigong (Chi Kung) is the Chinese name for the practice of cultivating life force energy. Throughout its over 5,000 year history Qigong has been found to have countless health benefits such as increasing core strength, blood flow, bone density, enzyme activity, serum lipid levels, cardiovascular, endocrine and immune functions. It reduces stress, hypertension, and risk of stroke, cures asthma, and has anti-cancer and anti-aging effects. When emitted from a Qigong master, Chi has been scientifically verified to aid in seed germination, increase the growth of plants and various cell cultures, and reduce the size of malignant tumors. When measurements are taken between a skilled Qigong master and receiver, amazingly both show identical blood pressure, respiration, skin conductivity, EEG, and heart rate variability. (Kenneth M. Sancier PhD "Multifaceted Health Benefits of Medical Qigong")

Doctors at the Philadelphia Biomedical Rescarch Institute have performed a number of experiments testing life force energy with fascinating results. Working in conjunction with Japanese Ki Master Kozo Nishino, the Philadelphia BioMed doctors created several experiments to test the efficacy of Ki healing. In their first experiment doctors took control blood samples of 21 volunteers, assayed the activity of their NK (natural killer) cells, and tested stress levels. Next the volunteers attended a 90 minute Ki breathing session led by Master Nishino. Afterwards the volunteers were tested again and the results were significant. The NK cell

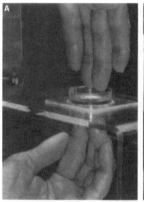

activity of 17 volunteers increased and stress hormone levels of all 21 decreased. PBRI doctors concluded that Ki breathing *"can effectively enhance the immunoregulatory system and reduce stress even after one class which indicates that the method would help improve the health of its practitioners if they continue to practice it."*

Long term students of Pranayama/Ki breathing have been found to consistently have higher bone density rates than the average population. This fact spurred a second experiment to test the effect of Ki energy on osteoblastic (bone forming) and osteoclastic (bone dissoluting) cells. First they had Master Nishino send Ki from his hands into 2 petri dishes of osteoblastic bone marrow cells for 5 and 10 minutes respectively. Next the cells were seeded in Fetal Bovine Serum, cultured for 72 hours, then counted. The dish given 5 minutes of Ki increased cell production by 6%, and the dish given 10 minutes of Ki increased cell production by 12%, both of which are quite significant. For the osteoclastic cells they

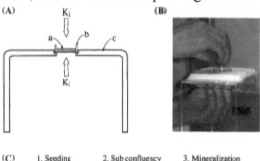

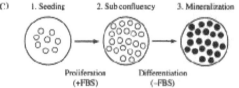

had Master Nishino send Ki from his hands into 2 petri dishes of bone marrow for 5 and 10 minutes, then added parathyroid hormone to stimulate resorption and counted the cells one week later. This time the difference between the 5 and 10 minute samples was insignificant, but the difference between the control dishes and Ki infused dishes was radical. After 7 days the Ki infused dishes contained approximately 38% less osteoclastic cells. Doctors at Philadelphia BioMed concluded that such results suggest that Pranayama/Ki therapy can indeed help heal and prevent degenerative bone diseases like osteoporosis.

In a third experiment PBRI doctors tested the effects of Qigong on cancer. This time they used human liver carcinoma cells, subjected them to 5 and 10 minute Ki sessions, cultured them overnight, then measured cell numbers, protein concentration per cell, mRNA expressions and regucalcin synthesis. Compared with the control (non-treated) cells, they found the Ki-exposed cultures contained 30.3% and 40.6% less cancer cells, and the protein content per cell in the Ki-exposed cultures were 38.8% and 62.9% higher respectively. They found that the mRNA expression for "c-myc," a tumor stimulator gene, was decreased and regucalcin, which suppresses DNA synthesis, was increased.

"We undertook this study to obtain objective and scientific evidence as to whether or not a 'Ki-effect' could inhibit the growth of cultured cancer cells ... Our molecular biological studies and mathematical model analysis demonstrated that Ki-energy inhibited cancer cell division. The data also indicate that the Ki-effects involve some form of infrared radiation from the human body. This study suggests the possibility that Ki-energy may be beneficial for cancer patients because it suppresses cancer cell growth, and at the same time, it stimulates immune functions of the patients." -Onishi T, Nishino K, Tsurusaki Y, Yamaguchi M, "Growth Inhibition of Cultured Human Liver Carcinoma Cells by Ki-Energy (Life Energy): Scientific Evidence for Ki-Effects on Cancer Cells"

"Cancer is one of the leading causes of death among human beings. Most current treatments for cancer ... come with significant drawbacks, including toxicity, costs and potential harm to both mood and immune function. Therefore, an effective non-pharmacological therapy for  *cancer with less cost and no side effects could have a major impact on cancer treatment. Qigong therapy shows promise in treating cancer and preliminary studies report immediate improvement without side effects and even complete remission in patients who engaged in ongoing practice ... Studies on Qigong and it's curative effect on cancer have demonstrated consistent results for its inhibitory effect on cancer growth and metastasis, in both in vitro and in vivo studies, as well as in clinical observation ... Our review suggests that this therapy should be seriously examined and be considered as an important supplement to conventional cancer treatment and other chronic diseases ... Unlike other alternative medicines, which are only able to cope with symptoms, Qigong therapy focuses on the entire body and its health system. Our review suggests that Qigong therapy may actually stop and prevent cancer growth, and help patients recover from many different diseases at the same time."* –Kevin Chan and Raphael Yeung, "A Review of Qigong Therapy For Cancer Treatment"

For their final study, the PBRI team designed an experiment suggested by their Ki-expert Kozo Nishino. Since most Ki cultivation techniques involve deep breathing and breathe regulation, Kozo Nishino believed that mitochondria (cells' respiratory power plants) may play a key role in maintaining vitality and health. To test the hypothesis the team used isolated rat liver mitochondria and applied Ki energy as before. The results showed that Ki had a very

126

beneficial effect protecting mitochondria, maintaining cellular metabolism, and decreasing the occurrence of unnecessary apoptosis (programmed cell death). Using infrared and visible range filters they also observed that Ki-effects involve near-infrared radiation with a wavelength range between 0.8 and 2.7 μm.

"We are demonstrating that so-called 'Ki-energy' is a natural phenomenon, and therefore, it can be analyzed by rigorous scientific and objective investigations. A 'breathing method' developed by a Japanese Ki-expert, Kozo Nishino, stimulated immune activity of practitioners and lowered their stress levels. We then reported that his Ki-energy inhibited cell division of cultured human carcinoma cells. Since 'breathing' is directly related to oxygen respiration, he has long proposed that mitochondria may play a key role in maintaining vitality and health. This led us to undertake the project to explore a possible relationship between Ki-energy and mitochondrial function." -Onishi T, Nishino K, "Ki-Energy (Life-Energy) Protects Isolated Rat Liver Mitochondria from Oxidative Injury"

More verification for Ki/Chi's medical efficacy has come with Harvard professor Dr. Herbert Benson's recent studies involving the Relaxation Response and gene expression. The Relaxation Response (RR) is the physiological counterpoint to the Fight or Flight (FF) stress response. RR is characterized by decreased oxygen consumption and increased nitric oxide and carbon dioxide elimination, reduced blood pressure, heart and respiration rate, alterations in cortical/subcortical brain regions, and low psychological distress; FF is characterized by the exact opposite. Various forms of meditation, yoga, deep breathing, tai chi, qigong, repetitive prayer, progressive muscle relaxation, and other techniques all elicit this Relaxation Response. Acting through the same underlying mechanism, practitioners of these various disciplines all share (what would otherwise be) very unique physiological profiles and gene expression changes.

"Changes in the activation of these same genes have previously been seen in conditions such as post-traumatic stress disorder; but the relaxation response-associated changes were the opposite of stress-associated changes and were much more pronounced in the long-term practitioners." -Dr. Herbert Benson, "Genomic Counter-Stress Changes Induced by the Relaxation Response"

Dr. Benson's team took blood samples and assessed transcriptional profiles from three groups: long-term practitioners of various RR techniques (5-10 years), short-term practitioners (8 weeks), and a control group of healthy non-practitioners. They found that the expressions of 2,209 genes were significantly different between the long-term practitioners and the non-practitioners, and the expressions of 1,561 genes were similarly significantly different between the short-term practitioners and non-practitioners. More specifically, the results showed that long-term (and short-term to a lesser degree) cultivation of RR changes the expression of genes involved with inflammation, programmed cell death, the treatment of free radicals, cellular metabolism, and response to oxidative stress.

"It is becoming increasingly clear that psychosocial stress can manifest as system-wide perturbations of cellular processes, generally increasing

oxidative stress and promoting a pro-inflammatory milieu. Stress associated changes in peripheral blood leukocyte expression of single genes have been identified. More recently, chronic psychosocial stress has been associated with accelerated aging at the cellular level. Specifically, shortened telomeres, low telomerase activity, decreased anti-oxidant capacity and increased oxidative stress are correlated with increased psychosocial stress and with increased vulnerability to a variety of disease states." -Dr. Herbert Benson, "Genomic Counter-Stress Changes Induced by the Relaxation Response"

"My studies, along with those of several researchers in the USA, revealed that Transcendental Meditation elicited physiological changes that were the exact opposite to the stress response. Virtually every indicator of stress, from heart rate and blood pressure to body chemistry and brain activity, changed in the opposite direction during meditation. Herbert Benson of Harvard Medical School dubbed this the 'relaxation response,' and almost overnight meditation became respectable. Doctors began recommending it to patients; teachers encouraged students to take it up; even city business people took lessons on the quiet." -Peter Russell, "From Science to God"

Similar studies of Chinese Qigong, Indian Pranayama, and Japanese Johrei practitioners have also gleaned similar results. Published in the 2005 "Journal of Alternative and Complement Medicine," doctors at the Texas Center for Immunology performed "Genomic Profiling of Neutrophil Transcripts in Asian Qigong Practitioners." They found that long-term Qigong practitioners had enhanced immunity, down-regulated cellular metabolism, and apoptotic gene alteration in favor of rapid resolution of inflammation. The lifespan of normal neutrophils (white blood cells) was prolonged while the lifespan of inflammatory neutrophils was decreased. Doctors concluded that Qigong practice seems to regulate immunity, metabolic rate, and cell death at the transcriptional (DNA/RNA) level.

India's Institute of Medical Sciences published their findings regarding gene expression profiling of Pranayama practitioners in the 2008 "Journal of Psychosomatic Research." Much like the Qigong study, doctors found that long-term Pranayama practitioners showed effects on immunity, aging, cell death, and stress reduction through transcriptional regulation. Compared to a control group of 42 healthy non-practitioners, 42 Pranayama masters showed better antioxidant status at the RNA level, higher enzyme activity, better stress regulation and immune function (due to prolonged life span of lymphocytes by up-regulation of anti-apoptotic/pro-survival genes).

Johrei is a Japanese spiritual practice much like Reiki, Qigong, or Pranayama which utilizes life force energy as a healing modality. A group of scientists lead by Dean Radin exposed cultured astrocyte brain cells to repeated Johrei sessions and found that they flourished and grew much faster than control astrocytes. By doing nothing but focusing a certain type of intention/concentration onto these cells, they flourished compared to the non-treated cells. In other words, cultivation of life force energy results in increased brain cell growth.

"Research on Mind-Body approaches is accelerating. One of a number of characteristics of Mind-Body practice is the purposeful elicitation of the Relaxation Response (RR). The various forms of practices which elicit the RR include Tai Chi, Qi Gong, Yoga, meditation, repetitive prayer, breathing exercises, progressive muscle relaxation, biofeedback, guided visualization, affirmation, etc. These methods tend to trigger

physiological and perhaps energetic mechanisms that move the body into a state of deep rest. It appears that this can literally change how genes behave in response to stress. Mind-Body practices that produce the Relaxation Response have been used by people across cultures for thousands of years to prevent and treat disease and generate states of mind that foster greater performance and intuitive insight. Recently, a number of studies have turned toward investigation of the effect that Mind-Body practice can have on genetic expression. In research on natural healing, functional maximization and holistic, complementary and integrative medicine there has been a growing trend away from simply studying disease mechanisms and outcomes, toward the study of the subtle factors that predispose individuals for sustainable wellbeing as well as for disease. Gene expression is an emerging arena wherein the total continuum – from wellbeing to disease – can be effectively investigated." –Roger Jahnke MD, "Researching the Benefits of Mind-Body Practice by Investigating Genetic Expression"

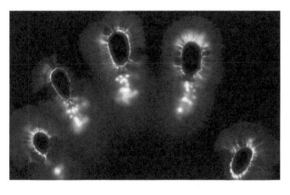

In 1939 Russian scientist Semyon Kirlian accidentally discovered that if an object on a photographic plate is subjected to a strong enough electrical charge, an image is created on the plate. By photographing the coronal discharge that occurs between an electrically grounded object and the electrode generating the field, the sparks captured on film show multi-colored, multi-frequency energy waves ranging from below infrared to above ultraviolet. These images have since become known as Kirlian photography or Biofield electrography.

Kirlian photography has now been studied and tested extensively in many reputable laboratories around the world and has shown consistent color/shape/frequency correlations with various emotional and physical states. For example, UCLA Neuropsychiatric Institute's Dr. Thelma Moss has recorded consistent patterns

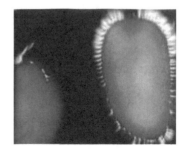

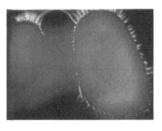 correlating fingertip coronas with specific emotions. Healthy, happy, relaxed subjects regularly exhibit quarter-inch wide blue and white coronas, while stressed, anxious, or nervous subjects consistently exhibit blotchy red coronas. In another study she found that when photographed together close friends generate brighter and more convergent coronas than strangers. Being photographed with strict authority figures produces smaller coronas, while being photographed with unassuming, unintimidating people produces larger coronas. When two people place their fingers on the same film, both images always come out clearly, but, if they look into each other's eyes while the photo is taken, one of the fingerprints is blanked out and disappears!

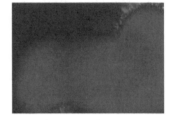

Dr. Moss' strange findings sparked interest at the US Heuristic Institute where they performed their own Kirlian/biofield experiments with intimate couples. When partners were instructed to place their fingers on the film and focus unpleasant, unloving thoughts towards one another their coronal patterns did not merge at all. When the couples focused pleasant, loving thoughts towards one another their patterns began to merge. And when they kissed each other during the photographs, their coronal boundaries dissolved into one. Some people were even able to

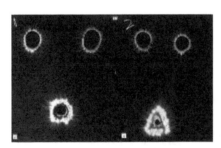 withhold their coronas by tensing all the muscles in their bodies. In experiments with Dr. J. L. Hickman, psychic Uri Geller was able to consciously direct the shape of his fingertip coronas, making circles, squares, straight lines, and triangles at will.

"The German magazine Esotera describes an interpersonal study conducted with Kirlian photography. Two individuals in a psychiatrist's office were asked to put their fingers next to each other and take a picture. They were asked to return once a week for three weeks. The Kirlian photos revealed the man to be very attracted to this woman (large, expansive corona in her direction), but her corona discharge

indicated that she did not feel an attraction towards him (small, tight corona). The second week revealed the man to be extremely persistent and it looked as if she might be more responsive (slightly converging coronas). The third week shows two bright, happy coronas blending ... and we are told that they are living happily ever after." -"Kirlian Photrapy as an Art and Science" documentary, International Kirlian Research Association

Dr. Moss also conducted experiments showing that cancerous tissue is easily distinguished from healthy tissue using Kirlian imaging. In one study she was able to separate 100 healthy control rats from 100 other rats injected with cancer simply by the dramatic difference in corona emanations. Romanian Dr. Loan Dumitrescu also used Kirlian imaging to detect cancer tissue. He screened 6,000 industrial workers for cancer and found 47 malignant tumors while conventional doctors found only 41. By analyzing the coronal discharge channels, their geometry, color, and energetics he was able to detect cancer better than traditional imaging and laboratory tests.

Various studies involving plant coronas have gleaned interesting information as well. For example, the viability of seeds can be determined by Kirlian images since fertile seeds show much larger coronal ejections than dead seeds. Healthy seeds have a deep blue aura, and as root tips sprout they show up pinkish-red indicating where the most active growth is taking place. Researchers also found that dew forms on plant leaves in exactly the same locations as maximum flare patterns. They found that male plant stamens always come out blue, while the female ovary photographs are always gold. And most impressively, when a leaf is torn in half then photographed, the outline of the entire leaf is still clearly visible in its discharge pattern!

"Physical evidence of the energy body exists and a number of different sources document it. The first of these is Russian engineer Semya Kirlian

who discovered that living tissue emits electromagnetic force fields that show up on photosensitive paper ... Using his photographic technique, a leaf with a portion of it cut out still shows the outline of its missing part. Even though it is not there, physically, the photograph shows an outline as if it was. This prompts suggestions that Kirlian photography reveals the energy body. Kirlian photographs show energy emanating from the body. A picture of a hand, for example, depicts the fingers illuminated by energy. If two people touch fingertips, the energy appears to fight until both people accept the presence of the other. Another interesting case involves people who have amputated feet and legs. These people frequently report intense pain originating from phantom limbs. When a person places their hand on the area of pain, where the missing limb would be, and massages it as if there was a hand or limb there the pain stops. At the point of death the human body inexplicably loses several ounces of weight. Studies have also shown that when photographed with light sensitive film, for an amount of nanoseconds, less than a second, a large illumination expands from the body and disappears upon death. These examples all point toward the conclusion that a separate body or being composed of energy inhabits the physical human body." -Eric Pepin, "Handbook of the Navigator" (160-161)

The bioelectric fields captured by Kirlian photographs are postulated by many to be an expression of the "aura" representing our chi/life force energy. Psychics, mystics, and shamans the world over in traditions including Christian, Chinese, Japanese, Egyptian and Tibetan have all talked about being able to see a faint multi-colored corona or halo around people's physical bodies/heads. This aura emanates from the "energy body" which exists within and permeates the physical body. Healthy, positive, and spiritual people are said to have glowing white/gold auras, while unhealthy, negative, or immoral people have more subdued darker colored auras. Each person's aura is said to be unique but constantly changing based on thoughts, mood, disease, environment, and other factors. Experiments with Kirlian photographs and bioelectrography have proved very consistent with ancient definitions of the aura.

"One mystical phenomenon that appears to involve the ability to see reality's frequency aspects is the aura, or human energy field. The notion that there is a subtle field of energy around the human body, a halo-like envelope of light that exists just beyond normal human perception, can be found in many ancient traditions. In India, sacred writings that date back over five thousand years refer to this life energy as prana. In China, since the third millennium B.C., it has been called ch'i and is believed to be the energy that flows through the acupuncture meridian system. Kabbalah, a Jewish mystical philosophy that arose in the sixth century B.C., calls this vital principle nefish and teaches that an egg-shaped bubble of iridescence surrounds every human body. In their book Future Science, writer John White and parapsychologist Stanley Krippner list 97 different cultures that refer to the aura with 97 different names." -Michael Talbot, "The Holographic Universe" (165)

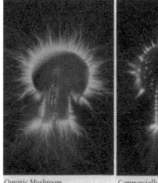

Organic Mushroom   Commercially Grown Mushroom.

"The Aura is also an extremely accurate indicator of Spiritual attainment. Highly Spiritually evolved people will be instantly recognizable by a vivid, clean, dynamic aura, the most prominent feature of which is an intense bright golden yellow area extending from and around the crown of the head. Sometimes the aura can be so intense it can even be viewed

by people not usually possessing the ability of auric vision. It is also this intense golden aura around the head of highly Spiritual people that gives rise to the so called 'halo,' as often for example depicted

Slightly Cooked Organic Tomato (Kirlian Image)   Raw Organic Tomato (Kirlian Image)

135

around the head of Jesus or a saint." -Adrian Cooper, "Our Ultimate Reality" (195)

Skeptics claim that Kirlian photography is merely capturing variances in pressure, humidity, temperature, voltage etc. and not some mystical aura. It is true that New Age fairs and internet sites sell "aura cameras" often marketing them as "Kirlian cameras." These are indeed misleading and serve no practical purpose beyond that of a mood ring. However, electrophysiological studies have shown that corona emanation of true Kirlian photographs does not relate to temperature, perspiration, galvanic skin response, vasoconstrictions or dilations. While it may be easy for some to discount 97 traditions around the world and their descriptions of the aura, it is much harder to discount Dr. Moss and Dr. Dumitrescu's amazing work with cancer detection or the Heuristic Institute's results involving couples.

"The greatest advance in the utilization of Kirlian photography was made by the efforts of the German Dr. Peter Mandel who was trained as an acupuncturist. He observed that by treating disease states with acupuncture points the corresponding deficiencies in the Kirlian photograph would change. After years of research Dr. Mandel has developed a diagnostic and treatment program based on Kirlian analysis. Disease states are caused by energy blockages. The Kirlian photograph helps to determine the overall energy flow of the body and locations of energy blockage which are manifested in the disease state. Dr. Mandel has categorized types of energy patterns on the Kirlian into endocrine, toxic and degenerative. Endocrine is the pre-disease state. The patient has symptoms but there is no discernable pathology. The Kirlian can be extremely valuable in locating the area of blockage. The second type of disturbance in the energy pattern is the toxic state. This is when there tissue changes develop such as inflammation, congestion and blockages of energy flow

in the body. The third type is the degenerative type where the body begins to show destructive tissue changes." -Dr. Edward Kondrot, "Kirlian Photography"

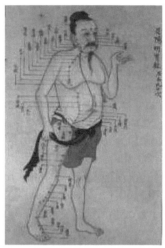

Acupuncture is a 3,000+ year old traditional Chinese therapy that involves inserting tiny needles into various vital energy points throughout the human body. Hundreds of these "acupoints" connect to 12 main chi/life energy channels known as "meridians." Each meridian is related to and named after a specific organ or function, the main 12 being the lung, colon, stomach, spleen, heart, intestine, triple warmer, pericardium, bladder, gallbladder, kidney and liver meridians. Through skillful application and combination of acupoint needles, blockages of chi flow are overcome and healthy energy balance is restored to the body.

"Many traditions worldwide have perceived the manifestation of consciousness through various levels of energetic frequencies. Eastern healing techniques continue this holistic tradition, where disease is treated as a blockage or imbalance in the flow of a life-force energy. Almost all non-Western approaches to medicine speak of a life force, such as the prana of the Indian tradition and the chi of the Chinese tradition. These forces are said to vivify a biological entity at birth and to withdraw on its death. The importance of very low-energy electromagnetic fields associated with the body's energy flows is being recognized and progressively measured. These energy flows take particular pathways that Eastern medicine has long identified as the meridians. Just as the arterial system carries blood around our bodies, such meridians are deemed to carry both the subtle and the electromagnetic component of these energies. Around our bodies and distributed along these meridians are approximately a thousand points that are the nodes for such energies where they may be accessed via the skin. The Chinese tradition of acupuncture uses extremely fine needles

137

inserted painlessly into the skin at these points to free energy blockages, accelerate wound healing, control pain, and stimulate energy flow in the meridian system." -Ervin Laszlo and Jude Currivan, "Cosmos" (120)

Using Kirlian electrography, acupuncturist Dr. Peter Mandel showed that he could stimulate various acupoints to cause bigger, brighter coronas to appear at other nodes along the same meridian. By needling tonification points on one foot and sedation points on the other, he could increase the luminescence of one foot while nearly extinguishing the other. One of his patients with a sprained ring 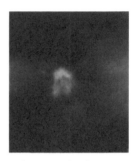 finger displayed a huge reddish corona emanating from the sprain, but after just a few minutes of acupuncture treatment it shrunk back to normal size/color and healed completely within the day.

"Research has also shown that painkilling endorphins and the steroid cortisol are released through the body when the [acupuncture] points are stimulated at low frequency, and important mood-regulating neurotransmitters like serotonin and norepinephrine, at high frequency ... Yet other research has proved that acupuncture can cause blood vessels to dilate and increase blood flow to distant organs in the body. Other research demonstrates the existence of meridians as well as the effectiveness of acupuncture for a variety of conditions. Orthopaedic surgeon Dr. Robert Becker, who performed a great deal of research on electromagnetic fields in the body, designed a special electrode recording device which would roll along the body like a pizza cutter. After many studies it showed up electrical charges on the same places on every one of the people tested, all corresponding to Chinese meridian points." -Lynne McTaggart, "The Field: The Quest for the Secret Force of the Universe," (55)

Modern medicine has long been aware of an electrical phenomenon present in the body known as "the Current of Injury." When skin tissue undergoes trauma or microscopic damage, such as when skin cells are pierced by acupuncture needles, they begin leaking electrically charged ions into the surrounding tissue. This creates a weak electrical battery-like charge which stimulates a healing response from the nearby cells.

In the 1950s, Japanese Dr. Yoshio Nakatani and German Dr. Reinhold Voll both independently verified electronically that within a few millimeters of each acupoint there is a significant decrease in the skin's electrical resistance compared with non-acupoints. They also proved that there are measurable differences between healthy and unhealthy patient's overall resistance levels.

In 1971 New York Times reporter James Reston became a firm believer in acupuncture's efficacy. While traveling around China James became ill with appendicitis and doctors performed a complete appendectomy using only acupuncture for an anesthetic. In the popular article he wrote afterwards, James mentioned interviewing one brain tumor patient who was eating oranges and conversing with him while his skull was wide open! Some people have claimed acupuncture's analgesic properties are merely an expression of the placebo effect, but this has been proven erroneous due to the fact that many animals have also responded to the analgesic properties of acupuncture, not to mention that it works 75% of the time compared to the placebo effect's 30%.

"The effectiveness of acupuncture for pain relief is now supported by a growing number of studies. Neuroscientist Bruce Pomeranz was the first to show that acupuncture triggers the production of endorphins – our body's natural 'feel-good' hormones. The use of functional MRI technology to scan brain patterns by a number of researchers, including Zang-Hee Cho at the University of California, Irvine, has shown in recent years that acupuncture desensitizes pain controls in our brain. Indeed, so powerful is its ability to reduce pain that it has been used to enable open-

heart surgery to be performed without anesthetic." -Ervin Laszlo and Jude Currivan, "Cosmos" (121)

University of Toronto Dr. Bruce Pomeranz discovered by activating small myelinated nerve fibers, acupuncture sends impulses to the spinal chord, midbrain, pituitary, and hypothalamus resulting in endorphin release. When Pomeranz pre-treated rats with Naloxone, an endorphin blocker, acupuncture's pain relieving properties disappeared, suggesting that endorphin release caused by acupuncture stimulus is the key mechanism behind its pain relieving effects.

In 1992 at the Necker Hospital in Paris, Dr. Jean-Claude Darras and Dr. Pierre de Vernejoul explicitly confirmed the existence of the meridian system with their famous experiment. They injected harmless radioactive tracers into acupoints of 300 volunteers then tracked their migration using gamma cameras. Whenever tracers were injected to non-acupoints they quickly disbursed and disappeared, but when injected into actual acupoints, the tracers migrated steadily along the traditional Chinese meridian paths. They also found that the tracers moved more slowly around diseased organs and faster around healthy organs, confirming the notion of illness resulting from obstructions in the body's chi flow.

"This is a computer-enhanced version of an image produced at the Necker Hospital in Paris in a joint study with the Cytology Laboratory at the Military Hospital. They injected a radioactive tracer into acupuncture points and then took the photograph with a gamma camera to see where it would go. It followed the pattern of the acupuncture meridian system. Not only does this confirm the existence of the meridian network, which 'modern medicine' has long dismissed and ridiculed, but the study also established another crucial fact. It found that the slower the energy (or chi to the Chinese) passed through the meridians, the less healthy was the person involved. When the energy was flowing at optimum speed and

balance the subject was in good health. How can this be? Because the energy, the chi, is information that includes details about a problem or imbalance, and the instructions on how to respond. If people were taking too long to tell you that a problem existed and too long to pass your response to those at the scene, what would happen? The problem would not get fixed and would probably worsen as a result.

This is one reason why people who are ill are more vulnerable to other illnesses. The chi also carries instructions to maintain balance and harmony and, again, when this communication is affected, so is the balance and harmony, and the body becomes diseased." –David Icke, "The David Icke Guide to the Global Conspiracy" (7)

In 2003 the World Health Organization assessed and compiled a list of over 100 ailments for which acupuncture treatment has proven effective. Just a small sampling of these include allergies, arthritis, depression, dysentery, dysmenorrhoea, epigastralgia, headache, hypertension, hypotension, labor pain, leucopenia, lower back pain, nausea, neck pain, sciatica, sprains, and stroke.

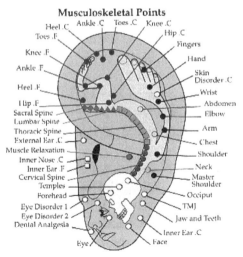

In acupuncture there is the concept of "the little man in the ear" which is an acupoint diagram of the whole human body that fits within the ear and affects meridians connecting 40 organs/systems throughout the body. In reflexology there are similar acupressure concepts and diagrams of the feet and hands showing how points in these extremities connect to organs/systems throughout the body. This once again demonstrates the holographic nature of our bodies and matter in general; the part reflected in the whole, and the whole reflected in all parts.

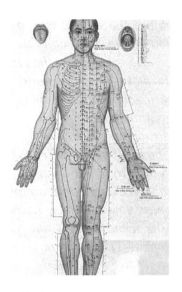

"How can reflexology and acupuncture find points throughout the body that relate to all the organs and other functions? How can you massage, or insert a needle at a point on the foot, hand or ear and affect the liver, stomach or heart? It seems crazy if you accept the official explanations of the human form, but it makes perfect sense when you know the body is a hologram. Remember that one of the amazing properties of holograms is that every part is a smaller version of the whole. Far from being a mystery that the whole body can be found in the foot, hand or ear, it is the way it must be if the body is a hologram. An entire body can be grown from a single cell because every cell is a smaller version of the whole and contains all the information contained in the whole." –David Icke, "Infinite Love is the Only Truth, Everything Else is Illusion" (96)

"We human beings consider ourselves to be made up of 'solid matter.'

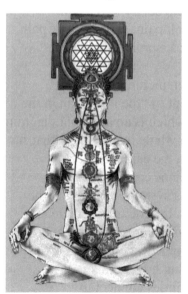

Actually, the physical body is the end product, so to speak, of the subtle information fields, which mold our physical body as well as all physical matter. These fields are holograms which change in time (and are) outside the reach of our normal senses. This is what clairvoyants perceive as colorful egg-shaped halos or auras surrounding our physical bodies." -Itzhak Bentov, "Stalking the Wild Pendulum"

Also connected and intertwined with the meridian system is the "chakra" system which runs from the base of the spine up to the top of the head. Chakra is Sanskrit for "wheel," and signifies the 7 main energy centers in the body, each of which is located along the spinal column and corresponds directly to a major nerve ganglia, endocrine gland, or internal organ. These focal points of subtle energy have been measured electromagnetically and produce ten-fold stronger biofields than non-chakra points. They have physical manifestations but also extend into the energy body affecting us emotionally, psychologically, and spiritually as well. Briefly, the 7 chakras are as follows:

Muladhara, the red root chakra, is located in the perineum and relates to the gonads, adrenal medulla, and the pubococcygeus muscle that controls ejaculation. Psychologically the root chakra controls security, survival, and the fight-or-flight response.

Swadhisthana, the orange sacral chakra, is located in the sacrum and relates to the testes/ovaries, the genitourinary system and the adrenals. Psychologically the sacral chakra controls sexuality, relationships, violence, addictions, pleasure, creativity, and enthusiasm.

Manipura, the yellow solar plexus chakra, is located in the solar plexus and relates to the metabolic and digestive systems, the pancreas and adrenal cortex. Psychologically the solar plexus chakra controls power, will, fear, anxiety, and introversion.

Anahata, the green or pink heart chakra, is located at the thymus in the middle of the chest and relates to the immune, circulatory, and endocrine systems, responsible for fending off disease, blood flow, and maturation of T-cells. Psychologically the heart chakra controls love, compassion, rejection, equilibrium and well-being.

Vishuddha, the blue throat chakra, is located at the thyroid, which produces the thyroid hormone responsible for growth and maturation. Psychologically the throat chakra is related to communication and growth through expression.

Ajna, the indigo third eye chakra, is located at the pineal gland at the geometric center of the brain. The pineal gland is light sensitive and produces melatonin which regulates sleep and dream states. Psychologically the third eye chakra is related to intuition and clarity of mind.

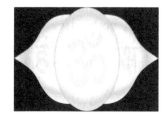

Sahasrara, the violet crown chakra, is located at the crown of the head and relates to the pituitary gland which secretes hormones to control the endocrine system and connects to the central nervous system via the hypothalamus. Psychologically the crown chakra is related to beingness, pure consciousness, and karma.

"Of the seven primary chakras that are deemed to mediate the awareness and energies of our personal energy field, five are considered to align primarily along the main meridians up our spine, one is between and slightly above our eye level, and the last sits at the crown of our head. Associated with nerve plexuses and the endocrine system of our bodies, which secretes and regulates hormonal balances, the chakras – as viewed by Eastern traditions – have a primary role in the mediation of consciousness. The electronic recordings of the human

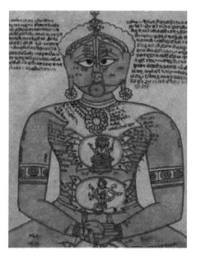

biofield were found to be strongest over the chakras. When the signal from the nervous system's alternating field was filtered out, at frequencies above 500 cycles per second, the continuous low-intensity direct field seemed to be around ten times as high as the field through which the body's nervous system is controlled, although its intensity is less than half that of a resting muscle." -Ervin Laszlo and Jude Currivan, "Cosmos" (125)

Psi Science

Psi Science is the rigorous on-going scientific pursuit of experimenting and testing the validity and reliability of so-called psychic or paranormal phenomena. Common psi abilities include such things as mind-to-mind connections (telepathy), mind-over-matter interactions, (psychokinesis), perceiving distant places, people, objects, or events (clairvoyance), perceiving the future (precognition), prophetic dreams, déjà vu, spiritual healing, the power of prayer and intention, intuition, gut feelings, and the sense of being stared at.

"There are words for psi experiences in every language, from Arabic to Zulu, Czech to Manx Gaelic. The universality of the words reflects the fact that these phenomena are basic to human experience. And indeed psi experiences have been reported by people in all cultures, throughout history, and at all ages and education levels." -Dean Radin, "Entangled Minds" (6)

A meta-analysis of every psi experiment performed and published (in the English language) over the past century was recently conducted by Dean Radin, senior scientist at the Institute of Noetic Sciences. Statistically analyzing the data from all 1,019 controlled studies produced the astonishing result of 1.3×10^{104} to 1 against chance –

that is:
1,300,000,000,000,000,000,000,000,000,000,000,000,000,000,000,0
00,000,000,000,000,000,000,000,000,000,000,000,000,000,000,000,
000,000 to 1 odds against the results being due to coincidence.

"After a century of increasingly sophisticated investigations and more than a thousand controlled studies with combined odds against chance of 10^{104} to 1, there is now strong evidence that some psi phenomena exist. While this is an impressive statistic, all it means is that the outcomes of these experiments are definitely not due to coincidence. We've considered other common explanations like selective reporting and variations in experimental quality, and while those factors do moderate the overall results, there can be little doubt that overall something interesting is going on. It seems increasingly likely that as physics continues to refine our understandings of the fabric of reality, a theoretical outlook for a rational explanation for psi will eventually be established." -Dean Radin, "Entangled Minds" (275)

Scientists, psychologists, academic institutions and governments have been conducting psi research with consistently positive results for over a century yet wide-spread acceptance of the existence of such phenomena is curiously absent. In 2002, a review of the 57 most popular introductory psychology textbooks in common use at Universities showed that 24 contained no mention of psi whatsoever, and the 33 that did devoted an average of only 2.4 pages to the subject. Not only is the voluminous amount of available psi research mysteriously absent from the textbooks, but the second most often cited references come from the magazine, Skeptical Inquirer.

"This should make your hair stand up. It's like trying to sustain a serious scientific discussion based on citations from tabloids ... If this is the type of scholarly information being fed to impressionable psychology students, it's not surprising that whole generations of future academic psychologists assume there's nothing to it." -Dean Radin, "Entangled Minds" (289-90)

"I assume that the reader is familiar with the idea of extrasensory perception ... telepathy, clairvoyance, precognition and psychokinesis. These disturbing phenomena seem to deny all our usual scientific ideas. How we should like to discredit them! Unfortunately the statistical evidence is overwhelming. It is very difficult to rearrange one's ideas so as to fit these new facts in." -Alan Turing

Simply stated, there is no place in the old Newtonian/Darwinian models for the existence of psi, and this more than anything is likely responsible for the lack of mass acceptance of psi as a genuine phenomenon. In a material Universe where mind is merely an emergent evolutionary mechanism, such abilities as clairvoyance and precognition must be cast aside as superstition or coincidence. Regardless, valid psi science continues its march forward while the skeptical establishment and its indoctrinated minions religiously defend the dogma of their crumbling material worldview.

"Pick up practically any scientific or scholarly journal and you'll quickly find that researchers are always engaged in vigorous debates and controversies. The moment a discipline collapses into a single set of beliefs, constructs, or even methods, it's no longer science, it's religion." -Dean Radin, "Entangled Minds" (283)

"When a belief is widely held in the face of overwhelming evidence to the contrary, we call it a superstition. By that criterion, the most egregious superstition of modern times, perhaps of all time, is the 'scientific' belief in the non-existence of psi." -Thomas Etter

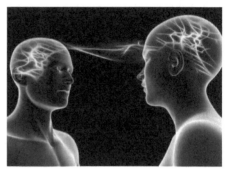

The term "telepathy" was coined in 1882 by Frederic Myers, founder of the Society for Psychical Research, during his investigation into what was formerly known as "thought transference." Reports and documented cases of thought transference abound in almost every culture dating back for millennia, but during the 20th century, the scientific method was applied and repeatable experiments were performed which proved, with combined odds against chance of trillions to one, that telepathy is indeed a genuine phenomenon.

The most common method of testing perceptual-psi (ESP/telepathy) is to isolate a test subject from a hidden target object or person placed at a distance and see if the test subject can accurately describe the target or mentally influence the other person. Hundreds of variations have been performed on experiments following this basic design:

"A classic experiment in telepathy was reported in 1923 by Dr. H. I. F. W. Brugmans and his colleagues in the Department of Psychology at the University of Groningen, The Netherlands. In this experiment, a 23 year-old physics student named Van Dam was investigated for his claimed telepathic abilities. He was placed inside a curtained booth, blindfolded, and asked to place his arm under the curtain to select one square on a 6 x 8 checkerboard placed on a table next to the curtain. The target square Van Dam was attempting to select was determined randomly by the experimenter on each trial. An assistant experimenter knew the target square and tried to mentally influence Van Dam's arm movements to guide him to select the correct target square ...

The results of the experiment were extremely significant, with 60 successes out of 187 trials rather than the 4 expected by chance. That's associated with odds against chance of 121 trillion to 1." -Dean Radin, "Entangled Minds" (82-3)

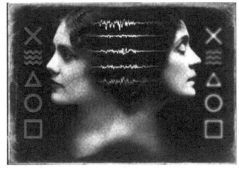

"*A second classic experiment that has withstood the test of time is the ESP card test, as popularized by J. B. Rhine's Parapsychology Laboratory at Duke University. This test involved cards imprinted with one of five symbols: circle, square, wavy lines, star and triangle ... In a typical experimental run, the deck was thoroughly shuffled and then one person would select each card in turn and try to mentally send the symbol on that card to a distant person. This technique made it possible to collect hundreds of trials quickly, in a wide variety of environments, and under controlled conditions ... Rhine's 1940 book, Extrasensory Perception After Sixty Years combined his 60 years of ESP research, 188 different experiments with thousands of trials, in which even the most highly controlled studies had odds against chance of 375 trillion to 1.*" -Dean Radin, "Entangled Minds" (84-5)

Hubert Pearce (left) calling down through a pack of 25 Zener cards (five sets shuffled), before taking a card off. I am recording his calls.

In 1933, Hubert E. Pearce Jr., a student of J.B. Rhine's at Duke University introduced himself saying that he had inherited his mother's clairvoyant abilities and would be willing to scientifically test and verify his skills. For the next seven months, Rhine worked with Pearce devising, performing, and documenting the now famous Pearce-Pratt distance telepathy tests at his Duke Parapsychology Lab. The experiment consisted of 700 runs through 25-card ESP decks with Pearce acting as the telepathic receiver while another student, Gaither Pratt, was the sender. Pratt simply laid down one card per minute and concentrated on it, while Pearce, from another building on campus, attempted to telepathically read and/or clairvoyantly see each card. After

1,850 trials, Pearce guessed the correct card 558 times (32%), which is 188 times above chance expectation (20%). Though this 12% difference may not sound like much, it is associated with odds against chance of 10,000,000,000,000,000,000,000,000,000 to 1.

Another popular and often replicated psi experiment is known as the "Ganzfield" telepathy test. In a ganzfield test, Participant A sits in a comfortable, reclining chair, wears headphones playing pink noise (peaceful waterfall sound), has halved

ping-pong balls placed over their eyes, and a soft red light shined on them. This type of sensory deprivation results in a dreamy state of awareness in which the subject becomes more open to mental suggestions/impressions. Once Participant 1 is fully immersed in this "ganzfield condition," Participant 2 sits in another room watching a freeze-frame picture on a TV screen and attempts to telepathically send that image to Participant 1. Later, Participant 1 comes out of the ganzfield state, discusses their impressions, is shown 4 images, and must choose which one they think Participant 2 was sending them.

"From 1974 through 2004 a total of 88 ganzfield experiments reporting 1,008 hits in 3,145 trials were conducted. The combined hit rate was 32% as compared to the chance-expected 25%. This 7% above-chance effect is associated with odds against chance of 29,000,000,000,000,000,000 (or 29 quintillion) to 1." -Dean Radin, "Entangled Minds" (120)

"The modern ganzfield experiment is as close to the perfect psi experiment as anyone knows how to conduct. Until recently, the ganzfield experiments were largely unknown outside of the discipline of parapsychology. Then, in 1994, psychologists Daryl Bem from Cornell University and Charles Honorton from the University of Edinburgh published a meta-analysis of ganzfield studies in Psychological Bulletin, a well-regarded academic psychology journal. That paper provided strong evidence for a genuine psi effect. Bem and Honorton's review of

earlier ganzfield studies estimated an effect with overall odds against chance of 48 billion to 1." -Dean Radin, "Entangled Minds" (117-8)

In Upton Sinclair's 1930 book Mental Radio he cataloged a series of picture-drawing telepathy experiments performed in collaboration with his ESP-gifted wife Mary Craig Sinclair. During these tests Upton or friends/family would sketch a small object and then Mary, in another room, another house, or even miles away, would mentally perceive the image and reproduce the sketch herself. Mental Radio contains scores of these sketches which show incredible similarities far beyond what anyone would expect by chance. In conclusion to these experiments, Upton Sinclair wrote, *"there isn't*

a thing in the world that leads me to [write this book] except the conviction which has been forced upon me that telepathy is real, and that loyalty to the nature of the universe makes it necessary for me to say so ... It is foolish to be convinced without evidence, but it is equally foolish to refuse to be convinced by real evidence."

"A second example of picture-drawing experiments is described in the book Mind to Mind, published in 1948, by French researcher Rene Warcollier ... Warcollier was already convinced that telepathy existed through the work of Rhine and others, so his books primarily explored how it worked ... He noted that images were not transmitted like photographs but were 'scrambled, broken up into component elements which are often transmuted into a new pattern.' What Warcollier demonstrated is compatible with what modern cognitive neuroscience has learned about how visual images are constructed by the brain. It implies that telepathic perceptions bubble up into awareness from the unconscious and are probably processed in the brain in the same way that we generate images in dreams. And thus

telepathic 'images' are far less certain than sensory-driven images and subject to distortion." -Dean Radin, "Entangled Minds" (92-93)

A third picture-drawing experiment was conducted in 1941 at Cambridge University by psychologist Whatley Carington. He recruited 250 students to attempt to replicate sketches in a series of 5 experiments, with 10 drawings each, for a total of 50 targets. By the end of the study Carington had collected 2,200 student sketches which he then cross-matched with the original 50 possible targets. Amazingly he found 1,209 drawings (55%) were similar to the targets! And this is from 250 different students with no particular ESP gifts or previous experience.

Another telepathy test that has been scientifically investigated for nearly a century is the sense of being stared at. In a typical study of this sort, Participant 1 stands with his back turned to Particpant 2, who stands a few meters behind him. Next Partcipant 2 flips a coin to decide whether he will stare at the back of Participant 1's head for 10 seconds, or look away for 10 seconds. After the 10 seconds pass, Participant 1 records their impression, yes or no, and the coin is flipped again for the next trial.

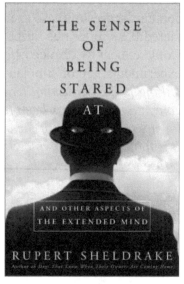

"British biologist Rupert Sheldrake has popularized experiments based on this simple design ... and under more controlled conditions, such as those involving use of blindfolds, no trial-by-trial feedback, and even more secure conditions such as having [participants] stare through a window from a distance. I found 60 such experiments involving a total of 33,357 trials from publications cited by Sheldrake and others. The overall success rate in these experiments was 54.5% where chance expectation is 50%. The overall odds against chance are a staggering 202 octodecillion (that's 20,200,000,000,000,000,000,000,000,000,000,000,000,000,000,000, 000,000,000) to 1." -Dean Radin, "Entangled Minds" (127)

In over a dozen scientific experiments over the last 45 years, using EEG and MRI brain scanning technology, pairs of identical twins have been separated into different rooms, and one of them subjected to visual or emotional stimulus which is then found to register on both of their brains simultaneously. This has also been shown to happen (with a lower correlation rate) between family, friends, and complete strangers as well.

"The design used in these electroencephalograph or 'EEG correlation' experiments asks, in effect, whether poking one person will produce an ouch response in a distant partner. It's not recommended to poke people in the brain, so instead we use a stimulus like a flashing light to cause one of the brains to jump electrically in a predictable way, and then we look at the other, distant brain to see if it's jumping at the same time." - Dean Radin, "Entangled Minds" (136)

"Psychophysiologist Jacobo Grinberg-Zylberbaum and his colleagues from the National Autonomous University of Mexico reported a series of studies in which they claimed to detect simultaneous brain responses in the EEGs of separated pairs of people. One of their studies was published in the journal Physics Essays, stimulating another round of replication attempts. In 2003, a successful replication was reported in Neuroscience Letters by EEG specialist Jiri Wackermann and his colleagues ... Wackermann's team concluded that 'We are facing a phenomenon which is neither easy to dismiss as a methodological failure or a technical artifact nor understood as to its nature. No biophysical mechanism is presently known that could be responsible for the observed correlations between EEGs of two separated subjects.' Another successful replication, this time reported by Leanna Standish of Bastyr University and her colleagues, was recently reported in the medical journal Alternative Therapies in Health and Medicine. They conducted an EEG correlation experiment with the receiving participant located in a functional magnetic resonance imaging (fMRI) scanner ... They found a highly significant increase in brain activity (odds against chance of 14,000 to 1) in the receiving person's visual cortex (in the back of the brain) while the distant partner was viewing a

flickering light. The same group later successfully replicated this finding." -Dean Radin, "Entangled Minds" (137-8)

The man who invented the EEG, Hans Berger, actually became interested in the brain and the powers of the human psyche after a telepathic experience he had in early adulthood. It began when one day, as a soldier during a military training exercise, he was thrown off his horse and nearly trampled by a horse-drawn cannon: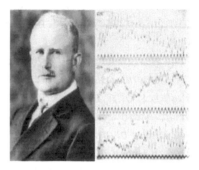

"Miraculously, the driver of the artillery battery managed to stop the horses just in time. The accident left Hans thoroughly shaken but without serious injury. At that very moment, many miles away in his family's home, Hans's older sister was suddenly overwhelmed with an ominous certainty that something bad had happened to Hans. She anxiously insisted that their father contact him, and so he did via telegram. That evening, when Hans received the telegram, he was initially concerned, as he had never before received a telegram from his father. Then, upon reading his sister's urgent concern about his well-being, he knew that his feelings of intense fear earlier in the day had somehow reached his sister. Many years later, Hans wrote, 'This is a case of spontaneous telepathy in which at a time of mortal danger, and as I contemplated certain death, I transmitted my thoughts, while my sister, who was particularly close to me, acted as the receiver.'" -Dean Radin, "Entangled Minds" (22)

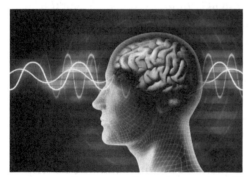

"If telepathy is a real fact, it is very possible that it is operating at every moment and everywhere, but with too little intensity to be noticed, or else it is operating in the presence of obstacles which neutralize the effect at the same moment that it manifests itself. We produce electricity at every moment, the atmosphere is continually electrified, we move among magnetic currents, yet millions of human beings lived for thousands of years without having suspected the existence of electricity. It may be the same with telepathy." -French philosopher and Nobel laureate Henri

Bergson in presidential address to the Society for Psychical Research in London, May 1913

One of the most well-researched and fascinating branches of psi science is active-psi or Psychokinesis (PK). Also known as Telekinesis and mind over matter, PK is the ability to mentally influence a physical system or object. The most common method to test for active-psi is to isolate a volunteer from a target such as an inanimate object or a random system like a coin toss, dice roll or radioactive decay, then see if the person can mentally influence the target in a repeatable manner.

"The dice-tossing experiment is the epitome of simplicity. A die face is chosen in advance, then one or more dice are tossed while a person wishes for that face to turn up. If the person's intention matches the resulting die face, then a 'hit' is scored. If more hits are obtained than expected by chance over many dice tosses, that's evidence for PK. In 1989, when psychologist Diane Ferrari and I were at Princeton University, we used meta-analysis to assess the combined evidence for PK effects in dice experiments. We searched all the relevant English-language journals for the dice experiments published from the 1930s to 1989 ... We found 73 relevant publications, representing the efforts of 52 investigators from 1935 to 1987. Over that half-century, some 2,500 people attempted to mentally influence 2,600,000 dice throws in 148 different experiments, and just over 150,000 dice-throws in 31 control studies where no mental influence was applied to the dice ... The odds that the dice studies were due to chance alone were 10^96 to 1 (that's 10 with 96 zeros after it). By contrast, the results of control experiments were well within chance expectation. So something else was clearly going on." -Dean Radin, "Entangled Minds" (149)

When self-professed so-called rational, logically-minded "skeptics" hum and haw about the amazing findings in psi-science, I like to visually show them the odds against chance of various controlled and peer-reviewed studies. Dean Radin and Diane Ferrari's meta-analysis of psychokinetic dice experiments yielded a ratio of 10,000,000,000,000,000,000,000,000,000,0 00,000,000,000,000,000,000,000,000,000,0 00,000,000,000,000,000,000,000,000,000,0 00,000,000 to 1 odds against chance. On what grounds can such "rational skeptics" claim these odds to be mere coincidence?

"If all this is true, then why aren't the casinos going out of business? And why don't prayers work more reliably? The truth is that no one knows – yet. These experiments suggest that mind and matter are indeed related to a small degree that is statistically repeatable under controlled conditions. But we've barely scratched the surface of a phenomenon that's still profoundly mysterious. So offering answers to all the 'but why' questions evoked by these data, given our present state of knowledge, is terribly premature. I think a more reasonable question to ask at this point is: If the results of the dice experiments suggest a genuine mind-matter interaction, then there ought to be corroborating evidence from similar experiments using other types of physical targets. And there is." -Dean Radin, "Entangled Minds" (153)

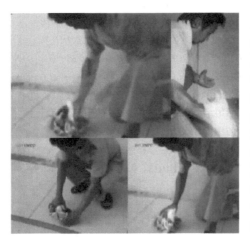

Another popular type of PK experiment involves using Random Number Generators (RNGs) which are simple machines that electronically generate up to thousands of random 0's or 1's (heads or tails) every second moving an indicator light either one step clockwise or one step counterclockwise. A volunteer then attempts to mentally influence the RNG outputs by willing more clockwise results (like "heads" known as the "high aim condition") or more counterclockwise results (like "tails" called the "low aim condition"). In 1997, after 12 years of RNG experiments at their Princeton Engineering Anomalies Research Laboratory (PEAR Lab), lead engineer Robert Jahn and his team formally published their findings. It seems when volunteers mentally intended for high aim conditions, the RNG outputs invariably drifted more clockwise above chance expectation. When volunteers intended for low aim conditions, the outputs drifted more counterclockwise above chance expectation. And when withdrawing all mental influence, the RNGs maintained an average baseline/control condition well within chance expectation. They found that couples working in tandem affected the output more substantially than individuals, and intimate couples affected the output six-fold. In their final meta-analysis the PEAR team's RNG experiments yielded 35,000,000,000,000 to 1 odds against chance that their volunteers can and did indeed intentionally influence the machines.

"For nearly 30 years at the Princeton Engineering Anomalies Research (PEAR) Laboratory, engineer Robert Jahn, his colleague Brenda Dunne, and their team have investigated whether volunteers could affect the random sequences of 0s and 1s produced by electronic RNGs ... The results showed conclusively that such influence is real. What's important to note is that they demonstrated that couples working together are able to affect the RNG outcomes substantially more than either can do as individuals. And for a couple who are emotionally bonded, the effects are six times those measured for each of them. In summarizing their vast archive of experimental results demonstrating nonlocal human awareness, Jahn has said, 'If people do not believe us after all the results we have produced, then they never will.'" -Ervin Laszlo and Jude Currivan, "Cosmos" (89)

Since 1997 the Global Consciousness Project has taken collective PK testing to a whole new level by placing RNGs all over the world which run automatically and incessantly in the background as indicators of collective mind-matter occurrences. The idea is that since RNGs are designed to generate pure randomness, any fluctuations in that randomness (i.e. sudden coalescent movement) can be observed and correlated with various global phenomena. The Global Consciousness Project began rather by accident when a dozen consciousness researchers with RNGs set up throughout the USA and Europe noticed a sudden coalescence in combined outputs during Princess Diana's world-wide live televised funeral.

"These studies rely on the fact that RNGs are designed to generate pure randomness, technically known as entropy, and that fluctuations in entropy can be detected using simple statistical procedures. If it turns out that the recorded entropy decreases when one of these random generators is placed near groups engaged in high focused attention, like a group meditation or a deeply engaging spiritual ritual, then we can infer something about the presence of coherent minds possibly infusing the environment with an ordering 'field' that reduces entropy." - Dean Radin, "Entangled Minds" (182)

As of 2008 the Global Consciousness Project had over 65 active RNGs all over the world covering 6 continents and collected data from 185 events of global interest. These events tested and verified by independent analysts included natural disasters, celebrity deaths, mass meditations, outbreaks of war/peace, new year celebrations, sporting events and many other occurrences with global influence. The world-wide level of coalescent RNG output during these 185 events showed a clear deviation from control/baseline outputs with odds against chance of 36,400 to 1.

"Perhaps the most dramatic event examined by the project so far occurred on September 11, 2001. On that day of infamy, now known as 9/11, we found numerous striking changes in the randomness network ...

In examining the results of this analysis, we noticed that something unusual happened one day. On September 11, 2001, the curve deviated wildly as compared to all the other days we examined. As it happened, this curve peaked nearly two hours before a hijacked jet crashed into World Trade Tower 1 in New York City at 8:46 a.m. EDT, and it dropped to its lowest point around 2 p.m., roughly eight hours later. There's no easy answer for why the peak in this curve occurred before the terrorist attacks unfolded, although it is reminiscent of the data obtained in the presentiment experiments ... The huge drop in this curve within an eight-hour period was the single largest drop for any day in the year 2001 ... What caused this large change? Did the massive coherence of mind on that day induce a massive coherence that was reflected in the RNGs? It appears so." -Dean Radin, "Entangled Minds" (202-4)

After 9/11 the Global Consciousness Project published an article in the Foundation of Physics Letters Journal focusing on the anomalous data gathered on that fateful day. They proved with odds against chance of 1,000,000 to 1 that an "autocorrelation," such as mass change in attention or emotion, caused the normally random output to behave in a dramatically non-random way.

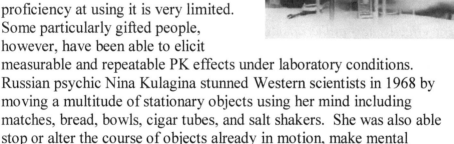

Scientifically and mathematically it has been documented and proven beyond reasonable doubt that PK does exist. Unfortunately our collective understanding of how it works and our proficiency at using it is very limited. Some particularly gifted people, however, have been able to elicit measurable and repeatable PK effects under laboratory conditions. Russian psychic Nina Kulagina stunned Western scientists in 1968 by moving a multitude of stationary objects using her mind including matches, bread, bowls, cigar tubes, and salt shakers. She was also able stop or alter the course of objects already in motion, make mental impressions on film, and speed up or stop a frog's heart! Ingo Swann, a New York psychic can change the temperature of objects near him and affect the magnetic field of a magnetometer. In 2001 University of Arizona psychology professor Gary Schwartz conducted a large-scale spoon-bending experiment with his students resulting in over 60 bent forks and spoons.

Even if they don't believe in mind over matter, most people behave as though their thoughts do affect the world. Surveys have shown that the vast majority of the world's population prays and many throughout history have witnessed and testified to the power of prayer. The majority of such prayers essentially ask for God, the Universe, or Nature to "roll the dice favorably" in our direction, thus things like prayer and distance healing are also testable PK techniques.

"Randolph Byrd in 1988 attempted to determine in a randomized, double-blind trial whether remote prayer would have any effect on patients in a coronary care unit. Over 10 months, nearly 400 patients were divided into two groups, and only half (unbeknownst to them) were prayed for by a Christian prayer group outside the hospital. All patients had been evaluated, and there was no statistical difference in their condition before treatment. However, after treatment, those who'd been prayed for had significantly less severe symptoms and fewer instances of pneumonia and also required less assistance on a ventilator and fewer antibiotics than patients who hadn't been prayed for." -Lynne McTaggart, "The Field: The Quest for the Secret Force of the Universe," (186-7)

"The effectiveness of therapeutic touch has also been demonstrated in several studies. For example, Dr. Janet Quinn, an associate professor and assistant director of nursing research at the University of South Carolina at Columbia, decided to see if therapeutic touch could lower the anxiety levels of heart patients. To accomplish this she devised a double-blind study in which one group of nurses trained in the technique would pass their hands over a group of heart patients' bodies. A second group with no training would pass their hands over the bodies of another group of heart patients, but without actually performing the technique. Quinn

found that the anxiety levels in the authentically treated patients dropped 17 percent after only five minutes of therapy, but there was no change in anxiety levels among the patients who received the 'fake' treatment. Quinn's study was the lead story in the Science Times section of the March 26, 1985, issue of the New York Times." -Michael Talbot, "The Holographic Universe" (173)

In 1998 Dr. Elisabeth Targ and Fred Sicher designed a famous double-blind study on the effects of remote healing for advanced AIDS patients. They selected 20 patients with the same T-cell counts and the same degree of illness, and then subjected 10 of them to various distance healing modalities for 6 months. Since it was double-blind, neither patients nor doctors knew who was being healed, and all information was kept in sealed envelopes. Only the healers themselves knew their targets, and to remove any individual bias, the healers had a weekly rotation guaranteeing that the healing effect itself (not one particular variety of it) was studied.

"After four months of searching, Fred and Elisabeth had their healers – an eclectic assortment of forty religious and spiritual healers all across America, many highly respected in their fields ... several Christian healers, a handful of evangelicals, one Jewish kabbalist healer and a few Buddhists. A number of others were trained in non-religious healing schools, such as the Barbara Brennan School of Healing Light, or worked with complex energy fields, attempting to change colors or vibrations in a patient's aura. Some used contemplative healing or visualizations; others worked with tones and planned to sing or ring bells on behalf of the patient, the purpose of which, they claimed, was to reattune their chakras, or energy centers. A few worked with crystals. One healer, who'd been trained as a Lakota Sioux shaman, intended to use the Native American pipe ceremony. Drumming and chanting would enable him to go into a trance during which he would contact spirits on the patient's behalf. They also enlisted a Qigong master from China, who said that he would be sending harmonizing qi

energy to the patients ... Collectively, the healers had an average of 17 years of experience in healing and reported an average of 117 distant healings apiece." -Lynne McTaggart, "The Field: The Quest for the Secret Force of the Universe," (188-89)

After 6 months, 4 of the original 20 patients had died, and several were becoming more ill, but several more were regaining health. When the files were opened, it turned out that the 4 patients who died and the patients with declining health were all in the control group. The 10 patients who received a weekly rotation of various remote healings all had improved overall health and T-cell counts.

"*Elisabeth was open-minded about it, but the conservative in her kept surfacing ... She remained fairly convinced that Native American pipe smoking and chakra chanting had nothing to do with curing a group of men with an illness so serious and so advanced that they were virtually certain to die. And then she saw her patients with end-stage AIDS getting better. During the six months of the trial period, 40 percent of the control population died. But all ten of the patients in the healing group were not only still alive but had become healthier, on the basis of their own reports and medical evaluations. At the end of the study, the patients had been examined by a team of scientists, and their condition had yielded one inescapable conclusion: the treatment was working.*" -Lynne McTaggart, "The Field: The Quest for the Secret Force of the Universe," (190)

Dr. Targ and Sicher decided to repeat the experiment this time with double the participants and control groups perfectly matched for age, degree of illness, personal habits and beliefs. Once again, after 6 months the treated group was overall healthier in all areas than the control group. The treated group had significantly fewer doctor visits, fewer hospitalizations, fewer AIDS-defining illnesses, lower severity of disease, and higher T-cell counts. Only 3 people in the treatment group had been hospitalized compared with 12 in the control group, and only 2 people in the treatment group developed new AIDS-defining illnesses compared with 12 in the control group.

"The results were inescapable. No matter which type of healing they used, no matter what their view of a higher being, the healers were dramatically contributing to the physical and psychological well-being of their patients ... In Elisabeth's study, it didn't seem to matter what method you used, so long as you held an intention for a patient to heal. Calling on Spider Woman, a healing grandmother star figure common in the Native American culture, was every bit as successful as calling on Jesus." -Lynne McTaggart, "The Field: The Quest for the Secret Force of the Universe," (192-3)

"My goal is simply to pave the way for free and fair scientific discourse on subjects that have previously been considered 'non-rational.' It's our responsibility as scientists and physicians to speak based on fact, not opinion. If there's a benefit to distant healing, physicians and patients should consider it along with all the other proven treatments for disease." -Dr. Elisabeth Targ

As highlighted in the Targ/Sicher studies, regardless of the patient's or healer's beliefs, or which modality is used, a significant, repeatable distance healing effect has been measured in peer-reviewed double-blind studies. It seems that the universal life force energy (the "Qi" in Qigong, the "Ki" in Reiki, and the "Prana" in Pranayama) regardless of what we call it, how we cultivate it, or what we believe about it, responds to our conscious will and generates a transmutable, transmittable healing effect.

163

"In the Copper Wall Project in Topeka, Kansas, a researcher named Elmer Green has shown that experienced healers have abnormally high electric field patterns during healing sessions. In his test, Green enclosed his participants in isolated rooms made with walls constructed entirely of copper, which would block electricity from any other sources. Although ordinary participants had expected electrical readings related to breathing or heartbeat, the healers were generating electrical surges higher than 60 volts during healing sessions, as measured by electrometers placed on the healers themselves and on all four walls. Video recordings of the healers showed these voltage surges had nothing to do with physical movement. Studies of the nature of the healing energy of Chinese Qigong masters have provided evidence of the presence of photon emission and electromagnetic fields during healing sessions. These sudden surges of energy may be physical evidence of a healer's greater coherence – his ability to marshal his own quantum energy and transfer it to the less organized recipient." -Lynne McTaggart, "The Field: The Quest for the Secret Force of the Universe," (194)

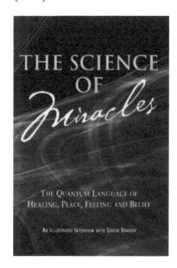

Gregg Braden, author of many books combining science and spirituality found one thing in common amongst all the monks, nuns, abbots, and shamans he interviewed. Having searched high mountain villages, remote monasteries, and forgotten holy texts looking for the commonality between various forms of prayer, meditation, and energy healing he came to one inescapable conclusion: The key is feeling. Much like the "Law of Attraction" one must first feel the inner sensations of peace, love, health, and abundance in order to attract and transmit that energy.

164

"In the spring of 1998, I had the opportunity to facilitate a combined research trip and pilgrimage into the highlands of central Tibet for 22 days. During that time the group and I found ourselves immersed in some of the most magnificent, rugged, pristine, and remote land remaining on the planet today. Along the way, we visited 12 monasteries, 2 nunneries, and some of the most beautiful humans that you could ever imagine including monks, nuns, nomads, and pilgrims. It was during that time that I found myself face-to-face with the abbot of one of the monasteries and got the chance to ask the question that we'd traveled so far and long to ask ... Through our translator, I asked him the same question that I'd asked every monk and nun we'd met throughout our pilgrimage. 'When we see your prayers,' I began, 'what are you doing? When we watch you intone and chant for 14 and 16 hours a day; when we see the bells, bowls, gongs, chimes, mudras, and mantras on the outside, what's happening to you on the inside?' A powerful sensation rippled through my body as the translator shared the abbot's answer. 'You've never seen our prayers,' he said, 'because a prayer cannot be seen ... What you've seen is what we do to create the feeling in our bodies. Feeling is the

prayer!' How beautiful, I thought. And how simple! Just as the late 20th century experiments had shown, it's human feeling and emotion that affect the stuff our reality is made of – it's our inner language that changes the atoms, electrons, and photons of the outer world." -Gregg Braden, "The Divine Matrix" (84)

"Perhaps mind and matter are like two sides of the same coin. To study such an effect, you could take a ribbon and write mind on the inside and matter on the outside. Now, as you wiggle the ribbon, you'll find very strong correlations between mind and matter, yet in a fundamental sense never the twain shall meet. Then one day, while you're distracted for a moment, a mischievous friend cuts your ribbon, creates a half-twist, and

carefully tapes it back together. Later you pick up the altered ribbon and proceed to ponder the abyss between mind and matter by absent-mindedly tracing a finger along the matter side of the ribbon. To your astonishment, you find that your finger ends up on the mind side! This is because the ribbon was transformed into a Mobius strip by your friend's half-twist, and this topological curiosity has only one side. The lesson is that sometimes simple twists in conventional concepts can unify things that appear to be quite different, like mind and matter. Some believe that consciousness may be the unifying 'substance' from which mind and matter arise." -Dean Radin, "Entangled Minds" (160)

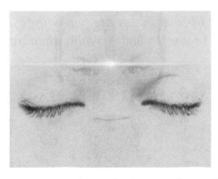

Clairvoyance, or as the intelligence agencies have renamed it, Remote Viewing, is the psychic ability to internally "see" and obtain information on a given target object, person, location or event across both space and time. Mystics, shamans, yogis, meditators, out-of-body experiencers, near-death experiencers, psychedelic users, people under hypnosis, and naturally gifted psychics have all reported the ability of clairvoyance for centuries. More recently however, experiments performed by the CIA, US Army, SRI and PEAR laboratories suggest that given proper training, everyone is capable of cultivating this skill of inner vision.

"Remote viewing is broadly speaking a controlled shifting of awareness performed from the normal waking state of consciousness ... Humans are all part of a collective Mind existing beyond the limitations of physical space and time. Anyone who is focused into this 'dimension', 'plane' or 'state,' which is a level of energy or vibration, either permanently or temporarily, can potentially project their consciousness anywhere within time or space in an instant. Remote viewing works therefore by means of the 'remote viewer' projecting, or tuning their consciousness into this spaceless and

timeless aspect of the universe." -Adrian Cooper, "Our Ultimate Reality" (130)

The term "Remote Viewing" was coined in the early 1970s by Stanford Research Institute's physicists Russell Targ and Harold Puthoff. In their experiments, one person (the "agent") would travel to a distant location randomly selected by computer, while another person (the "viewer") would attempt to clairvoyantly see and describe where the agent went. In Targ and Puthoff's initial experiments, one Soviet psychic was consistently able to accurately describe several locations, sometimes before the agent arrived, and sometimes before the computer had even made the selection! Throughout twenty years of research they carried out hundreds of successful tests using several different viewers and even demonstrated these feats on live television including on 60 Minutes and the Donahue show.

"*In these carefully controlled experimental tests spanning two decades, many different subjects sat in a windowless office, closed their eyes, and explored the world outside. These individuals were consistently able to experience and accurately describe distant scenes and events from coast-to-coast and even continent-to-continent, in both present and future time. The SRI experiments demonstrated unequivocal evidence for extrasensory perception and the existence of the nonlocal mind, outside the brain and body. The ability of human awareness to make remarkable connections apparently transcends the conventional limitations of time and space.*" - Russell Targ and Jane Katra, "Miracles of Mind" (6)

One day in 1973 Targ and Puthoff were contacted by Burbank, California Police Commissioner Pat Price who had been closely following their work and wanted to help. Price said that he had been practicing clairvoyance for years and successfully using it in his police work to catch criminals. Whenever dispatch reported a crime he would sit in his office, close his eyes, and psychically scan the city looking for someone matching the description. Once he pin-pointed their location in his mind's eye, he would send out a car to check, and actually succeeded in catching several criminals this way.

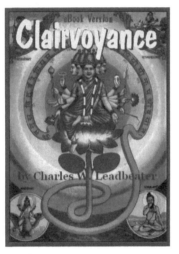

For Price's first informal experiment at SRI, Targ had him remotely view Puthoff who was on vacation. Sitting together in the Stanford lab each day, using Puthoff as the unwitting agent, Price described what he saw, recounting scenes of churches, market squares, and volcanic mountains all very characteristic of Central America. When Puthoff returned, he confirmed that his holiday was in Costa Rica and he had indeed visited churches, markets, and mountains on the very days that Price remotely viewed them.

"Price took over as chief remote viewer. Hal and Russ underwent nine trials with him, following their usual double-blind protocol of sealed target spots near Palo Alto – Hoover Tower, a nature preserve, a radio telescope, a marina, a toll plaza, a drive-in movie theater, an arts and crafts plaza, a Catholic church and a swimming pool complex. Independent judges concluded that Price had scored seven hits out of the nine. In some cases, like the Hoover Tower, Price even recognized it and correctly identified it by name. Price was noted for his incredible accuracy." -Lynne McTaggart, "The Field: The Quest for the Secret Force of the Universe," (153)

Through SRI the CIA got wind of Price's skills and initiated the now declassified Projects "GrillFlame" and "Scanate" in an attempt to clairvoyantly spy on sensitive targets. Price was given nothing but the

168

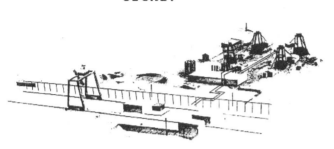

latitude and longitude of a remote location and asked to describe all details that he could see. With unwavering confidence Pat polished his glasses, sat back in his chair, closed his eyes and began recounting what he saw. It was a military airfield with a few buildings scattered around. There was a large 8 wheeled gantry set upon tracks, a big cluster of compressed gas cylinders at one end, and inside the buildings were masses of steel gores. Price then opened his eyes and drew pictures of the building layout, the cylinders, the gantry, and gores. When the results came back from CIA spy satellites and ground Intel, it turned out that the target site was indeed a Soviet military airfield and nuclear testing area in Semipalatinsk, Kazakhstan. The building layout, cylinders, 8 wheeled gantry, and even the steel gores inside were all confirmed to be just as Price described.

Sadly Pat Price died in 1975, but Targ and Puthoff continued their remote viewing projects and in 1978 met someone they later described as "the greatest natural

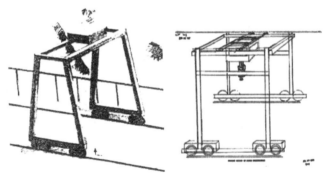

psychic ever to walk into our laboratory," US Army Special Projects Intelligence Officer Joe McMoneagle. A highly decorated and esteemed soldier, Joe McMoneagle had survived a near-death experience and had many out-of-body experiences which piqued his interest in remote viewing. He said the experience of leaving and looking down on his own body started him on his psychic journey and forever changed his metaphysics.

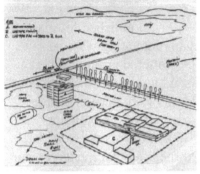

For his first experiment at SRI, Joe was told only that he would be viewing a "technological" target within 100 miles of the San Fransisco Bay Area (which is full of possible technological locations such as military bases, airports, factories, power plants, cell towers, linear accelerators, radar installations and radio telescopes). The actual target was the Lawrence Livermore Laboratory, the famous hydrogen bomb research facility directed by Edward Teller. Without hesitation Joe picked up his pencil and began drawing what he saw in his mind's eye: the multipurpose laboratory complex, segmented one-story buildings nearby, the six-story administration building, a T-shaped building, a cylindrical roofed building and a large parking lot. When Joe's drawing was finished it was independently deemed as 85% accurate.

"Joseph McMoneagle, remote viewer #001 in the U.S. Army's formerly Top Secret project codenamed GRILLFLAME, STARGATE, and other exotic names. McMoneagle has been repeatedly tested in numerous double-blind laboratory experiments and has been shown to have an ability to describe objects and events at a distance and in the future, sometimes in spectacular detail. In one experiment, all that McMoneagle knew was that a person he hadn't met before would be visiting a technological target, at a certain time, somewhere that could be reached within an hour's drive around Silicon Valley

in Northern California. The number and range of possible technological targets that one can get to in a short drive around Silicon Valley is gigantic. As it turned out, the target that the person arrived at was a particle beam accelerator, and that's what McMoneagle drew." -Dean Radin, "Entangled Minds" (292)

In perhaps his most impressive viewing session on record, Joe was given absolutely no feedback whatsoever about where the agent would be traveling and he was able to draw an astonishing resemblance independently verified as 94% accurate. The target was a windmill farm in the foothills of Livermore Valley, and that's exactly what Joe drew: Multiple wind generators, rotating blades, with poles scattered amongst the hills all connected in a grid.

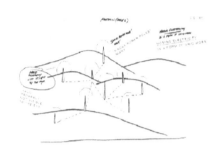

"Human beings, talented or otherwise, appear to have a latent ability to see anywhere across any distance. The most talented remote viewers clearly can enter some framework of consciousness, allowing them to observe scenes anywhere in the world. But the inescapable conclusion of their experiments is that anyone has the ability to do this, if they are just primed for it – even those highly skeptical of the entire notion ... Hal Puthoff gathered together nine remote viewers in total, mostly beginners with no track record as psychics, who performed in total over fifty trials. Again, an impartial panel of judges compared targets with transcripts of subject descriptions. The descriptions may have contained some inaccuracies, but they were detailed and accurate enough to enable the judges to directly match description with target roughly half the time – a highly significant result."

" -Lynne McTaggart, "The Field: The Quest for the Secret Force of the Universe," (155)

In her 1995 CIA funded evaluation of all Remote Viewing experiments conducted since 1970, Dr. Jessica Utts concluded that:

"Using the standards applied to any other area of science it is concluded

171

that psychic functioning has been well established. The statistical results of the studies examined are far beyond what is expected by chance. Arguments that these results could be due to methodological flaws in the experiments are soundly refuted. Effects of similar magnitude to those found in government-sponsored research at SRI and SAIC have been replicated at a number of laboratories across the world. Such consistency cannot readily be explained by claims of flaws or fraud."

In addition to SRI's studies, Princeton University's Engineering Anomalies Research (PEAR) Laboratory also conducted 25 years of remote viewing research with 653 trials involving 72 participants. Headed up by Dean of Engineering Robert Jahn and psychologist Brenda Dunne, in a 2003 meta-analysis they summarized their findings regarding the evidence for remote viewing. Their overall assessment showed with odds against chance of 33 million to 1, the results were definitely not due to luck or coincidence. Jahn and Dunne concluded, *"the overall results of these analyses leave little doubt, by any criterion, that the data contain considerably more information about the designated targets than can be attributed to chance guessing."*

"In the 1980s, I worked on a top secret psi research program for the U.S. government (now declassified). At the first research briefing I attended, I was shown examples of high-quality remote viewing obtained under exceptionally well-controlled circumstances. I asked in amazement, 'Why is psi still considered controversial by the scientific mainstream? Why not just conduct an experiment of 20 or 30 trials with this type of remote viewing skill? That ought to convince anyone that psi is real.' The answer, explained to me patiently by physicist Ed May, was simple. He said, 'You're making the rational man mistake.' He meant that we usually assume science is a rational process, but it's not ... The technical

term for one form of this irrational phenomenon is the 'confirmation bias.' This psychological quirk causes evidence supporting your beliefs to be perceived as plausible, and evidence challenging your beliefs to be perceived as implausible. Studies in social psychology have repeatedly demonstrated that journal reviewers invariably judge articles being submitted for publication according to their prior beliefs. Those who agree with a hypothesis tend to judge a paper reporting positive results

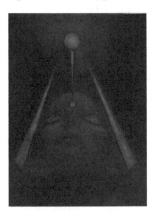

as an excellent piece of work, and those who disagree judge the very same paper as a flawed failure. The former referees recommend publication and the latter don't. The final decision is left up to the editor, so if the editor doesn't happen to agree with the paper's hypothesis then there's a good chance it won't appear in the journal. And then the evidence doesn't exist as far as the rest of the scientific community is concerned." -Dean Radin, "Entangled Minds" (101-2)

The ability of remote viewing raises some interesting questions and serious objections regarding the scientific materialist paradigm. Traditionally science has explained the miracle of sight as a purely material process taking place in the eyes and brain; however, this obviously conflicts with the research done at SRI and PEAR. Anyone trained in remote viewing or anyone who has experienced out-of-body travel and witnessed looking down upon their own sleeping body would have to agree that there must be something much more mystical and immaterial responsible for vision.

Life magazine once featured Rosa Kuleshova, a Russian girl who could read perfectly clearly using her fingertips. The Russian Academy of Science tested her repeatedly under controlled conditions and concluded that her abilities were genuine. Italian Doctor Cesare Lombroso wrote about a blind

patient who could see using her earlobe. Harvard Doctor David Eisenberg even published an article about two Chinese girls who can read using their armpits!

"Despite our unwavering conviction that we see with our eyes, reports persist of individuals who possess, 'eyeless sight,' or the ability to see with other areas of their bodies. Recently David Eisenberg, M.D., a clinical research fellow at the Harvard Medical School, published an account of two school-age Chinese sisters in Beijing who can 'see' well enough with the skin in their armpits to read notes and identify colors. In Italy the neurologist Cesare Lombroso studied a blind girl who could see with the tip of her nose and the lobe of her left ear. In the 1960s the prestigious Soviet Academy of Science investigated a Russian peasant woman named Rosa Kuleshova, who could see photographs and read newspapers with the tips of her fingers, and pronounced her abilities genuine ... Now, because every part of a hologram contains the whole, every part of the body - the hand, toe, knee - has the ability to pass frequency patterns to the brain, which it transforms into holograms that we can 'see'. This means that people really do have eyes in their backsides. I have heard some people speak of being able to see 360 degrees when they have entered altered states of consciousness that make them more attuned to these senses by withdrawing their focus from the five-sense consensus reality. All this is perfectly explainable from the holographic perspective." -Michael Talbot, "The Holographic Universe" (236-7)

Receiving direct knowledge or perception of the future, Precognition, is another common psi ability with a long-standing history. Precognition is usually achieved through prophetic dreams, during deep meditation, or spontaneously received as images in the mind's eye. The existence of this paranormal ability, however, once again goes against the Newtonian grain and strikes close to the heart of people's conceptions of time and

free will. Because if precognition is real, then the future must in some sense be pre-written and determined.

"Time is not at all what it seems. It does not flow in only one direction, and the future exists simultaneously with the past. The distinction between past, present, and future is only a stubbornly persistent illusion." -Albert Einstein

"Both in common experience and in physics, time has generally been considered to be a primary, independent and universally applicable order, perhaps the most fundamental one known to us. Now, we have been led to propose that it is secondary and that, like space, it is to be derived from a higher-dimensional ground, as a particular order." -David Bohm

"When asked to define time, the physicist John Wheeler once replied that time is what stops everything from happening at once. Scientists are still searching for a good definition, because the problem of time is that it doesn't appear to exist!" -Ervin Laszlo and Jude Currivan, "Cosmos" (68)

I have personally experienced Precognition on a few occasions but none as amazing or memorable as the following. During college I had what seemed to be a normal dream involving myself and my friend, wearing our typical attire, talking outside my dorm about what we wanted to do that day. Now I didn't remember even having the dream until the next day as my friend and I were approaching my dorm; every word she said started triggering the clearest, most mind-blowing déjà vu as the dream came flooding back to me. We were both wearing the same clothes I'd envisioned, we were standing in the same place, and every word she said was exactly as I had dreamt. Seizing the opportunity to test and manifest this amazing clarity of déjà vu I was experiencing, I quickly blurted out the entire next sentence that I knew she would be saying and matched her word for word in real time! Stunned at my simultaneous telepathic mocking, she abruptly stopped talking and I laughed uncontrollably trying to explain the whole thing.

That and other precognitive experiences forever changed my perception of the arrow of time. If time is truly linear then we can only remember the past and cannot in any way remember the future. But if it is impossible to remember the future, then what was my dream? How was I able to vividly see and remember the entire scenario in precise detail the night before it happened? I guarantee anyone who felt my paradigm-crushing déjà vu, would agree that this synchronicity was far beyond some quirky coincidence.

"Even our most ancient writings pay homage to the premonitory power of dreams, as is evidenced in the biblical account of Pharoah's dream of seven fat and seven lean cows ... The proximity the unconscious mind has to the atemporal realm of the implicate may also play a role. Because our dreaming self is deeper in the psyche than our conscious self – and thus closer to the primal ocean in which past, present, and future become one – it may be easier for it to access information about the future." -Michael Talbot, "The Holographic Universe" (210)

"One near-death experiencer described what he saw once the filter of human perception was lifted. He talked of seeing the 'panoramic view of life': ... everything from the beginning, my birth, my ancestors, my children, my wife, everything comes together simultaneously. I saw everything about me, and about everyone who was around me. I saw everything they were thinking now, what they thought then, what was

happening before, what was happening now. There is no time, there is no sequence of events, no such thing as limitation, of distance, of period, of time, of place. I could be anywhere I wanted to be simultaneously." – David Icke, "The David Icke Guide to the Global Conspiracy" (55)

President Lincoln dreamt of his own assassination a week before he died. British Aeronautics Engineer J.W. Dunne documented several prophetic dreams come true in his 1927 book "An Experiment with Time." There are even 19 documented cases of people who precognitively saw the sinking of the Titanic. Some by passengers who acknowledged their premonitions and survived, others by passengers who ignored their intuition and drowned, and others still by non-passengers.

Swedish scientist/mystic Emanuel Swedenborg had a gift for precognition and documented many independently verified examples. One evening, on June 19th, 1759 upon arriving at a dinner party in Goteborg, Swedenborg had a vision of Stockholm burning 300 miles away. He told everyone in attendance including the mayor about the blazing fire and that it had stopped only 3 doors from his home. The next day a messenger from Stockholm arrived and confirmed Swedenborg's incredible vision.

Dutch psychic Gerard Croiset was well-known for the several "chair tests" he accurately predicted. First the experimenter randomly selected a chair from the seating plan of some upcoming public event in a large theater, stadium, or auditorium anywhere in the world. There could be no reserved seating to prevent possible collusion or trickery. Then without telling him the name, the location or the event, knowing only the date and seating plan, Croiset consistently gave accurate and detailed descriptions of the people who would be sitting in any given chair. Over the course of 25 years numerous investigators in Europe and America were stunned by Croiset's accurate predictions including specifics like gender, dress, features, occupation, and personality.

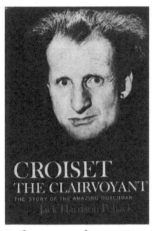

"For instance, on January 6, 1969, in a study conducted by Dr. Jule Eisenbud, a clinical professor of psychiatry at the University of Colorado Medical School, Croiset was told that a chair had been chosen for an event that would take place on January 23, 1969. Croiset, who was in Utrecht, Holland, at the time, told Eisenbud that the person who would sit in the chair would be a man five feet nine inches in height who brushed his black hair straight back, had a gold tooth in his lower jaw, a scar on his big toe, who worked in both science and industry, and sometimes got his lab coat stained by a greenish chemical. On January 23, 1969, the man who sat down in the chair, which was in an auditorium in Denver, Colorado, fit Croiset's description in every way but one. He was not five feet nine, but five feet nine and three-quarters."
-Michael Talbot, "The Holographic Universe" (207)

Psi-researcher Dean Radin highlighted the interesting case of Anne Ring in his "Entangled Minds" book. She sent him the following in a letter: *"Many years ago I had a very strange dream concerning my father. I dreamt that he was decorating the house (the way we do in England – or used to – with paper chains, holly, etc.). Except the decorations he was using were not the type used for Christmas. Suddenly he sat down on a chair and collapsed and he died. I woke up crying so loudly that it woke up my husband. I looked at the clock and it was exactly 2 a.m. California time. I told my*

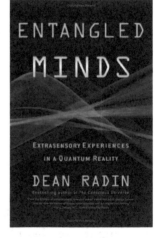

husband the dream and he just said, 'Well it's nothing, you are always having strange dreams, go back to sleep.' But the dream had disturbed me and it took a long while for me to get back to sleep. The following morning was Thanksgiving Day and as I was preparing the meal the telephone rang and it was my brother calling from London to say my father had died. It was a terrible shock because I had seen him in May of that year and he was in robust health (in fact, he had not ever been ill or in hospital in his life). I asked my brother when it had happened and he

178

replied that our stepmother had just called him and told him it had happened at 10 a.m. London time: The exact moment that I had the dream (2 a.m. California time). By the way, he was putting up decorations because it was his wedding anniversary to my stepmother and they were going to have a party that night."

"How shall we interpret this experience? Is it a poignant coincidence or is it a case of genuine clairvoyance? This was the one and only time Mrs. Ring ever had a dream like this, and it contained details and timings that matched real-world events. I've been told similar experiences by professors at major universities, by program directors at the NSF, and by generals in the Army. These are not naïve people prone to fantasy. They appreciate the difference between meaningless coincidence and genuinely exceptional events." -Dean Radin, "Entangled Minds" (105)

The most rigorous scientific study of dream psi ever took place at the Maimonides Medical Center in Brooklyn, New York. Over the course of several years, Psychologists Montague Ullman and Stanley Krippner ran hundreds of in-house and at-home dream sessions with thousands of volunteers. Experiments usually involved trying to predict random images chosen by computer and displayed overnight in a locked room at the dream lab. Each day volunteers attempted to dream of tomorrow's picture then recorded their impressions for Ullman and Krippner to cross-check. In 2003 when British psychologists Simon Sherwood and Chris Roe performed a meta-analysis of all the Maimonides dream psi results they found that the overall hit rate was associated with odds against chance of 22 billion to 1.

"In his work at the Dream laboratory at Maimonides Medical Center, Montague Ullman, along with psychologist Stanley Krippner and researcher Charles Honorton, produced compelling evidence that accurate precognitive information can also be obtained in dreams. In their study, volunteers were asked to spend eight consecutive nights at the sleep laboratory, and each night they were asked to try to dream about a picture that would be chosen at random the next day and shown to them. Ullman and his colleagues hoped to get one success out of eight, but found that some subjects could score as many as five 'hits' out of eight. For example, after waking, one volunteer said that he had dreamed of 'a large concrete building' from which a 'patient' was trying to escape. The patient had a white coat on like a doctor's coat and had gotten only 'as far as the archway.' The painting chosen at random the next day turned out to be Van Gogh's Hospital Corridor at St. Remy, a watercolor depicting a lone patient standing at the end of a bleak and massive hallway exiting through a door beneath an archway." -Michael Talbot, "The Holographic Universe" (206)

Other evidence such as psychic "forced-choice" experiments also supports the idea that we can see into the future. These entail having participants guess the outcome of future events with calculable possibilities like what playing card will turn up or what dice number will roll. In 1989 the Maimonides Center's Charles Honorton and Diane Ferrari published a meta-analysis of all forced-choice precognition experiments conducted since 1935. They found 309 studies with 50,000 participants totaling 2 million trials

where the time between prediction and event ranged from milliseconds to a year. The results were surprisingly positive with odds against chance of ten million billion billion to one.

One of the most convincing and astonishing proofs of precognition was discovered when University of Amsterdam's Dr. Dick Bierman hooked several poker players to electrodermal instruments to test learned responses in gambling addicts. He found that they all registered rapid changes in electrodermal activity just <u>before</u> being handed their cards. Not only this but the differences in EDA corresponded with the type of cards being drawn. When about to receive a bad hand participants showed physiological activity indicating a heightened fight or flight response. When about to receive a favorable hand their EDA calmed towards a relaxation response. This indicates that on a subconscious physiological level, somehow we already "know" the future.

Building on Bierman's work, Dean Radin also hooked volunteers up to electrodermal and other physiological instruments (heart rate, blood pressure, skin conductivity etc.) to test for recordable physical effects of anticipating future stimuli. In his experiment volunteers would click a mouse button, wait 5 seconds, view a random picture displayed on their monitor for 3 seconds, then watch as the screen went blank for 10 seconds and began again. The images randomly shown were either tranquil photos such as landscapes and nature scenes or disturbing photos such as autopsies and erotica.

"As expected, the participant's body would calm down immediately after he or she observed the tranquil scenes, and become aroused after being confronted by the erotic or disturbing. Naturally, study participants recorded the largest response once they'd seen the photos. However, what Radin discovered was that his subjects were also anticipating what they were about to see, registering physiological responses before

they'd seen the photo. As if trying to brace themselves, their responses were highest before they saw an image that was disturbing. Blood pressure would drop in the extremities about a second before the image was flashed." -Lynne McTaggart, "The Field: The Quest for the Secret Force of the Universe," (169)

"The idea of presentiment assumes that we are constantly and unconsciously scanning our future, and preparing to respond to it. If this is true, then whenever our future involves an emotional response, we'd predict that our nervous system would become aroused before the emotional picture appears ... As expected, skin conductance reacted 2 to 3 seconds after the presentation of an emotional stimulus, and the expected differences between the calm and emotional responses were clearly evident. But the presentiment effect, which was predicted to occur before the stimulus, was also observed ... The skin-conductance levels were virtually identical before the button press, but as soon as the button was pressed they began to diverge in accordance with the future stimulus." -Dean Radin, "Entangled Minds" (166-7)

 Nobel laureate Kary Mullis had the opportunity to participate in Dean Radin's presentiment experiment and was quite impressed with the results. He went on National Public Radio's May 1999 Science Friday program afterwards stating, *"I could see about 3 seconds into the future. It's spooky. You sit there and watch this little trace, and about three seconds, on average, before the picture comes on, you have a little response in your skin conductivity which is in the same direction that a large response occurs after you see the picture. Some pictures make you have a rise in conductivity, some make you have a fall. He's done that over and over again with people. That, with me, is on the edge of physics itself, with time. There's something funny about time that we don't understand because you shouldn't be able to do that."*

In 2004 psychophysiologist Rollin McCraty replicated Bierman and Radin's experiments and published his results in the Journal of Alternative and Complementary Medicine. With odds against chance of

1000 to 1 he found that heart rate significantly slowed before future disturbing pictures and that the brain responded differently before the two different types of stimuli.

"Lest we forget what's going on in this experiment, it's useful to be reminded what these results mean: The brains of both men and women were activated in specific areas before erotic pictures appeared, even though no one knew in advance that those pictures were about to be selected. In other words, the brain is responding to future events. Given the controversial nature of this claim, Bierman discussed in detail alternative explanations for these results ... He concluded that the fMRI results were valid, and in agreement with the other studies based on skin-conductance and heart and brain measures ... When you step back from the details of these studies, what you find is a spectacular body of converging evidence indicating that our understanding of time is seriously incomplete. These studies mean that some aspect of our minds can perceive the future. Not infer the future, or anticipate the future, or figure out the future. But actually perceive it." -Dean Radin, "Entangled Minds" (179)

In ordinary states of consciousness and without the aid of technology most people are able to remember the past but not the future. This has led to the philosophical idea of an "arrow of time" shooting from past to future with us riding along the present. In altered states of consciousness or with the aid of technology, however, many people, myself included, have been able to experience and remember future events in detail. Perhaps then it is more likely that time, as our ancient ancestors believed, is cyclic and infinite, not straight and finite. It seems that ultimately, our consciousness exists outside of this time/space/matter explicate hologram and therefore under the right conditions has the ability to access and experience anything in the implicate. Physicist David Bohm concurred and wrote that, *"when people dream of accidents correctly and do not take the plane or ship, it is not the actual future that they were seeing. It was merely something in the present which is implicate and moving toward making that future. In fact, the future they saw differed from the actual future because they altered it. Therefore I think it's more plausible to say that, if these phenomena exist, there's an anticipation of the future in the implicate order in the present. As they used to say, coming events cast their shadows in the present. Their shadows are being cast deep in the implicate order."*

"Such incidents strongly suggest that the future is not set, but is plastic and can be changed. But this view also brings with it a problem. If the future is still in a state of flux, what is Croiset tapping into when he describes the individual who will sit down in a particular chair seventeen days hence? How can the future both exist and not exist? Loye provides a possible answer. He believes that reality is a giant hologram, and in it the past, present, and future are indeed fixed, at least up to a point. The rub is that it is not the only hologram. There are many such holographic entities floating in the timeless and spaceless waters of the implicate, jostling and swimming around one another like so many amoebas. 'Such holographic entities could also be visualized as parallel worlds, parallel universes,' says Loye. Thus, the future of any given holographic universe is predetermined, and when a person has a precognitive glimpse of the future, they are tuning into the future of that particular hologram only. But like amoebas, these holograms also occasionally swallow and engulf each other, melding and bifurcating like the protoplasmic globs of energy that they really are. Bohm's and Loye's descriptions seem to be two different ways of trying to express the same thing – a view of the future as a hologram that is substantive enough for us to perceive it, but malleable enough to be susceptible to change. Others have used still different words to sum up what appears to be the same basic thought. Cordero describes the future as a hurricane that is beginning to form and gather momentum, becoming more concrete and unavoidable as it approaches. Ingo Swann, a gifted psychic who has produced impressive results in various studies, including Puthoff and Targ's remote-viewing research, speaks of the future as composed of 'crystallizing possibilities.' The Hawaiian kahunas, widely esteemed for their precognitive powers, also speak of the future as fluid, but in the process of 'crystallizing,' and believe that great world events are crystallized furthest in advance, as are

184

the most important events in a person's life, such as marriage, accidents, and death." -Michael Talbot, "The Holographic Universe" (211-212)

"Time, then, is much like a hologram that already stands complete; it's a subjective sensory effect of a progressively moving point of view. There's no beginning or end to a hologram, it's already everywhere, complete – in fact, the appearance of being 'unfinished' is part of its completeness. Even the phenomenon of 'unfoldment' itself reflects a limited point of view: There is no enfolded and unfolded universe, only a becoming awareness. Our perception of events happening in time is analogous to a traveler watching the landscape unfold before him. But to say that the landscape unfolds before the traveler is merely a figure of speech – nothing is actually unfolding; nothing is actually becoming manifest. There's only the progression of awareness ... In fact, this is a holographic universe. Each point of view reflects a position that's defined by the viewer's unique level of consciousness ... A hologram, we might say, is in and of itself a process. There's nothing fixed in a three-dimensional hologram. And what then of a four-dimensional hologram? It would include all possible instances of itself simultaneously. To change seems to be to move through time, but if time itself is transcended, then there's no such thing as sequence. If all is now, there's nothing to follow from here to there." -David R. Hawkins, M.D., Ph.D., "Power Vs. Force" (232-239)

Out-of-Body Experiences

An out-of-body experience is a condition usually occurring spontaneously during meditation, deep sleep, hypnosis, shamanic trance, sensory-deprivation, anesthesia, extreme illness or trauma, in which one finds themselves outside their physical body, yet remaining fully conscious and perceiving everything normally. Robert Monroe describes it as *"an altered state of consciousness in which the subject feels that his mind or self-awareness is separated from his physical body and this self-*

awareness has a vivid and real sense about it, quite different from a dream."

The experience typically begins by finding yourself floating over or standing next to your physical body, perceiving normally, but with a great feeling of lightness and power. You may see your physical body lying on the bed or you may just rise straight up through the ceiling. You may have a ghostly, astral body which can fly around or you may be a point of pure consciousness which can travel instantaneously to wherever you think about.

"Some individuals describe themselves as amorphous clouds, energy patterns, or pure consciousness; others experience distinct feelings of having a body which is, however, permeable, invisible, and inaudible for those in the phenomenal world. Sometimes there is fear, confusion, and a tendency to return to the physical body; sometimes there are ecstatic feelings of timelessness, weightlessness, peace, serenity, and tranquility. Some individuals in this state show concern about the fate of their physical bodies; others feel totally indifferent." -Stanislav Grof & Joan Halifax, "Human Encounter with Death" (154)

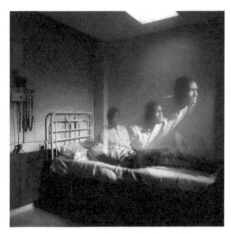

"You can move through space (and time) slowly or apparently somewhere beyond the speed of light. You can observe, participate in events, make willful decisions based upon what you perceive and do. You can move through physical matter such as walls, steel plates, concrete, earth, oceans, air, even atomic radiation without effort or effect. You can go into an adjoining room without bothering to open the door. You can visit a friend three thousand miles away. You can explore the moon, the solar system, and the galaxy if these interest you. Or you can

enter other reality systems only dimly perceived and theorized by our time/space consciousness." –Robert Monroe, "Far Journeys" (3-4)

Most OBEs have common features. They all typically begin while in an altered state of consciousness your awareness shifts to a point outside your physical body. The physical body is usually seen dormant on the bed (or wherever you left it) while a second, astral body is seen attached to your new space of awareness. This light, ghostly body can pass through walls or solid objects, float/fly around, and is sometimes even seen by other people.

"In the OOBE, the individual is near-totally conscious ... Most if not all of your physical sensory perception is replicated. You can 'see,' 'hear,' and 'touch' - the weakest seem to be smell and taste. Your perspective is from a position outside your physical body, near or distant. In a near state, it is usually from a location impossible for you to 'be' with your physical body, such as floating against the ceiling. In a far location, it could be in Paris when you know you are in New York physically. You can observe events taking place, but you cannot change or significantly affect them. You can verify the authenticity of such events subsequently if you so desire." –Robert Monroe, "Far Journeys" (265)

OBE's have been reported throughout history by people of all ages and cultures. The soul-body or astral-body was known as the "ka" to ancient Egyptians, the "siddhi" to Indians, and the "bardo-body" to Tibetans. OBEs are the main subject matter, described in detail in the Egyptian and Tibetan Books of the Dead. St. Paul seems to describe an OBE in second Corinthians chapter twelve. Ernst

Hemmingway wrote about witnessing his soul leave his physical body and float around after being hit by shrapnel in 1918.

"Aldous Huxley, Goethe, D. H. Lawrence, August Strindberg, and Jack London all reported having OBEs. They were known to the Egyptians, the North American Indians, the Chinese, the Greek philosophers, the medieval alchemists, the Oceanic peoples, the Hindus, the Hebrews, and the Moslems. In a cross-cultural study of 44 non-Western societies, Dean Shiels found that only three did not hold a belief in OBEs. Erika Bourguignon looked at 488 world societies – or roughly 57 percent of all known societies – and found that 437 of them, or 89 percent, had at least some tradition regarding OBEs ... Dr. Robert Crookall, a geologist at the University of Aberdeen and an amateur parapsychologist, investigated enough cases to fill nine books on the subject. " -Michael Talbot, "The Holographic Universe" (230)

"It is quite well known, for example, that many cultures attribute to shamans the capacity to fly out of the body. In fact, a shaman cannot be anointed as such unless he has that capacity. According to Eliade, such flights express 'intelligent understanding of secret things, metaphysical truths, symbolic meaning, transcendence, and freedom.'" –Robert Monroe, "Far Journeys" (278)

Many surveys have also been conducted in recent years testing the prevalence of the OBE phenomenon. In 1954 Dr. Hornell Hart of Duke University surveyed 115 of his students and found that 27 of them had experienced an OBE at least once. A 1966 study by Celia Green showed that 19% of students asked at Southampton University had had one. A 1968 Green15 survey reported that 34% of 380 Oxford undergraduates had experienced an OBE. Palmer and

Dennis' 1975 study randomly selected a group of 1,000 students and townspeople in a small Virginia town resulting in 25% of the students, and 14% of the townspeople answering affirmatively. Erlendur Haraldsson's random survey of 902 adults found 8% had been out of their bodies at least once. And a 1980 survey by Dr. Harvey Irwin at the University of New England in Australia found 20% of his 177 had experienced out-of-body travel. All results pooled together, it seems an average of about 1 in 7 people experiences an OBE at least once during their lives.

"First, OOBEs are a universal human experience, not in the sense that they happen to large numbers of people, but in that they have happened all through recorded history, and there are marked similarities in the experience among people who are otherwise extremely different in terms of cultural background. One can find reports of OOBEs by housewives in Kansas which closely resemble accounts of OOBEs from ancient Egyptian or oriental sources. Second, the OOBE is generally a once-in-a-lifetime experience, seemingly experienced by 'accident.' Illnesses sometimes bring it about, especially illnesses which are almost fatal. Great emotional stress sometimes brings it about. In many cases, it simply happens during sleep without our having any idea of what might have caused it. In very rare instances it seems to have been brought about by a deliberate attempt. Third, the experience of an OOBE is usually one of the most profound experiences of a person's life, and radically alters his beliefs. This is usually expressed as, 'I no longer [merely] believe in survival of death or an immortal soul, I <u>know</u> that I will survive death.' The person feels that he has directly experienced being alive and conscious without his physical body, and therefore knows that he possesses some kind of soul that will survive bodily death." –Robert Monroe, "Journeys Out of the Body" (7)

In Robert Monroe's book "Far Journeys" he shares many recorded accounts of OBEs including the following: *"When I was approximately ten years old I was living together with my older brother at my uncle's house, a major in the U.S. Army Medical Corps. One day I was reclined on my bed quite awake and was looking at the ceiling beams of the old Spanish building where the living quarters were located. I was saying to myself many questions such as what was I doing there and who was I. All of a sudden I get up from the bed and start walking toward the next room. At that moment I felt a strange sensation in me; it was a sensation of weightlessness and a strange mix of a sense of a feeling of joy. I turned*

back in my steps in order to go back to bed when to my big surprise I saw myself reclined on the bed. This surprising experience at that very small age gave me the kind of a jerk which, so to say, shook me back to my body." (276-7)

When talking about these subjects at work I found that one of my colleagues, while under anesthesia for an operation, found himself out-of-body hovering against the ceiling in the corner of the Operating Room where he watched his body and the surgeons perform the entire procedure. It turns out this is actually a fairly common occurrence. Dr. Michael Rawlings recorded the account of one patient who remembered what the doctor was wearing and what he did during an emergency procedure, which was seemingly impossible because the patient was in a coma at the time.

"Out-of-body experience also eventually became a relatively common subject, as more and more surgical patients reported that they witnessed their entire operations and heard everything that was said in the operating room." - David R. Hawkins, M.D., Ph.D., "Power Vs. Force" (258)

"Experiencing an OBE during cardiac arrest is relatively common, so common that Michael B. Sabom, a cardiologist and professor of medicine

*at Emory University and a staff physician at the Atlanta Veterans'
Administration Medical Center, got tired of hearing his patients recount
such 'fantasies' and decided to settle the matter once and for all."* -
Michael Talbot, "The Holographic Universe" (232)

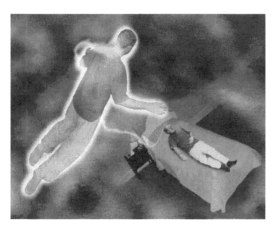

Dr. Sabom interviewed 32 chronic cardiac patients who reported having an OBE during their heart attack and the results forever changed his mind about this phenomenon. He asked them to describe exactly what they remembered happening during the procedure while they were out-of-body:

"26 gave correct but general descriptions, 6 gave highly detailed and accurate descriptions of their own resuscitation, and 1 gave a blow-by-blow accounting so accurate that Sabom was stunned. The results inspired him to delve even deeper into the phenomenon ... he has now become an ardent believer and lectures widely on the subject." -Michael Talbot, "The Holographic Universe" (232)

In conclusion to his research, Dr. Sabom stated: *"[There appears] to be no plausible explanation for the accuracy of these observations involving the usual physical senses. The out-of-body hypothesis simply seems to fit best with the data at hand."*

"There are many people who have reported OBEs in which they saw things that really did happen. The most common of these are the descriptions by patients undergoing surgery, who claim to have witnessed the whole procedure from outside their body. Some have reported details of the procedure that they could not have possibly known, such as where the doctors put gall stones that were removed. Some patients have

accurately repeated conversations that went on during the surgery. Skeptics may dismiss such cases by theorizing that some subconscious part of the patient still had cognitive abilities during the operation, and assuming that somehow the patient accessed this subconscious memory when they awoke. This theory cannot explain the less common cases where OBE subjects have reported what was happening in a different room. These seem to suggest that the subject could actually see some part of physical reality." –Robert Peterson, "Out of Body Experiences" (86)

My fiancé Petchara has also experienced OBEs many times periodically throughout her life. Always during sleep, having drifted off into the subconscious realms, there comes a self-reflexive moment where she finds herself floating in her room with a light-body while fully aware that her physical body is asleep on the bed. From there she usually leaves through the closed window by her bed and floats over the roofs/houses/roads in her village. On many occasions she has astrally projected to the houses of classmates, houses she had never visited before, and remembered specific details which were later confirmed true by her shocked classmates. During one OBE she found herself at her friend Tan's house and saw orange stairs, a street sign, a van parking lot on one side and a small wooded area on the other, all subsequently confirmed true by Tan. Another time she found herself apparently outside her friend Oil's new condo, face to face with a "do not enter" sign on the door and a large swimming pool on the left, both later confirmed to be true. Not long after meeting me, she astrally traveled to my old house in America where my parents still live and accurately reported the outline, white color, gray tin roof, garage, shelving and flower beds.

"I had a spontaneous OBE as a teenager, and after recovering from the shock of finding myself floating over my body and staring down at myself asleep in bed, I had an indescribably exhilarating time flying through walls and soaring over the treetops. During the course of my bodiless journey I even stumbled across a library book a neighbor had lost and

was able to tell her where the book was located the next day." -Michael Talbot, "The Holographic Universe" (231)

In Dr. Stanislav Grof's book "The Holotropic Mind" he shares the account of one Cuban woman who, during cardiac arrest in a Miami hospital, found herself out-of-body back at her old home in Cuba. She recovered from the heart attack, but came back to her body very agitated about what she had seen while astrally in Cuba. The people now living in her old home had moved everything around, changed furniture, and painted the fence a shade of green which she hated; all of which were subsequently verified and documented by her curious attending physician.

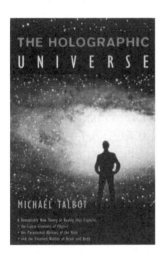

In Michael Talbot's "The Holographic Universe" he shares the story of Kimberly Clark, a Seattle hospital social worker who never took OBEs seriously until an incident with a coronary patient named Maria. One day Maria went into cardiac arrest and found herself hovering against the ceiling watching the doctors and nurses tending to her body. She watched for a while and then found herself distracted by something over the emergency room driveway. As soon as she thought about this, she was instantly there hovering outside the hospital:

"As soon as she 'thought herself' there, she was there. Next Maria 'thought her way' up to the third floor of the building and found herself 'eyeball to shoelace' with a tennis shoe. It was an old shoe and she noticed that the little toe had worn a hole through the fabric. She also noticed several other details, such as the fact that the lace was stuck under the heel. After Maria finished her account she begged Clark to please go to the ledge and see if there was a shoe there so that she could confirm whether her experience was real or not. Skeptical but intrigued ... she went up to the third floor and ... found a room where she pressed her face against the glass and looked down and saw the tennis shoe. Still, from her vantage point she could not tell if the little toe had worn a place

in the shoe or if any of the other details Maria had described were correct. It wasn't until she retrieved the shoe that she confirmed Maria's various observations. 'The only way she would have had such a perspective was if she had been floating right outside and at very close range to the tennis shoe,' states Clark, who has since become a believer in OBEs. 'It was very concrete evidence for me.'" -Michael Talbot, "The Holographic Universe" (231-232)

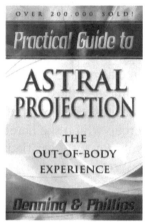

"In some instances of OOBEs the description of what was happening at a distant place is correct and more accurate than we would expect by coincidence. Not the majority, by any means, but some. To explain these we must postulate either that the 'hallucinatory' experience of the OOBE was combined with the operation of ESP, or that in some sense the person really was 'there.' The OOBE then becomes very real indeed. The fact that most of our knowledge about OOBEs comes from reports of once-in-a-lifetime experiences puts us at two serious disadvantages. The first of these is that most people cannot produce an OOBE at will, so this precludes the possibility of studying them under precise laboratory conditions. The second disadvantage is that when a person is suddenly thrust for a brief period of time into a very novel environment he may not be a very good observer." –Robert Monroe, "Journeys Out of the Body" (8)

OBEs are generally sporadic or once-in-a-lifetime phenomena so scientifically verifying their authenticity is an elusive task. However, with the help of many skilled astral projectors, OBEs have indeed been scientifically documented in the lab. For instance, in one experiment, parapsychologist Charles Tart wrote a five-digit number on a pad of paper then kept it in a locked room. In another room an experienced astral traveler laid down, shifted consciousness to her astral body, floated through the wall and accurately reported the number. In another series of experiments, psychologists Janet Lee Mitchell and Karlis Osis set up a special room for OBE trials at the American Society for Psychical Research in New York. They placed certain images, objects, and colored geometric patterns in various places around the room, locked it, and then had skilled astral projectors from many places across the country project in and record what they saw. Many of the participants were able to correctly identify everything in the room. In another series of experiments, Dr. Robert Morris, director of research at the Psychical Research Foundation in North Carolina, used pets to detect the astral presence of their owners. For example, during one experiment, a kitten belonging to seasoned astral traveler Keith Harary would always stop meowing and start purring whenever Keith astrally projected into the room.

"Some people have mastered the ability well enough to leave their body at will. One of the most famous of these individuals is a former radio and television executive named Robert Monroe ... Monroe began keeping a written journal of his experiences, carefully documenting everything he learned about the out-of-body state. He discovered he could pass through solid objects and travel great distances in the twinkling of an eye simply by 'thinking' himself there. He found that other people were seldom aware of his presence, although the friends whom he traveled to see while in this 'second state' quickly became believers when he accurately described their dress and activity at the time of his out-of-body visit. He also discovered that he was not alone in his pursuit and occasionally bumped into other disembodied travelers." -Michael Talbot, "The Holographic Universe" (233)

"As an example of a real-time projection experience, I think of my nephew Matt's two-week visit back in 1991. During this time, apart from many other activities, I coached Matt on projection. A few days before he was due to leave, while meditating late at night, I clearly saw Matt's projected real-time double float through the wall and come into the room I was sitting in. He waved cheerfully at me and I slowly waved back at him, without breaking my entranced state - no mean feat in itself - immensely pleased that Matt had finally managed to get out of his body.

195

Matt floated about the room, seemingly having some difficulty with movement and directional control, but apparently thoroughly enjoying himself. He soon floated out of my sight and that was the last I saw of him that night. The next morning Matt was very excited about his first conscious-exit projection. He vividly remembered using my technique and feeling heavy vibrations, then leaving his body, moving through the wall and seeing me, and us waving at each other." –Robert Bruce, "Astral Dynamics" (8)

I have also personally experienced a mild OBE. Once while meditating during a magic mushroom trip my center of awareness shot up to about 5 feet above my head. I could see and hear normally, but the vantage point was no longer from my physical eyes and ears; it was from a point well above them, making me feel like a sitting giant. It only lasted for a few moments, but that experience of clearly seeing/hearing from a point far above my physical eyes/ears was enough to shatter my already waning materialist worldview.

"Considered as a whole the evidence seems unequivocal. Although we are taught that we 'think' with our brains, this is not always true. Under the right circumstances our consciousness – the thinking, perceiving part of us – can detach from the physical body and exist just about anywhere it wants to. Our current scientific understanding cannot account for this phenomenon, but it becomes much more tractable in terms of the holographic idea. Remember that in a holographic universe, location is itself an illusion. Just as an image of an apple has no specific location on a piece of holographic film, in a universe that is organized holographically things and objects also possess no definite location; everything is ultimately nonlocal, including consciousness. Thus, although our consciousness appears to be localized in our heads, under certain conditions it can just as easily appear to be localized in the upper corner of the room, hovering over a grassy lawn, or floating eyeball-to-shoelace with a tennis shoe on the third-floor ledge of a building … If the idea of a nonlocal consciousness seems difficult to grasp, a useful analogy can once again be found in dreaming. Imagine that you are dreaming you are attending a crowded art exhibit. As you wander among

the people and gaze at the artworks, your consciousness appears to be localized in the head of the person you are in the dream. But where is your consciousness really? A quick analysis will reveal that it is actually in everything in the dream, in the other people attending the exhibit, in the artworks, even in the very space of the dream. In a dream, location is also an illusion because everything – people, objects, space, consciousness, and so on – is unfolding out of the deeper and more fundamental reality of the dreamer." -Michael Talbot, "The Holographic Universe" (234)

Near-Death Experiences

Another fascinating phenomenon closely related to the OBE is the NDE or Near-Death Experience. The NDE is essentially the ultimate OBE occurring at the moment of physical death. Throughout history people who have died and later been resuscitated report the same story of consciousness leaving their physical body, entering a realm of love and light, meeting angelic beings, and watching their entire lives flash before their eyes. Slight differences exist in various accounts of NDEs, but these pale next to the incredible universal similarities. The typical NDE is as follows:

"*A man is dying and suddenly finds himself floating above his body and watching what is going on. Within moments he travels at great speed through a darkness or a tunnel. He enters a realm of dazzling light and is warmly met by recently deceased friends and relatives. Frequently he hears indescribably beautiful music and sees sights – rolling meadows, flower-filled valleys, and sparkling streams – more lovely than anything he has seen on earth. In this light-filled world he feels no pain or fear*

and is pervaded with an overwhelming feeling of joy, love, and peace. He meets a 'being (and/or beings) of light' who emanates a feeling of enormous compassion, and is prompted by the being(s) to experience a 'life review,' a panoramic replay of his life. He becomes so enraptured by his experience of this greater reality that he desires nothing more than to stay. However, the being tells him that it is not his time yet and persuades him to return to his earthly life and reenter his physical body."
-Michael Talbot, "The Holographic Universe" (240)

"*A man is dying and, as he reaches the point of greatest physical distress, he hears himself pronounced dead by his doctor. He begins to hear an uncomfortable noise, a loud ringing or buzzing, and at the same time feels himself moving very rapidly through a long dark tunnel. After this, he suddenly finds himself outside of his own physical body, but still in the immediate physical environment, and he sees his own body from a distance, as though he is a spectator. He watches the resuscitation attempt from this unusual vantage point and is in a state of emotional upheaval. After a while, he collects himself and becomes more accustomed to his odd condition. He notices that he still has a 'body' but one of a very different nature and with very different powers from the physical body he has left behind. Soon other things begin to happen. Others come to meet and to help him. He glimpses the spirits of relatives and friends who have already died, and a loving, warm spirit of a kind he has never encountered before - a being of light - appears before him. This being asks him a question, nonverbally, to make him evaluate his life and helps him along by showing him a panoramic, instantaneous playback of the major events of his life. At some point he finds himself approaching some sort of barrier or border, apparently representing the limit between earthly life and the next life. Yet, he finds that he must go, back to the earth, that the time for his death has not yet come. At this point he resists,*

for by now he is taken up with his experiences in the afterlife and does not want to return. He is overwhelmed by intense feelings of joy, love, and peace. Despite his attitude, though, he somehow reunites with his physical body and lives." –Dr. Raymond Moody, "Life After Life" (34)

Considering the fact that "hallucination" is the usual skeptical argument against NDEs, it is important to note that the main features are amazingly consistent. The "hallucination" always begins by finding oneself in a non-physical body somewhere near your now lifeless physical body. At this point your consciousness becomes more expansive than ever, all sensation and perception becomes incredibly lucid, you can hear the thoughts and feel the feelings of everyone around, and you can travel at the speed of thought. Eventually the physical world begins to fade as you proceed to float through a luminous tunnel, walk up a long staircase, cross a narrow bridge or other such transitional, archetypal scene. In Greek mythology all newly deceased souls crossed the river Styx on a ferry boat from the world of the living to Hades, the world of the dead. After transitioning from the world of the living, you begin to see or feel the presence of deceased friends/relatives, angels, so-called "light-beings" who communicate telepathically and send overwhelming emanations of love. You are then shown a full spectrum playback of your entire life accurate to the finest detail which you re-experience from this space of expanded consciousness able to think, feel, and fully understand not only yourself

but everyone you have ever interacted with in life. You feel the betrayal of a cheated spouse, understand your enemies, realize your true friends, and so on; you feel and experience the consequences of your actions on everyone else.

Ultimately you are told or decide to come back to the world of the living and find yourself stuck in your physical body right at the moment of your resuscitation. This seems like quite a coherent, meaningful, and oft-repeated sequence of events to be so casually labeled "hallucination."

"It was nothing like an hallucination. I have had hallucinations once, when I was given codeine in the hospital. But that had happened long before the accident which really killed me. And this experience was nothing like the hallucinations, nothing like them at all ... I tried to tell my minister, but he told me I had been hallucinating, so I shut up ... I tried to tell my nurses what had happened when I woke up, but they told me not to talk about it, that I was just imagining things. So, in the words of one person: you learn very quickly that people don't take to this as easily as you would like for them to. You simply don't jump up on a little soapbox and go around telling everyone these things." –Dr. Raymond Moody, "Life After Life" (34-6)

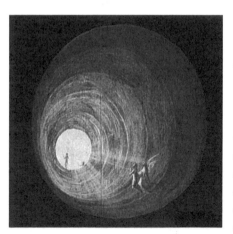

"Some people later choose to relate their NDE experiences to doctors, relatives and friends, however it is likely the vast majority do not, often believing for example they will not be believed or worse are considered to have been hallucinating due to the anesthetic or other medical factors associated with the medical situation, or suffering from after-effects arising from the physical condition leading to the NDE. Other people are afraid to relate NDE experiences on the basis they might be considered to be mentally deranged or will be ridiculed. To most people experiencing an NDE, relating the experience to others seems pointless, the experience itself being so intensely profound and personal. Research

has proven however that literally millions of people have experienced an NDE, most of which are described as deeply profound, life changing experiences." -Adrian Cooper, "Our Ultimate Reality" (394)

Regardless of many so-called experts claiming the contrary, no near-death experiencer ever considers their NDE to have been a hallucination. In fact, universally, NDErs report the experience to be "more real than this reality" and "like returning home." Not to mention, during the NDE, these patients are indeed clinically dead and showing zero brain activity  which fundamentally sets NDEs apart from traditional "hallucinations." Furthermore, there are hundreds of documented cases in which NDErs come back to life and report in detail actual events that occurred while they were "dead" and out of body! This obviously conflicts with the notion that NDEs are mere hallucinations.

 *"Although the orthodox view of NDEs is that they are just hallucinations, there is substantial evidence that this is not the case. As with OBEs, when NDEers are out-of-body, they are able to report details they have no normal sensory means of knowing. For example, Moody reports a case in which a woman left her body during surgery, floated into the waiting room, and saw that her daughter was wearing mismatched plaids. As it turned out, the maid had dressed the little girl so hastily she had not noticed the error and was astounded when the mother, who did not physically see the little girl that day, commented on the fact. In another case, after leaving her body, a female NDEer went to the hospital lobby and over heard her brother-in-law tell a friend that it looked like he was going to have to cancel a business trip and instead be one of his sister-in-law's pall bearers. After the woman*

recovered, she reprimanded her astonished brother-in-law for writing her off so quickly." -Michael Talbot, "The Holographic Universe" (241)

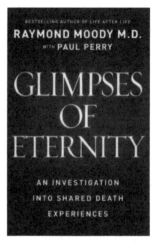

"Several doctors have told me, for example, that they are utterly baffled about how patients with no medical knowledge could describe in such detail and so correctly the procedure used in resuscitation attempts, even though these events took place while the doctors knew the patients involved to be 'dead.' In several cases, persons have related to me how they amazed their doctors or others with reports of events they had witnessed while out of the body. While she was dying, for example, one girl went out of her body and into another room in the hospital where she found her older sister crying and saying, 'Oh, Kathy, please don't die, please don't die.' The older sister was quite baffled when, later, Kathy told her exactly where she had been and what she had been saying, during this time." –Dr. Raymond Moody, "Life After Life" (40)

To date there are hundreds of independently verified and documented cases in which NDErs have come back to life accurately reporting events that happened in other rooms / buildings / places while they were "dead." Even more astonishing, there are several cases in which <u>blind</u> NDErs have gained sight while out of body and given detailed visually accurate accounts of their surroundings! NDE researcher Dr. Elisabeth Kubler-Ross interviewed many such clinically blind patients who were able to see perfectly while "dead" and out of body. She wrote that, "*to our amazement, they were able to describe the color and design of clothing and jewelry the people present wore.*"

"Raymond Moody, Kenneth Ring, Michael Sabom, Elisabeth Kubler-Ross, and other highly respected researchers, have repeatedly confirmed that people in near-death situations have had out-of-body-experiences

(OOBEs), during which they were able to witness events happening in other rooms or even distant places. These accounts have been objectively verified by independent observers. The ultimate challenge to Newtonian science in this area of research has been the discovery that clinically blind people experiencing OOBEs describe scenes that are visually accurate, though after recovering from the disease or trauma that caused the near-death experience they are not able to see." -Stanislav Grof, "The Holotropic Mind" (133-134)

If NDErs are clinically dead and all brain activity has ceased, yet they still retain regular memory and cognitive function, then the orthodox explanation of consciousness arising from the brain must be incorrect. If OBErs and NDErs are comatose with their eyes closed (or blind), yet they still experience regular vision while out-of-body, then the orthodox explanation of sight arising from eyes must also be incorrect. Moreover, not only do NDErs retain their sight, memory, and cognitive functioning, but they universally report them to be expanded and deepened. This strongly suggests that consciousness, the ability to see, remember, and have an inner witness to the external world is intangibly inherent in nature and not created by or confined to biological structures. It suggests that our brains, eyes, and nervous systems act not as creators of consciousness, but rather as receiver/transmitters of consciousness. It suggests that consciousness is an objective, omnipresent, omniscient, omnipotent underlying field of awareness received and transmitted by various subjective biological organisms in various degrees on various frequencies. It suggests that we all channel Objective Universal Mind (God) into subjective packets of awareness to experience and participate in creation.

"People who have 'near death' or 'out-of-body' experiences describe how they could still see while they were looking down at their bodies lying on the operating table or wherever. If we see with our eyes, or indeed even

our brain, how come we can see without them?" –David Icke, "Infinite Love is the Only Truth, Everything Else is Illusion" (107)

Dr. Raymond Moody is the psychologist/medical doctor who actually coined the term "near-death experience" in his 1975 book Life After Life. After conducting interviews and an in-depth study of 150 patients who had clinically died and come back, Dr. Moody became a firm believer in life after death. Since then he has written nearly a dozen more intriguing books on the subject. His research identifies nine experiences common to almost all NDEs:

-Hearing sounds such as buzzing
-Feeling absolute peace and painlessness
-Having an out-of-body experience
-Traveling through a tunnel
-Rising into the heavens
-Seeing angels or dead relatives
-Meeting a spiritual being such as God
-Seeing a review of one's life
-Feeling reluctant to return to life

Dr. Moody's research also focuses on the after-effects NDEs have on people mentally, emotionally, and spiritually. His patients came back from their near-deaths with many epiphanies, new paradigms and lifestyle changes, all of them positive. For instance most NDErs came back with a more jovial, relaxed demeanor, a more sincere, loving, forgiving, appreciative attitude, and became less worldly and more intuitive, less materialistic and more spiritual.

"One of the most important aspects of Moody's study is his discussion of the effects the death experiences had on the lives of these individuals. They felt that their lives had broadened and deepened. They developed serious interest in ultimate philosophical and spiritual issues, and started pursuing quite different values in life than before. Existence suddenly appeared much more precious, and much more emphasis was put on a

full experience of the present moment, on the here and now. There were deep changes in the concept of the relative importance of the physical body and the mind; rarely, this was associated with the development of psychic abilities." -Stanislav Grof & Joan Halifax, "Human Encounter with Death" (156)

"*One last piece of evidence of the reality of the NDE is the transformative effect it has on those who experience it. Researchers have discovered that NDEers are almost always profoundly changed by their journey to the beyond. They become happier, more optimistic, more easygoing, and less concerned with material possessions. Most striking of all, their capacity to love expands enormously. Aloof husbands suddenly become warm and affectionate, workaholics start relaxing and devoting time to their families, and introverts become extroverts. These changes are often so dramatic that people who know the NDEer frequently remark that he or she has become an entirely different person. There are even cases on record of criminals completely reforming their ways, and fire-and-brimstone preachers replacing their message of damnation with one of unconditional love and compassion. NDEers also become much more spiritually oriented. They return not only firmly convinced of the immortality of the human soul, but also with a deep and abiding sense that the universe is compassionate and intelligent, and this loving presence is always with them.*" -Michael Talbot, "The Holographic Universe" (268-9)

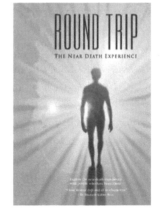

Perhaps the most amazing and fascinating aspect of NDEs is that no one ever wants to come back to life, and once they do, they lose all fear of death! The beauty, the wonder, the feelings of absolute bliss and contentment experienced on "the other side" are so compelling that everyone wishes nothing more than to stay. Inevitably though, once they do come back, they are never again afraid to die. NDErs are not afraid to die because they have personally experienced the continuation of consciousness beyond physical death and this gnosis alleviates any fear. Dr. Moody commented on this phenomenon, saying that, *"As one might reasonably expect, this experience has a profound effect upon one's attitude towards physical death, especially for those who had not previously expected that anything took place after death. In some form or another, almost every person has expressed to me the thought that he is no longer afraid of death."* Here are just a few testimonies from Dr. Moody's patients:

1) *"I am thoroughly convinced that there is life after death, without a shadow of a doubt, and I am not afraid to die. I am not. Some people I have known are so afraid, so scared. I always smile to myself when I hear people doubt that there is an afterlife, or say, 'When you're dead, you're gone.' I think to myself, 'They really don't know.' I've had many things happen to me in my life. In business, I've had a gun pulled on me and put to my temple. And it didn't frighten me very much, because I thought, 'Well, if I really die, if they really kill me, I know I'll still live somewhere.'"*

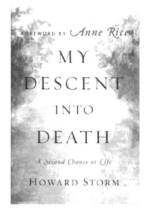

2) *"When I was a little boy I used to dread dying. I used to wake up at night crying and having a fit. My mother and father would rush into the bedroom and ask what was wrong. I told them that I didn't want to die, but that I knew l had to, and asked if they could stop it. My mother would talk to me and tell me, 'No, that's just the way it is and we all have to face it.' She said that we all had to do it alone and that when the time came we would do it all right. And years later after my mother died I would talk about death with my wife. I still feared it. I didn't want it to come. But since this experience, I don't fear death. Those feelings vanished. I don't feel bad at funerals anymore. I kind of rejoice at them, because I know what the dead person has been through."*

3) *"Now, I am not afraid to die. It's not that I have a death wish or want to die right now. I don't want to be living over there on the other side*

now, because I'm supposed to be living here. The reason why I'm not afraid to die, though, is that I know where I'm going when I leave here, because I've been there before." –Dr. Raymond Moody, "Life After Life"

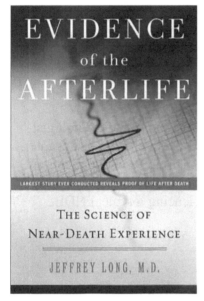

Dr. Moody comments that, *"The reason why death is no longer frightening, as all of these excerpts express, is that after his experience a person no longer entertains any doubts about his survival of bodily death. It is no longer merely an abstract possibility to him, but a fact of his experience."* Many of Dr. Moody's patients have actually ceased using the word "death" altogether, insisting that if by "death" one means "the annihilation of consciousness," then death is a misnomer – it does not exist. Moody seems to agree with this assertion as evidenced by the title of his first NDE book, "Life After Life." One of his patients stated, *"Some say that we are not using the word 'death' because we are trying to escape from it. That's not true in my case. After you've once had the experience that I had, you know in your heart that there's no such thing as death. You just graduate from one thing to another - like from grammar school to high school to college."*

"NDE, OBE and astral projection are all experiences reproducing what will happen to each and every person at the point of physical death, resulting in a profound knowing of the truth of the higher realities and the continuation of life after the death of the physical body. Anyone enjoying these experiences will profoundly know beyond any doubts the state known as 'death' is not final but is rather the continuation of a much greater adventure, the next stage in life as an immortal spiritual being of the multi-dimensional universe." -Adrian Cooper, "Our Ultimate Reality" (397)

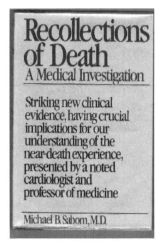

Recollections of Death
A Medical Investigation

Striking new clinical evidence, having crucial implications for our understanding of the near-death experience, presented by a noted cardiologist and professor of medicine

Michael B. Sabom, M.D.

In 1981 Gallup performed a telling poll which found that eight million adult Americans (over 5% of the population) had experienced an NDE! This massive figure means that if NDEs are mere hallucinations as the orthodox establishment would have us believe, then they are absolutely epidemic mass hallucinations affecting millions and millions. Is this even plausible?

In 1982 Dr. Michael Sabom, the cardiologist-OBE-skeptic-turned-believer from last chapter, collated 5 years of interviews with patients brought back to life after clinical death. Out of these 78 patients, 40% of them without being prompted reported experiencing a typical NDE.

"What Sabom discovered, much to his surprise, was the level of commonality expressed by those who reported NDEs – one that has remained consistent throughout all such subsequent research. Often the experience involves the person traveling through a tunnel to an all-encompassing light that innately feels loving and blissful, to be met by departed loved ones or archetypal or iconic figures. There's an expansion of awareness regularly accompanied by a nonjudgmental but frank life review. And sometimes – appearing to be by personal choice and other times by a gentle but firm mandate – the person is made to return to his or her life often with the profound sense of having to complete a mission." -Ervin Laszlo and Jude Currivan, "Cosmos" (146)

Dr. Sabom found there was no difference in religious convictions between NDErs and non-NDErs, nor was there any difference in being previously aware of the existence of such experiences. In fact, more patients who had NDEs were previously unaware of the existence of NDEs, than those who were already aware of them. Dr. Sabom's research concluded that NDEs happen regardless of expectation, religion, culture or creed.

"NDEers also have no unique demographic characteristics. Various studies have shown that there is no relationship between NDEs and a person's age, sex, marital status, race, religion, and/or spiritual beliefs, social class, educational level, income, frequency of church attendance, size of home community, or area of residence. NDEs, like lightning, can strike anyone at any time. The devoutly religious are no more likely to have an NDE than nonbelievers." -Michael Talbot, "The Holographic Universe" (240)

In 1990 pediatrician Dr. Melvin Morse first became interested in the NDE phenomenon after interviewing 12 young children recently resuscitated from cardiac arrest and 8 of them reporting NDEs. Over the next 10 years Dr. Morse interviewed every cardiac arrest survivor at his hospital. Time and time again, he heard the same story recounted. The patients found themselves outside their physical bodies, watched the doctors scramble to resuscitate them, were drawn into a mystical tunnel, and greeted by angelic light beings.

"Dr. Melvin Morse, a pediatrician in Seattle, Washington, first became interested in NDEs after treating a seven year-old drowning victim. By the time the little girl was resuscitated she was profoundly comatose, had fixed and dilated pupils, no muscle reflexes, and no corneal response ... Despite these odds, she made a full recovery and when Morse looked in on her for the first time after she regained consciousness she recognized him and said that she had watched him working on her comatose body. When Morse questioned her further she explained that she had left her body and passed through a tunnel into heaven where she had met 'the Heavenly Father.' The Heavenly Father told her she was not really meant to be there yet and asked if she wanted to stay or go back. At first she said she wanted to stay, but when the Heavenly Father pointed out that that decision meant she would not be seeing her mother again, she changed her mind and returned to her body. Morse was skeptical but fascinated and from that point on set out to learn everything he could about NDEs." -Michael Talbot, "The Holographic Universe" (242-243)

Dr. Pim Van Lommel is another leading cardiologist who became convinced there is life after death due to hearing the NDE accounts of so many patients. In 2001 he interviewed 344 heart patients at his Netherlands hospital who had been clinically dead for at least 5 minutes. 62 of them (or 18%) reported having lucid OBEs or NDEs, and could recall in detail specifics of what happened during their time spent "dead" out of body. Since 2001, Van Lommel has resigned his post as practicing cardiologist to pursue his research into NDEs.

"Dutch cardiologist Pim van Lommel produced a massive study of near-death experiences that supported the whole concept of life after death, as well as raising questions about DNA, the collective unconscious and the idea of 'karma'. His findings were published in the British medical journal, The Lancet. Van Lommel's interest was sparked 35 years ago when a patient told him about her near-death experience, but his serious study only began after he later read a book called Return from Tomorrow in which the American doctor, George Ritchie, detailed his own experience of 'near-death'. Van Lommel began to ask all his patients if they

remembered anything during their cardiac arrests." –David Icke, "The David Icke Guide to the Global Conspiracy" (23)

In one popular case, a female NDEer found herself moving towards the light at the end of the tunnel and saw a friend of hers coming back the other way! As they passed each other, the friend telepathically communicated that he had died but was being sent back. Confused, the woman continued down the tunnel only to eventually be sent back herself. Upon resuscitation, she discovered that her friend had suffered cardiac arrest at approximately the same time and vividly remembered seeing and communicating with her as well! Here are a few quotes from some of Van Lommel's other patients about their NDEs:

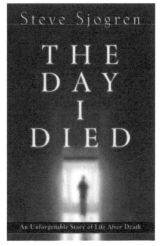

1) *"I became 'detached' from the body and hovered within and around it. It was possible to see the surrounding bedroom and my body even though my eyes were closed. I was suddenly able to 'think' hundreds or thousands of times faster, and with greater clarity, than is humanly normal or possible. At this point I realized and accepted that I had died. It was time to move on. It was a feeling of total peace - completely without fear or pain, and didn't involve any emotions at all."*

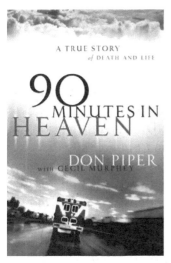

2) *"I was looking down at my own body from up above and saw doctors and nurses fighting for my life. I could hear what they were saying. Then I got a warm feeling and I was in a tunnel. At the end of that tunnel was a bright, warm, white, vibrating light. It was beautiful. It gave me a feeling of peace and confidence. I floated towards it. The warm feeling became stronger and stronger. I felt at home, loved, nearly ecstatic. I saw my life flash before me. Suddenly I felt the pain of the accident once again and shot back into my body. I was furious that the doctors had brought me back. This experience is a blessing for me, for now I know for sure that body and soul are separated, and that there is life after death. It has convinced me that consciousness lives on beyond the grave. Death is not death, but another form of life."*

3) *"[During my NDE] I saw a man who looked at me lovingly, but whom I did not know. [Later] At my mother's deathbed, she confessed to me that I had been born out of an extramarital relationship, my father being a Jewish man who had been deported and killed during the Second World War, and my mother showed me his picture. The unknown man that I had*

seen years before during my near-death experience turned out to be my biological father."

Dr. Van Lommel notes in his research that at the moment of their "deaths" not only are NDErs conscious, but their consciousness becomes more expansive than ever. They are able to think hundreds of times clearer/quicker than normal and remember every detail of their lives since childhood, yet all the while they are clinically dead and showing zero brain activity! This raises the obvious philosophical question, if consciousness is merely a by-product of brain activity, as the scientific-materialist establishment would have us believe, then how is it possible for millions of people to experience these phenomena? Whether they are authentic visits to the afterlife or merely hallucinations, either way, NDEs defy the orthodox theory that consciousness arises from brain activity.

Just like Dr. Moody, Dr. Van Lommel found that his patients lost all fear of death after coming back from their NDEs, and the reason for this, Dr. Van Lommel says, *"is because they have experienced that their consciousness lives on, that there is continuity. Their life and their identity don't end when the body dies. They simply have the feeling they're taking off their coat."*

"The NDE may climax with a merging into an indescribably loving and powerful white light that emanates from the divine, holy, and sacred. This leads to a mystical or spiritual experience in which time and space lose all meaning. Those who undergo an NDE feel embraced by something much greater than themselves, or anything they previously could have imagined: the 'source of all existence.' There's a certainty that consciousness exists after death. Those who reach the mystical level of the NDE emerge with a greater appreciation for life, less fear of death, and a reorientation of their priorities to less material and more spiritual

pursuits. The sense of reality of what near-death experiencers see and feel is undeniably certain, and it's common to hear expressions like 'it was more real than real.' It is difficult for those 'coming back' from an NDE to describe it; they often say it is 'beyond language.'" -Dr. Rick Strassman, "DMT – The Spirit Molecule" (220-1)

My good friend Chris Wilshaw from the TaoWow blog (www.taowow.blogspot.com) experienced an NDE while traveling abroad in India many years ago. Near the end of his  visit, he became very ill, weak, and unable to keep down food for over a fortnight, after which he died. Chris wrote of that fateful evening:

"At some point that night I knew for sure I was dying. I knew when I was close to death. I knew the point I had accepted death. I knew, for certain, as with all of these stages, each one, what they were and what they meant. And I knew when I was dead. The bliss and completeness were un-put-into-wordable and I have accepted that now years on. The experience is with me now but language does not exist to paint it."

 During his NDE (which he emphasizes was a <u>Death</u> Experience, not a <u>Near-Death</u> Experience) Chris went through most of Dr. Moody's 9 stages. He did not hear any buzzing or beautiful music, but did feel absolute peace and completeness, lifted out of his physical body, traveled through a tunnel upward to the heavens, and met some notable astral beings: He encountered a man painting statues of ancient deities who claimed to be the inventor of Hinduism; he sat in silent meditation with the Buddha; he interacted with a female Gaia entity; and finally *"reached a point of no beings, no separations, and pure completeness – no room for God, no duality."* Amazingly when Chris came back into his body the next morning, he was completely healthy, had a full appetite, and felt all his energy replenished. Now looking back at his NDE, he recounts a few basic truths that were shown to him:

"The basics of the truths that were clearly made to me that night are that: All is this, one, perfect. Life and death are nothing but ideas. The idea of separate self is an idea. We are like nodes of a complete net and each node is the whole net, but for this experience only sees as far as the next few nodes – beyond that is mystery, yet beyond that is infinity and if anything is infinite, it is also you. You're infinite, you are me as I am you as we are one. The one. Life and death are not separate but one action. The 'universe,' the 'infinite,' whatever you call it, is living, it has beings. These beings 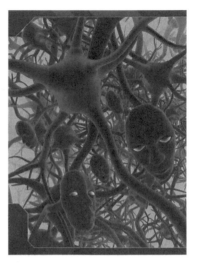 *come and go, but their coming and going are not life or death. An infinite number of beings have been born and will be born. An infinite number of beings have died and will die. Yet in all of this living and dying, the infinite had no beginning and will have no end. And that infinite, is you."*

As for overcoming the fear of death, I asked Chris, "are you less afraid or unafraid of death now?" to which he replied, *"What people fear is the thought of those left behind and the dissolution and end of their ego. Death is easy for the one who dies and hard on the ones left behind. It would be a great gift to let every person on earth know that when someone dies, this is not sad and not an end – that way both of these fears could be removed: No concern for those left behind and no last wrestling with the ego. The NDE is a very powerful experience that does clear up these human concerns. It would indeed be a gift if it could be given. Death is not an end and is no bad thing. If I died now I would die peacefully and in bliss."*

Dr. Moody only recently coined the term "Near-Death Experience" in the 1970s, but the NDE phenomenon has a long-standing history with documented examples going back thousands of years.

"Like OBEs, NDEs appear to be a universal phenomenon. They are described at length in both the eighth-century Tibetan Book of the Dead and the 2,500 year-old Egyptian Book of the Dead. In Book X of The Republic Plato gives a detailed account of a Greek soldier named Er, who came alive just seconds before his funeral pyre was to be lit and said that he had left his body and went through a 'passageway' to the land of the dead. The venerable Bede gives a similar account in his eighth-century work A History of the English Church and People, and, in fact, in her recent book Otherworld Journeys Carol Zaleski, a lecturer on the study of religion at Harvard, points out that medieval literature is filled with accounts of NDEs."* -Michael Talbot, "The Holographic Universe" (240)

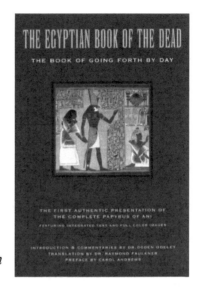

In Book X of The Republic, Plato recounted the story of a Greek soldier named Er who died on the battlefield and came back to life almost ten days later just as his body was about to be incinerated. Er awoke with a start and began describing what he had seen on the other side. He said his soul left his physical body and joined with a group of other spirits who led him upwards through a "passage way" (tunnel?) to the afterlife. There the other souls were taken by divine light beings and shown detailed life reviews. Er himself was shown many sights, but not his life review, and was ultimately sent back and told to inform others on Earth about what he experienced in the afterlife realm. Amazingly this two and a half thousand year old story sounds exactly like modern NDE accounts.

"According to Plato, the soul comes into the physical body from a higher and more divine realm of being., For him it is birth which is the sleeping and the forgetting, since the soul, in being born into the body, goes from a state of great awareness to a much less conscious one and in the meantime forgets the truths it knew while in its previous out-of-body state. Death, by implication, is an awakening and remembering. Plato remarks that the soul that has been separated from the body upon death can think and reason even more clearly than before, and that it can recognize things in their true nature far more readily. Furthermore, soon after death it faces a 'judgment' in which a divine being displays before the soul all the things - both good and bad - which it has done in its life and makes the soul face them." –Dr. Raymond Moody, "Life After Life" (46)

Plato's mentor Socrates' belief in the afterlife was so strong that he actually looked forward to his own death with curiosity and excitement. Socrates said that death was simply the separation of soul from body and an awakening from "illusion to reality," this 5-sense world being the illusion, and "reality" existing on the higher non-physical planes. This is consistent also with the Egyptian and Tibetan Books of the Dead which suggest that immediately following death we assume a "ka" or "bardo" spiritual body which transcends the ordinary limitations of time, space, and matter.

"In the Tibetan account the mind or soul of the dying person departs from the body. At some time thereafter his soul enters a 'swoon' and he finds himself in a void - not a physical void, but one which is, in effect, subject to its own kind of limits, and one in which his consciousness still exists. He may hear alarming and disturbing noises and sounds, described as roaring, thundering, and whistling noises, like the wind, and usually finds himself and his surroundings enveloped in a grey, misty illumination. He is surprised to find himself out of his physical body. He sees and hears his relatives and friends mourning over his body and preparing it for the funeral and yet when he tries to respond to them they neither hear nor see him. He does not yet realize that he is dead, and he is confused. He asks himself whether he is dead or not, and, when he finally realizes that he is,

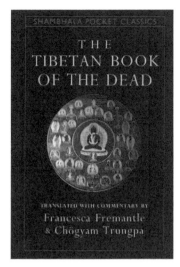

wonders where he should go or what he should do. A great regret comes over him, and he is depressed about his state. For a while he remains near the places with which he has been familiar while in physical life. He notices that he is still in a body-called the 'shining' body - which does not appear to consist of material substance. Thus, he can go through rocks, walls, and even mountains without encountering any resistance. Travel is almost instantaneous. Wherever he wishes to be, he arrives there in only a moment. His thought and perception are less limited; his mind becomes very lucid and his senses seem more keen and more perfect and closer in nature to the divine. If he has been in physical life blind or deaf or crippled, he is surprised to find that in his 'shining' body all his senses, as well as all the powers of his physical body, have been restored and intensified. He may encounter other beings in the same kind of body, and may meet what is called a clear or pure light. The Tibetans counsel the dying one approaching this light to try to have only love and compassion towards others. The book also describes the feelings of immense peace and contentment which the dying one experiences, and also a kind of 'mirror' in which his entire life, all deeds both good and bad, are reflected for both him and the beings judging him to see vividly. In this situation, there can be no misrepresentation; lying about one's life is impossible. In short, even though The Tibetan Book of the Dead includes many later stages of death which none of my subjects have gone so far as to experience, it is quite obvious that there is a striking similarity between the account in this ancient manuscript and the events which have been related to me by twentieth-century Americans." –Dr. Raymond Moody, "Life After Life" (48)

The Bible also contains stories of typical near-death experiences such as Paul on the road to Damascus. Paul was a persecutor of Christians until receiving his famous vision and conversion. Acts 26 describes how Paul saw a "light from heaven, above the brightness of the sun, shining round about me." He then heard the voice of Jesus speaking to him asking "why persecutest thou me?" The voice then tells Paul that he has appeared to him for a purpose, to make him a minister and a witness of God.

"This episode obviously bears some resemblance to the encounter with the being of light in near death experiences. First of all, the being is endowed with personality, though no physical form is seen, and a 'voice' which asks a question and issues instructions emanates from it. When Paul tries to' tell others, he is mocked and labeled as 'insane.' Nonetheless, the vision changed the course of his life: He henceforth became the leading proponent of Christianity as a way of life, entailing love of others." –Dr. Raymond Moody, "Life After Life" (44)

1 Corinthians 15 gets even more specific regarding the life after death state. It is asked "How are the dead raised up? And with what body do they come?" to which it is answered that there are both terrestrial bodies and celestial bodies, natural bodies and spiritual bodies. In death, the scripture says "we shall not all sleep, but we shall all be changed. In a moment, in the twinkling of an eye … the dead shall be raised incorruptible."

"Interestingly, Paul's brief sketch of the nature of the 'spiritual body' corresponds very well with the accounts of those who have found

themselves out of their bodies. In all cases, the immateriality of the spiritual body - its lack of physical substance - is stressed, as are its lack of limitations. Paul says, for example, that whereas the physical body was weak and ugly, the spiritual body will be strong and beautiful. This reminds one of the account of a near-death experience in which the spiritual body seemed whole and complete even when the physical body could be seen to be mutilated, and of another in which the spiritual body seemed to be of no particular age, i.e., not limited by time." –Dr. Raymond Moody, "Life After Life" (44-5)

In 1688, the "Leonardo da Vinci of his era," Swedish mystic Swedenborg was born. He spoke nine languages and was a successful mathematician, politician, astronomer and businessman. He built watches and microscopes, invented prototypes for the submarine and airplane, and wrote books on diverse subjects ranging from physics and chemistry to color theory and metallurgy.

"Throughout all of this he also meditated regularly, and when he reached middle age, developed the ability to enter deep trances during which he left his body and visited what appeared to him to be heaven and conversed with 'angels' and 'spirits.' That Swedenborg was experiencing something profound during these journeys, there can be no doubt. He became so famous for this ability that the queen of Sweden asked him to find out why her deceased brother had neglected to respond to a letter she had sent him before his death. Swedenborg promised to consult the deceased and the next day returned with a message which the queen confessed contained information only she and her dead brother knew. Swedenborg performed this service several times for various individuals who sought his help, and on another occasion told a widow where to find a secret compartment in her deceased husband's desk in which she found some desperately needed documents. So well known was this latter incident that it inspired the

German philosopher Immanuel Kant to write an entire book on Swedenborg entitled Dreams of a Spirit-Seer." -Michael Talbot, "The Holographic Universe" (257-8)

Swedenborg's descriptions of his out of body experiences in the afterlife realm, just like Plato's, the Bible's, and the Egyptian/Tibetan Books of the Dead all closely parallel descriptions given by modern day near-death experiencers. He mentions going through a tunnel, being greeted by telepathic loving angels, seeing landscapes more beautiful than earth, and being subjected to an extensive life review. All in all, Swedenborg wrote nearly 20 volumes about his out of body experiences. On his deathbed Swedenborg was asked if there was anything he wanted to recant, to which he replied, *"Everything that I have written is as true as you now behold me. I might have said much more had it been permitted to me. After death you will see all, and then we shall have much to say to each other on the subject."*

"How is it, we might well ask ourselves, that the wisdom of Tibetan sages, the theology and visions of Paul, the strange insights and myths of Plato, and the spiritual revelations of Swedenborg all agree so well, both among themselves and with the narratives of contemporary individuals who have come as close as anyone alive to the state of death?" –Dr. Raymond Moody, "Life After Life" (50)

Shamans the world over throughout history have spoken of visiting the "spirit world" or "after-life realm" regularly, conversing with sentient entities and deceased souls, then bringing visions and messages back to the living tribesmen. They believe that in the other realm one possesses a subtle body, it is populated by many spiritual teachers, and it is a world created by the thoughts and imaginations of many people. Amazonian shamans use the psychedelic brew Ayahuasca to transport them into this

220

realm. The Persian Sufis enter a deep trancelike meditation in order to visit this "land where spirits dwell." And the Australian aboriginals regularly enter this realm during group meditations called "dream-time."

"The picture of reality reported by NDEers is remarkably self-consistent and is corroborated by the testimony of many of the world's most talented mystics as well. Even more astonishing is that as breathtaking and foreign as these subtler levels of reality are to those of us who reside in the world's more 'advanced' cultures, they are mundane and familiar territories to so-called primitive peoples. For example, Dr. E. Nandisvara Nayake Thero, an anthropologist who has lived with and studied a community of aborigines in Australia, points out that the aboriginal concept of the 'dreamtime,' a realm that Australian shamans visit by entering a profound trance, is almost identical to the afterlife planes of existence described in Western sources. It is the realm where human spirits go after death, and once there a shaman can converse with the dead and instantly access all knowledge. It is also a dimension in which time, space, and the other boundaries of earthly life cease to exist and one must learn to deal with infinity. Because of this, Australian shamans often refer to the afterlife as 'survival in infinity.'" -Michael Talbot, "The Holographic Universe" (265-6)

Virtually all of the world's shamanic traditions describe a spirit world or alternate dimension reached during states of altered consciousness which they maintain is where souls travel after physical death. Shamans are experts at navigating these inner realms and they regularly use deep meditation, ecstatic dance, ingestion of entheogens and other methods of shifting consciousness in order to enter them. In many tribes the pre-requisite to becoming a shaman is having a near-death experience!

The Seneca, the Sioux, the Yakut, the Zulu, the Kikuyu, the Guajiro, the Mu Dang, the Eskimos and many other tribal societies all have traditions of shamans assuming the role after a life-threatening illness brings them face-to-face with the afterlife spirit world.

"Most non-Western cultures have religious and philosophical systems, cosmologies, ritual practices, and certain elements of social organization that make it easier for their members to accept and experience death. These cultures generally do not see death as the absolute termination of existence; they believe that consciousness or life in some form continues beyond the point of physiological demise. Whatever specific concepts of afterlife prevail in different cultures, death is typically regarded as a transition or transfiguration, and not as the final annihilation of the individual. Mythological systems have not only detailed descriptions of various afterlife realms, but frequently also complex cartographies to guide souls on their difficult posthumous journeys." -Stanislav Grof & Joan Halifax, "Human Encounter with Death" (2)

University of Toronto Psychology professor Joel Whitton has successfully used hypnosis to regress dozens of patients to the time before their birth and published his findings in the book "Life Between Life." In this between life state his patients universally reported all the classic features of NDEs including passage through a tunnel, entering a light-filled realm outside of space and time, encountering deceased relatives or spirit guides, and being subjected to an extensive life review.

"The message from deep trance is that life after death is synonymous with life before birth and that most of us have taken up residence in this other world many, many times as disembodied entities. Subconsciously, we are just as familiar with discarnate existence as we are with the Earth plane - the next world is both the state we have left behind in order to be born

and the state to which we return at death. As the wheel of life revolves, birth and death happen repeatedly in the evolution of the individual. Death is no more than the threshold of consciousness that separates one incarnation from the next. Truly there is life between lives. Subjects, whose religious backgrounds are as varied as their initial prejudices for or against reincarnation, have testified consistently that rebirth is fundamental to the evolutionary process in which we are enveloped. At death, they say, the soul leaves the body to enter a timeless, spaceless state. There, our most recent life on Earth is evaluated and the next incarnation is planned according to our karmic requirements." -Dr. Joel Whitton, "Life Between Life"

Several NDE researchers such as Dr. Kenneth Ring, author of "Life at Death," have pointed out that the Holographic Universe model offers a way of understanding these experiences as ventures into the more frequency-like aspects of reality. For instance, many patients describe their experiences as entering a realm of "higher vibrations," or "frequencies," where everything is made of light and sound. The sounds are described as "celestial music" more like a "combination of vibrations" than actual sounds, and the lights are described as "more brilliant than any on Earth," but despite their intensity do not hurt the eyes. Dr. Ring believes these and other observations provide evidence that the act of dying involves our consciousness being shifted away from the ordinary explicate world of appearances into the implicate holographic reality of pure frequency.

"Ring is not alone in his speculations. In the keynote address for the 1989 meeting of the International Association for Near-Death Studies (IANDS), Dr. Elizabeth W. Fenske, a clinical psychologist in private practice in Philadelphia, announced that she, too, believes that NDEs are journeys into a holographic realm of higher frequencies. She agrees with Ring's hypothesis that the landscapes, flowers, physical structures, and so forth, of the afterlife dimension are fashioned out of interacting (or interfering) thought patterns. 'I think we've come to the point in NDE research where it's difficult to make a distinction between thought and

light. In the near-death experience thought seems to be light,' she observes." -Michael Talbot, "The Holographic Universe" (246)

Another decidedly "holographic" feature of NDEs is the commonly repeated notion that, in the afterlife realm, time and space as we know them cease to exist. NDErs have reported that, *"it has to be out of time and space. It must be, because the experience cannot be put into a time thing"* and *"I found myself in a space, in a period of time, I would say, where all space and time was negated."* It seems inside this 4 dimensional holographic universe our consciousness experiences the explicate movement of space and the passage of time using a holographic physical body to navigate.

Outside the hologram, however, consciousness experiences the implicate at-one-ment of all space, time, and matter. Many have reported that in the afterlife realm they didn't even have a body unless they were thinking. One NDEr said, *"If I stopped thinking I was merely a cloud in an endless cloud, undifferentiated. But as soon as I started to think, I became myself."*

"In addition to those mentioned by Ring and Fenske, the NDE has numerous other features that are markedly holographic. Like OBEers, after NDEers have detached from the physical they find themselves in one of two forms, either as a disembodied cloud of energy, or as a hologram-like body sculpted by thought. When the latter is the case, the mind-created nature of the body is often surprisingly obvious to the NDEer. For example, one near-death survivor says that when he first emerged from his body he looked 'something like a jelly fish' and fell lightly to the floor like a soap bubble. Then he quickly expanded into a ghostly three-dimensional image of a naked man. However, the presence of two women in the room embarrassed him and to his surprise, this feeling caused him suddenly to

become clothed ... That our innermost feelings and desires are responsible for creating the form we assume in the afterlife dimension is evident in the experiences of other NDEers. People who are confined in wheelchairs in their physical existence find themselves in healthy bodies that can run and dance. Amputees invariably have their limbs back. The elderly often inhabit youthful bodies, and even stranger, children frequently see themselves as adults, a fact that may reflect every child's fantasy to be a grown-up, or more profoundly, may be a symbolic indication that in our souls some of us are much older than we realize." - Michael Talbot, "The Holographic Universe" (246)

Perhaps the most holographic aspect of NDEs is the life review. Dr. Ring calls it *"a holographic phenomenon par excellence."* Many NDErs themselves have used the term "holographic" to describe the  experience. *"It was an incredibly vivid, wrap-around, three-dimensional replay of my entire life,"* said one NDEr, *"It's like climbing right inside a movie of your life,"* said another. *"Every moment from every year of your life is played back in complete sensory detail. Total, total recall. And it all happens in an instant. The whole thing was really odd. I was there; I was actually seeing these flashbacks; I was actually walking through them, and it was so fast. Yet, it was slow enough that I could take it all in."* Thus the experience is holographic both in its panoramic three-dimensionality and also in its incredible capacity for information storage. NDErs lucidly re-experience every single thought and emotion of not only their lives, but the thoughts and emotions of everyone else they ever came in contact with! They feel the joy of people who they treated kindly and the pain of people they treated poorly. No thought or emotion, theirs or anyone else's they ever knew remains private.

"In fact, the life review bares a marked resemblance to the afterlife judgment scenes described in the sacred texts of many of the world's great religions, from the Egyptian to the Judeo-Christian, but with one crucial difference. Like Whitton's subjects, NDEers universally report that they are never judged by the beings of light, but feel only love and acceptance in their presence. The only judgment that ever takes place is self-judgment and arises solely out of the NDEer's own feelings of guilt and repentance. Occasionally the beings do assert themselves, but instead of behaving in an authoritarian manner, they act as guides and counselors whose only purpose is to teach. This total lack of cosmic judgment and/or any divine system of punishment and reward has been and continues to be one of the most controversial aspects of the NDE

among religious groups, but it is one of the most oft reported features of the experience. What is the explanation? Moody believes it is as simple as it is polemic. We live in a universe that is far more benevolent than we realize. That is not to say that anything goes during the life review. Like Whitton's hypnotic subjects, after arriving in the realm of light, NDEers appear to enter a state of heightened or meta-conscious awareness and become lucidly honest in their self-reflections. It also does not mean that the beings of light prescribe no values. In NDE after NDE they stress two things. One is the importance of love. Over and over they repeat this message, that we must learn to replace anger with love, learn to love more, learn to forgive and love everyone unconditionally, and learn that we in turn are loved. This appears to be the only moral criterion the beings use. The second thing the beings emphasize is knowledge. Frequently NDEers comment that the beings seemed pleased whenever an incident involving knowledge or learning flickered by during their life review. Some are openly counseled to embark on a quest for knowledge after they return to their physical bodies, especially knowledge related to self-growth or that enhances one's ability to help other people." - Michael Talbot, "The Holographic Universe" (250)

"Many dying individuals have reported encounters with other beings, such as dead relatives or friends, 'guardian spirits,' or spirit guides. Particularly common seem to be visions of a Being of Light, which usually appears as a source of unearthly light, radiant and brilliant, yet showing certain personal characteristics

such as love, warmth, compassion, and a sense of humor. The communication with this Being occurs without words, through an unimpeded transfer of thoughts. In the context of this encounter or outside of it, the dying individual can experience a partial or total review of his or her life, which almost always involves vivid colors and a three-dimensional, dynamic form. The message from this experience seems to be the realization that learning to love other people and acquiring higher knowledge are the most important values in human life." -Stanislav Grof & Joan Halifax, "Human Encounter with Death" (154-5)

People on their death beds will often speak of seeing angels, deceased friends/family, seeing bright warm lights of love, or having their entire lives flash before their eyes. These visions begin to reconcile traditional notions of "heaven" and the "afterlife" with the actual experiences of current and historical near-death experiencers. It appears the seeming finality of death truly is a physical phenomenon only and consciousness lives on forever.

"I would like to commence this section by emphatically stating an extremely important truth which everyone should know and understand beyond any possible doubt: There really is no such state as 'death.' What many people believe to be the finality of 'death' is

in fact no more and no less than the transition from one state of life and reality, that of the physical matter, to a state of life of a vastly finer density of the Universe." -Adrian Cooper, "Our Ultimate Reality" (145)

Entheogens

For millennia going back through the Greek, Egyptian and Vedic civilizations, the Aboriginals, the Mayan, the American Indians and various tribal societies, back to the most ancient cave and rock art worldwide we see proof that our ancestors had an intimate and extensive knowledge of both altered states of consciousness and the indigenous entheogenic plants which

help induce them. Ayahuasca, Ibogaine, Peyote, Magic Mushrooms and many other so-called "psychedelics" have long-standing histories, traditions and entire religions based around these sacraments. Nowadays due to intrusive and oppressive governments and their unlawful legal systems, the possession and use of most such entheogens has been

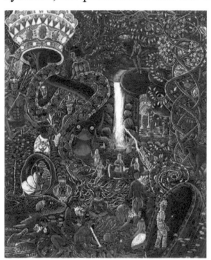

outlawed. And along with these plants, the altered states of consciousness achieved by their ingestion have also become outlawed.

In ancient societies and tribal cultures around the world their entheogenic sacraments have been referred to with names such as the "plant of souls," "the vine of death," or "the seeds of re-birth." They have often been symbolized by the phoenix rising from its own ashes or the coiled serpent eating its own tail. This is because a strong dose of certain entheogens essentially puts you through the entire death and rebirth experience. Your soul slowly separates from your physical body, detaches from this physical reality and gets a glimpse at the higher frequencies of the alterlife realm.

"In the Central African countries of Gabon, Cameroon and Zaire certain age-old ancestor cults still flourish in the twenty-first century. Their members share a common belief, based they say on direct experience, in the existence of a supernatural realm where the spirits of the dead may be contacted. Like some hypothetical dimension of quantum physics, this otherworld interpenetrates our own and yet cannot ordinarily be seen or verified by empirical tests. It is therefore a matter of great interest, with highly suggestive implications, that tribal shamans claim to have mastered a means, through the consumption of a poisonous shrub known locally as eboka or iboga, by which humans may reach the otherworld and return alive." -Graham Hancock, "Supernatural" (5)

"That these inner regions have been well traveled by shamanic peoples is evidenced by an experience anthropologist Michael Harner had among the Conibo Indians of the Peruvian Amazon. In 1960 the American Museum of Natural History sent Harner on a year-long expedition to study the Conibo, and while there he asked the Amazonian natives to tell him about their religious beliefs. They told him that if he really wished to learn, he had to take a shamanic sacred drink made from a hallucinogenic plant known as ayahuasca, the 'soul vine.' He agreed and after drinking the bitter concoction had an out-of-body experience in which he traveled to a level of reality populated by what appeared to be the gods and devils of the

Conibo's mythology. He saw demons with grinning crocodilian heads. He watched as an 'energy-essence' rose up out of his chest and floated toward a dragon-headed ship manned by Egyptian-style figures with blue-jay heads; and he felt what he thought was the slow, advancing numbness of his own death ... Is it possible that what we have been viewing as quaint folklore and charming but naïve mythology are actually sophisticated accounts of the cartography of the subtler levels of reality?

Kalweit for one believes the answer is an emphatic yes. 'In light of the revolutionary findings of recent research into the nature of dying and death, we can no longer look upon tribal religions and their ideas about the World of the Dead as limited conceptions,' he says. '[Rather] the shaman should be considered as a most up-to-date and knowledgeable psychologist." -Michael Talbot, "The Holographic Universe" (267-8)

Whether through entheogens, dreams, meditation, chanting, fasting, rhythmic dancing or drumming, sensory overload or deprivation, the prerequisite for accessing the netherrealms of the implicate order, the key to so-called "paranormal" or "supernatural" abilities, always lies in altered states of consciousness. By using various methods to shift awareness from the typical five-sense physical realm, our minds are able to access these higher frequencies and facets of consciousness well-known to our shamanic ancestors.

"Various techniques are used by a culture to expand the consciousness of an initiate by reducing or eliminating the psychological defenses that separate the world of the supernatural from the world of everyday reality. Such techniques include sleep deprivation, fasting, body mutilation, sonic and photic driving, social isolation, hyperactivity, group pressure,

suggestion, and, in some cases, psychedelic substances." -Stanislav Grof & Joan Halifax, "Human Encounter with Death" (192)

Czech medical doctor and psychiatrist, VISION 97 award winner, and founder of transpersonal psychology, Stanislav Grof has been working for the better part of five decades to improve the world's understanding of psychedelics. In his research Dr. Grof distinguishes between two pillar states of consciousness he refers to as hylotropic and holotropic. The normal, everyday experience of consensus reality is hylotropic whereas interpersonal states reflecting the wholeness and totality of existence are holotropic. In Vedic terms, Dr. Grof relates hylotropic consciousness to "namarupa" (name and form), the separate, individual, and ultimately illusory ego self, while holotropic consciousness relates to Atman-Brahman, the soul essence and divine true nature of the self.

"All the cultures in human history except the Western industrial civilization have held holotropic states of consciousness in great esteem. They induced them whenever they wanted to connect to their deities, other dimensions of reality, and with the forces of nature. They also used them for diagnosing and healing, cultivation of extrasensory perception, and artistic inspiration. They spent much time and energy to develop safe and effective ways of inducing them ... In one of my early books I suggested that the potential significance of LSD and other psychedelics for psychiatry and psychology was comparable to the value the microscope has for biology or the telescope has for astronomy. My later experience with psychedelics only confirmed this initial impression. These substances function as unspecific amplifiers that increase the cathexis (energetic charge) associated with the deep unconscious contents of the psyche and make them available for conscious processing. This unique property of psychedelics makes it

possible to study psychological undercurrents that govern our experiences and behaviours to a depth that cannot be matched by any other method and tool available in modern mainstream psychiatry and psychology. In addition, it offers unique opportunities for healing of emotional and psychosomatic disorders, for positive personality transformation, and consciousness evolution." -Stanislav Grof

Since the 1970s Dr. Grof has been using the psychedelic acid LSD with patients and volunteers in a clinical setting. The extraordinary results these sessions have had on people include: curing psychopathy, narcissism, character disorders and sexual deviations, overcoming addictions, alleviating physical or emotion pain, and dramatically changing concepts and attitudes toward death.  In many cases people had spontaneous glimpses of transpersonal, collective consciousness during which their awareness expanded beyond the normal boundaries of the ego and experienced what it was like to be other living beings, animals, plants, and objects. More than just an "out-of-body experience," the LSD often induced an "into-someone-or-something-else's-body experience."

"The common denominator of this otherwise rich and ramified group is the individual's feeling that his or her consciousness has expanded beyond the usual ego boundaries and has transcended the limitations of time and space. In 'normal' or usual state of consciousness, individuals experience themselves as existing within the boundaries of the physical body, and their perception of the environment is restricted by the physically determined range of the exteroceptors. Both internal perception (interoception) and perception of the environment (exteroception) are confined within the usual space-time boundaries. Under ordinary circumstances individuals vividly perceive

their present situation and their immediate environment; they recall past events and anticipate the future or fantasize about it. In transpersonal experiences occurring in psychedelic sessions, one or several of the above limitations appear to be transcended. In some instances individuals experience loosening of their usual ego boundaries; their consciousness and self-awareness seem to expand to include and encompass other people as well as elements of the external world. They can also continue experiencing their own identities, but at a different time, in a different place, or in a different context. In yet other cases people can experience a complete loss of their own ego identities and feel full identification with the consciousness of some other individual, animal, or even inanimate object." -Stanislav Grof & Joan Halifax, "Human Encounter with Death" (54-5)

Many of Dr. Grof's patients were able to tap into the consciousness of relatives, ancestors, and historical personages. For example one woman experienced what it was like to be her own mother at age three and re-lived a traumatic event from her childhood. She even gave such a precise description of her surroundings, the people, and the event, that it shocked her mother into admitting and confirming the incident which she had never shared with anyone. Another one of Dr. Grof's patients suddenly became convinced she was a prehistoric reptile and provided intricate details about how it felt to have her consciousness contained in such a form, like how she found the patch of colored scales on the side of the males' heads to be sexually arousing - a fact later confirmed by zoologists as being an important mating trigger in certain reptiles. Another patient suddenly found themselves in ancient Egypt and gave a complete account of their techniques of embalming and mummification including specifics like the size and shape of mummy bandages, a list of all the materials used, and the form and meaning of the amulets and sepulchral boxes seen during Egyptian funeral services.

"Other patients gave equally accurate descriptions of events that had befallen ancestors who had lived decades and even centuries before. Other experiences included the accessing of racial and collective memories. Individuals of Slavic origin experienced what it was like to participate in the conquests of Genghis Khan's Mongolian hordes, to dance in trance with the Kalahari bushmen, to undergo the initiation rites of the Australian aborigines, and to die as sacrificial victims of the Aztecs. And again the descriptions frequently contained obscure historical facts and a degree of knowledge that was often completely at odds with the patient's education, race, and previous exposure to the subject ... There did not seem to be any limit to what Grof's LSD subjects could tap into. They seemed capable of knowing what it was like to be every animal, and even plant, on the tree of evolution. They could experience what it was like to be a blood cell, an atom, a thermonuclear process inside the sun, the consciousness of the entire planet, and even the consciousness of the entire cosmos."* -Michael Talbot, "The Holographic Universe" (68-9)

In one remarkable case, Dr. Grof's patient found himself in a dimension inhabited by thousands of luminescent discarnate beings. One of them communicated with him telepathically and pleaded with him to contact a couple in the Moravian city of Kromeriz and tell them that their son Ladislav was well taken care of and doing just fine. He was even given their names, street address and telephone number. When Dr. Grof himself called the number, he asked to speak with Ladislav and the woman on the phone began to cry and said "our son is not with us any more; he passed away, we lost him three weeks ago."

"We are now beginning to learn that Western science might have been a little premature in making its condemning and condescending judgments about ancient systems of thought. Reports describing subjective experiences of clinical death, if studied carefully and with an open mind, contain ample evidence that various eschatological mythologies represent actual maps of unusual states of consciousness experienced by dying individuals. Psychedelic research conducted in the last two decades has resulted in important phenomenological and neurophysiological data indicating that experiences involving complex mythological, religious, and mystical sequences before, during, and after death might well represent clinical reality." -Stanislav Grof & Joan Halifax, "Human Encounter with Death" (159)

Shortly after his third LSD session, one of Dr. Grof's patients actually got into a bad accident during which he went through a typical near-death experience. Afterwards he stated that he found the experience of actually dying to be "extremely similar" to his psychedelic experiences. He emphasized how glad he was to have had the three LSD sessions before his accident because they were excellent training and preparation. "Without the sessions," he said, "I would have been scared by what was happening, but knowing these states, I was not afraid at all."

"Individuals who have suffered through the death-rebirth phenomenon in their psychedelic sessions usually become open to the possibility that consciousness might be independent of the physical body and continue beyond the moment of clinical death. This insight can be quite different from or even contrary to previous religious and philosophical beliefs.

Those who were previously convinced that death was the ultimate defeat and meant the end of any form of existence discovered various alternatives to this materialistic and pragmatic point of view. They came to realize how little conclusive evidence there is for any authoritative opinion in this matter and often began seeing death and dying as a cosmic voyage into the unknown." -Stanislav Grof & Joan Halifax, "Human Encounter with Death" (52)

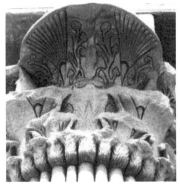 I have personally experimented with LSD and other entheogens periodically and have always found the experiences to be very healing and transformative. They have shown me directly how consciousness can exist outside the physical body, how we can see and hear without using our eyes and ears, they have taken me deep into my subconscious, exposed the illusion of personal identity, and given me a momentary but timeless experience of perfect bliss, contentment and complete at-one-ment with all that is. I remember telling my friend once during a mushroom trip, "I can't believe there aren't whole religions based around this experience!" Little did I know there are indeed many religions throughout the world based around the ingestion of an entheogenic sacrament.

"LSD subjects often arrive at the conclusion that no real boundaries exist between themselves and the rest of the universe. Everything appears to be part of a unified field of cosmic energy, and the boundaries of the individual are identical with the boundaries of existence itself. From this perspective the distinction between the ordinary and the sacred disappears, and the individual - who  *essentially is the universe - becomes sacralized. The universe is seen as an ever-unfolding drama of endless adventures in consciousness, very much in the sense of the Hindu lila, or divine play. Against the background of this infinitely complex and eternal cosmic drama, the fact*

of impending individual destruction seems to lose its tragic significance. In this situation death as we frequently see it - the end of everything, the ultimate catastrophe - ceases to exist. It is now understood as a transition in consciousness, a shift to another level or form of existence." -Stanislav Grof & Joan Halifax, "Human Encounter with Death" (57-8)

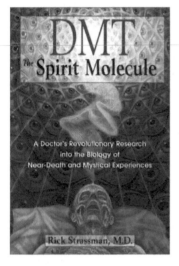

American medical doctor and psychiatrist, Rick Strassman, has also been working diligently to improve our understanding of entheogens, specifically dimethyltryptamine or DMT. In 1990 Dr. Strassman broke a 20 year prohibition on psychedelic experiments in America when he began his work giving intravenous doses of the world's strongest psychedelic to patients and volunteers. Like Dr. Grof's LSD subjects, Dr. Strassman's DMT subjects found the experience to be overwhelmingly positive with a myriad of long-term benefits.

"Volunteers reported a stronger sense of self, less fear of death, and greater appreciation of life. Some found they were better able to relax, and they pushed themselves a little less. Several volunteers drank less alcohol or noted they were more sensitive to psychedelic drugs. Others believed with greater certainty that there are different levels of reality." -Dr. Rick Strassman, "DMT – The Spirit Molecule" (274)

DMT is such a powerful psychedelic that it completely melts away the veil of this reality and transports consciousness into an entirely other dimension occupied by everything from advice-giving telepathic rainbows to body-snatching demonic gremlins. Whether your eyes stay open or closed, these so-called "hallucinations" completely immerse and ensconce themselves into your consciousness taking you out of your body and often out of this world. The effects then wear off after about 10 minutes when smoked, 30 minutes when injected, and after 3-4 hours when made into Ayahuasca.

Dr. Strassman's patients said in the long-term their DMT experiences made them more open-minded and laid-back, caused their thoughts and feelings to be better integrated and overlap more, lessened their fear of death, and gave them "*a more real sense of connectedness to everything and everyone.*" One of his patients named Elena said, "*most of my experiences fade with time. Not so with DMT. Outside me, not much is different. Inside, I rest in the comfort of knowing my soul is eternal and my consciousness endless.*" Another patient, Cleo, related how during her DMT trip, a cascading rainbow of colors telepathically communicated with her, telling her that she had been looking for God outside, but instead to go in, that God was in every cell of her body: "*The colors kept telling me things, but they were telling me things so I not only heard what I was seeing, but also felt it in my cells. I say 'felt,' but it was like no other 'felt,' more like a knowing that was happening in my cells. That God is in everything and that we are all connected, and that God dances in every cell of life, and that every cell of life dances in God. I am changed. I will never be the same. To simply say this almost seems to lessen the experience. I don't think that anyone hearing or reading this can truly grasp what I felt, can really understand it deeply and completely. The euphoria goes on into eternity. And I am part of that eternity.*"

Due to all the miraculous, revelatory, and other-worldly experiences shared by his DMT subjects, Dr. Strassman dubbed dimethyltryptamine "the spirit molecule." The parallels between classic mystical or "spiritual" experiences and what people experienced with the "spirit molecule" were too similar to ignore: During both DMT trips and mystical experiences time, space, and matter all become secondary to consciousness. The separation between self/non-self disappears and personal identity fades into identification with all of existence. Past, present and future all meld together into one timeless moment of eternity. Space is no longer

238

here or there but everywhere as one. There is only here now and travel happens at the speed of thought.

"In altered states of consciousness this new perception of the world becomes dominant and compelling. It completely overrides the everyday illusion of Newtonian reality, where we seem to be 'skin-encapsulated egos' existing in a world of separate beings and objects. In extreme forms of transpersonal perception we can experience ourselves as the whole biosphere of our planet or the entire material universe." -Stanislav Grof, "The Holotropic Mind" (88)

Further to their revelatory and spiritual experiences, many of Dr. Strassman's patients also reported experiencing a typical NDE while under DMT. They felt themselves lift out of their bodies, saw and entered tunnels of light, heard celestial music and encountered angels or light beings, felt absolute peace and painlessness and were reluctant to come back into their bodies. For example, one of his patients, Willow, described her experience saying, *"First I saw a tunnel or channel of light off to the right ... There was a sound like music, like a score, but unfamiliar to me, supporting the emotional tone of the events and drawing me in ...*

There were large beings in the tunnel, on the right side, next to me ... It was so much more real than life ... I felt strongly, 'This is dying and this is okay' ... I had a sense of dying, letting go and separating, after the beings in the tunnel helped me along. ... It's like a cosmic joke. If we all knew what was waiting for us, we'd all kill ourselves. That's why we stay in this form for so long, to figure that out. Everyone should try a high dose of DMT once ... That place is so full and so complete ... when I came back into my body it was so heavy and so confining."

239

"Her consciousness separated from her body, she moved rapidly through a tunnel, or tunnels, toward a warm, loving, all-knowing white light. Beings helped her on the way, and some even threatened to drag her down. Beautiful music accompanied her on the early stages of the journey. Time and space lost all meaning. She was tempted not to return, but realized she needed to share the incredible information she received with this world ... Her comment about everyone committing suicide if they knew how great the 'afterlife' is points out another similarity between Willow's experiences and those of 'naturally occurring' NDEs: That is, those who have had an NDE do not rush off to suicide. Rather, they reside in the knowledge that there is 'life after death,' and that transition loses its sting. Thus, they are able to live life more fully, because the fear of death that drives so many to distraction is now so much less." -Dr. Rick Strassman, "DMT – The Spirit Molecule" (226)

As mentioned earlier many entheogens have long been known to induce the death-rebirth experience and none are stronger than DMT. Several of Dr. Strassman's patients reported experiencing phenomena similar to what is outlined in the The Egyptian and Tibetan Books of the Dead, ancient texts regarding the process of death and the various states of consciousness the soul passes through on its afterlife journey. Elena shared that, *"more than once the DMT sessions gave me the gift of truly subjectively knowing the phenomenon described in 'Introductions to the Dead' in The Tibetan Book of the Dead."* Another of Dr. Strassman's

240

patients, Eli, said, "*I relaxed and the environment began to change noticeably. I knew I was going through the first bardo of death, that I had been here many times before and it was okay ... I had broken out of time and space ... I no longer fear death. It's like you're there one minute and then you're somewhere else, and that's just how it is ... These experiments are helping me in my reading of the Tibetan Book of Living and Dying. I know what it's like to be totally free.*" Another patient, Joseph, noted, "*I think the high dose is like death trauma. It knocks you out of your body ... This would be a good drug for people in a hospice program or the terminally ill to have some acquaintance with.*"

One of the most incredible facts about DMT is that it is endogenous to humans and produced by our pineal glands. The pineal gland, the only unpaired organ in the brain is located at the geometric center of the head

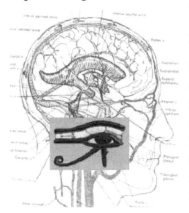

between the eyebrows. This mystical point, focused on during meditation, symbolized by the Hindu "bindi," is what Descartes famously called "the seat of the soul." It is also known as the "third-eye" because it can sense light and in certain birds, amphibians, and reptiles it even has a lens, cornea and retina. So why is this death-rebirth-inducing strongest psychedelic in the world produced inside our pineal glands? What exactly is its function?

"*DMT is closely related to serotonin, the neurotransmitter that psychedelics affect so widely. The pharmacology of DMT is similar to that of other well-known psychedelics. It affects receptor sites for serotonin in much the same way that LSD, psilocybin, and mescaline do. These serotonin receptors are widespread throughout the body and can be found in blood vessels, muscle, glands, and skin. However, the brain is where DMT exerts its most interesting effects. There, sites rich in these DMT-sensitive serotonin receptors are involved in mood, perception, and thought. Although the brain denies access to most drugs and chemicals, it takes a particular and remarkable fancy to DMT. It is not stretching the truth to suggest that the brain 'hungers' for it.*" -Dr. Rick Strassman, "DMT – The Spirit Molecule" (52)

In human embryos the pineal gland becomes visible and releases its first burst of DMT 49 days after conception. This is also the exact moment when an embryo becomes a fetus and the gender of the baby is determined. At birth there is another burst of DMT, then regularly every night for the rest of our lives during REM sleep our pineal glands excrete DMT and "trip" us out into various dream states. Finally the last and largest DMT burst of our lives happens at the moment of physical death.

"The human pineal gland becomes visible in the developing fetus at seven weeks, or forty-nine days, after conception. Of great interest to me was finding out that this is nearly exactly the moment in which one can clearly see the first indication of male or female gender. Before this time, the sex of the fetus is indeterminate, or unknown. Thus, the pineal gland and the most important differentiation of humanity, male and female gender, appear at the same time ... When our individual life force enters our fetal body, the moment in which we become truly human, it passes through the pineal and triggers the first primordial flood of DMT. Later, at birth, the pineal releases more DMT. In some of us, pineal DMT mediates the pivotal experiences of deep meditation, psychosis, and near-death experiences. As we die, the life-force leaves the body through the pineal gland, releasing another flood of this psychedelic spirit molecule." -Dr. Rick Strassman, "DMT – The Spirit Molecule" (61-9)

Traditional Chinese funerals are 49 days long. The Tibetan Book of the Dead states that it takes 49 days for a recently deceased soul to travel from one physical body into the next. It also contains 49 days worth of specific passages for friends and family to read aloud to assist the deceased in their transition. 49 days after Easter is Pentecost, the day when "tongues of fire" came into the temple and rested upon the heads of the elders. Symbolically this could mean their crown chakras were

illuminated, pineal glands functioning, and the spirit came down unto them, just as literally 49 days after conception, the fetal pineal gland begins functioning and the gender is determined. Are these 49s all just a coincidence or is this mystical number the time it takes for deceased souls to reincarnate? The Catholic Church celebrates the "Immaculate Conception" on December 8th, exactly 9 months before Mary's birthday, and celebrates the Incarnation of Christ on March 25th, exactly 9 months before Christmas. Is this why the death and conception of Jesus can happen simultaneously? Because we are all re-conceived (reincarnated) at the moment of our deaths and 49 days later our soul enters the embryo through a burst of pineal DMT?

"I already knew that the Tibetan Buddhist Book of the Dead teaches that it takes forty-nine days for the soul of the recently dead to 'reincarnate.' That is, seven weeks from the time of death of one person elapses until the life-force's 'rebirth' into its next body. I remember very clearly, several years later, feeling the chill along my spine when, reading my textbook of human fetal development, I discovered this same forty-nine day interval marking two landmark events in human embryo formation. It takes forty-nine days from conception for the first signs of the human pineal to appear. Forty-nine days is also when the fetus differentiates into male or female gender. Thus the soul's rebirth, the pineal, and the sexual organs all require forty-nine days before they manifest ... [Then] as we die, if near-death experiences are any indication, there is a profound shift in consciousness away from identification with the body. Pineal DMT makes available those particular non-embodied contents of consciousness. All the factors previously described combine for one final burst of DMT production: catecholamine release; decreased breakdown and increased formation of

DMT; reduced anti-DMT; and decomposing pineal tissue. Therefore, it may be that the pineal is the most active organ in the body at the time of death. Might we say that the life-force therefore exits the body through the pineal?" -Dr. Rick Strassman, "DMT – The Spirit Molecule" (81-2)

 It seems very likely that our souls enter and exit physical bodies via the pineal gland (third-eye). Robert Monroe, Robert Bruce and other out-of-body experts have reported the third-eye as the main contact point where consciousness enters or exits the physical body during OBEs. Several near-death experiencers talk about the "silver cord," a long, bright, elastic cable of light which extends from the third-eye of their physical body attached to their disembodied

consciousness wherever it goes. Rene Descartes noticed he could only think one thought at a time and guessed it must be the pineal gland, the only singular, unpaired organ in the brain responsible for these singular, unpaired thoughts. He even went so far as to call it "the seat of the soul" which certainly concurs with Dr. Strassman's findings. Both intravenous DMT injections and endogenous pineal DMT conclusively cause out-of-body near-death experiences and play a key role in the birth-death process.

"While the release of neuroprotective compounds near death certainly is a useful response, the psychedelic side effects are not as obviously beneficial. We must therefore wonder, are these spiritual properties a coincidence, or do they have a purpose? I suggest that near-death chemicals released by the brain are psychedelic for this reason: They must be. It is similar to asking why there is silicon in computer chips. Silicon works. It does the job. Near-death brain products are psychedelic because those are the properties consciousness requires at that time. Psychedelic compounds released near death mediate

consciousness exiting the body. This is their function and this is what they do. DMT is a spirit molecule, just as silicon is a chip molecule. Rather than just causing the mind to feel as if it were leaving the body, DMT release is the means by which the mind senses the departure of the life-force from it, the content of consciousness as it leaves the body." -Dr. Rick Strassman, "DMT – The Spirit Molecule" (326)

"Activation and opening of the transpersonal area in the unconscious of dying individuals can have far-reaching consequences for their concepts of death, their attitudes toward the situation they are facing, and their abilities to accept physical mortality ... Those who see themselves as an insignificant and impermanent speck of dust in an immense universe become open to the possibility that the dimensions of their own beings are commensurate with the macrocosm and microcosm. Consciousness here appears as a primary characteristic of existence, preceding matter and supraordinated to it, rather than being a product of physiological processes in the brain. It seems to be quite plausible that consciousness and awareness are essentially independent of the gross matter of the body and brain, and will continue beyond the point of physical demise. This alternative is experienced in a way that is at least as complex, vivid, and self-evident as the perception of reality in usual states of consciousness. The transcendental impact of these experiences is usually stronger in those individuals who, prior to entering the transpersonal realms, went through the experience of ego death and rebirth. The memory that consciousness emerged intact from this seemingly final annihilation constitutes a powerful emotional and cognitive model for understanding the process of actual death." -Stanislav Grof & Joan Halifax, "Human Encounter with Death" (56-7)

Ghosts

Contrary to Hollywood's many fanciful farcical depictions, ghosts are generally not monstrous, malicious, or even particularly mysterious; they are simply recently deceased disembodied souls lingering around the physical plane. In fact, the only difference between a ghost and a person in the OBE state is that an out-of-body traveler can return to their physical body whereas a ghost cannot. In death, the "silver cord" that connects astral travelers to their physical bodies, that life essence is

severed and the disembodied consciousness can no longer return. The Bible even mentions this in Ecclesiastes 12:6-7, "*Remember him – before the silver cord is severed, or the golden bowl is broken; before the pitcher is shattered at the spring, or the wheel broken at the well, and the dust returns to the ground it came from, and the spirit returns to God who gave it.*"

"*Although ghosts are very real they are almost always completely harmless. A ghost is after all quite simply a totally normal but deceased human being living within a more subtle body, but after having experienced physical death, for some reason they become trapped in the lowest part of the etheric plane closest to the physical world.*" - Adrian Cooper, "Our Ultimate Reality" (161)

There are many reasons why deceased souls fail to smoothly transition from out of their bodies and the physical plane. Some people dying from sudden accidents, murder, or heart attacks for example do not realize they have passed on. Other people simply will not accept that they have died and cannot return to the physical. Some are so attached to the material world and addictions like sex and power that they refuse to move on. Others are attached to certain relationships or harbor guilt they feel must be reconciled.

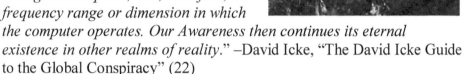

"The true nature of 'death' - in fact a seamless transition from life to life - was portrayed so well in the 1998 Robin Williams film, What Dreams May Come. It is simply a withdrawing from the biological computer, and, therefore, the frequency range or dimension in which the computer operates. Our Awareness then continues its eternal existence in other realms of reality." –David Icke, "The David Icke Guide to the Global Conspiracy" (22)

Several surveys have been taken during the past century in Great Britain and the United States which have concluded that between 10% and 27% of the general population claim to have had at least once in their life, a sensory perception, often visual, of another person who was not physically present (i.e. ghost, apparition). Many respondents gave startling accounts of recently (or sometimes long) deceased people appearing and even interacting with them. For example one Charlottesville, Virginia woman had told her sick mother on her death bed when she passed to try and give some signal that her soul lived on. Two days after her mother's death, just after returning from the funeral, she laid down and saw an apparition of her mother's head and shoulders float into the bedroom. She asked her mother if she was in heaven and her mother smiled and nodded. She asked if her father was there and again she smiled and nodded then dissipated and floated out the window.

Another woman related a similar story of the day following her husband's death seeing an apparition of him sitting in his favorite chair. He greeted her non-chalantly with a smile, asked her how she was doing, assured her he was doing fine then told her where to find the legal papers she would need for finalizing his estate.

"When the Soul of a deceased person remains in a particular locality, a house for example, the Soul is known as a 'ghost,' and the location inhabited by the ghost is considered to be 'haunted.' To a physical person living in a 'haunted' house the 'ghost' will often seem to carry out exactly the same series of actions every time it makes an appearance, often at the same physical time of day or night, for example 'stepping' on a creaky floor board, walking up the stairs, rattling door handles, moving items around, and even switching lights and other electric appliances on and off. This is possible because the Etheric Body is already relatively dense by comparison to the inner Astral and Mental bodies, and a ghost can sometimes achieve the necessary density approaching that of the physical world by absorbing large amounts of Etheric Energy from their surroundings, sufficient to influence the density of physical objects." -Adrian Cooper, "Our Ultimate Reality" (159-160)

My fiancé Petchara has seen ghosts as long as she can remember. As a child she lived in a house long haunted by a female ghost. She and several family members had experiences while wide awake feeling invisible footsteps on the bed nearly every night, hearing discarnate crying, screaming or laughter, and often seeing clear

248

apparitions of the same long-haired woman. Since then ghosts have regularly visited Petchara during her dream-states. The most noteworthy of these visits was from a schoolmate who she saw soaking wet sitting at the end of her bed one night. Pale and shivering she sat curled up asking over and over for a towel. Petchara found out the next day that her schoolmate had just drowned to death last night shortly before visiting her bedside.

"As I have already outlined, Infinite Awareness experiences this reality through the body-computer - akin to wearing a genetic spacesuit. Our lower levels of Awareness can, and mostly do, become confused and identify with the computer. When the  *computer (body) ceases to function - or 'dies' - our Awareness is released from the illusion and starts the process of remembering who it really is. This can be instant for those who were aware of their true identity before*  *'computer death', while for others it can take longer if their incarnate Awareness has become utterly dominated by its computer identity. It is for this reason that there are so many stories of 'ghosts' that 'haunt' locations where they once lived. What we call ghosts are often discarnate entities, aspects of Awareness, who are still identifying themselves with the computer they once occupied and they live in a limbo-land dimension very close to this one ... Instead of understanding what is happening at 'death' - when Infinite Awareness is released from the computer reality - 'ghosts' go on believing that the 'earthly' self is who they are. Some people call them 'earthbound souls' or 'lost souls'. Such is the identification with the former computer 'self' that they manifest as a mental projection of what they once looked like in physical form. It is what they called in the Matrix movies 'residual self-*

image'." –David Icke, "The David Icke Guide to the Global Conspiracy" (21)

David Icke related an interesting story after the death of his mother. Her funeral was due to begin at 11:30am the next week and every day before, during and even after the funeral several strange things happened. At precisely 11:30am each day the electrical equipment, TV, watches and mobile phones in his house would turn themselves on and off. One day

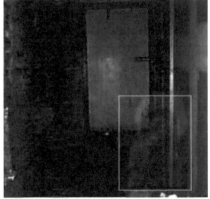

emergency services called him at 11:31 and asked why he had just rung them, when of course he had done no such thing.

"Often, a departed loved one will try to manifest signs to show that they have not ceased to be ... When we are operating on other dimensions the easiest way to have an influence in this world is via electrical equipment through a vibrational connection that affects electrical circuitry. People can stop watches by projecting their thoughts because thoughts are electrical and vibrational phenomena - hence 'brainwaves' - and they can be used to block the watch's electrical circuits. Such thought waves can also be projected from other dimensions into this one and have a similar effect. When this happens people will often say that a place is 'haunted'." –David Icke, "The David Icke Guide to the Global Conspiracy" (27)

In November 1967 in a haunted Rosenheim, Bavaria law office some of the best documented ghost/poltergeist activity was witnessed by over forty scientists and professionals. Over several days they recorded paranormal phenomena such as loud sounds from unknown sources, pictures on walls spinning around 360 degrees, light-bulbs dimming then brightening and exploding, electrical equipment spontaneously starting up or breaking down, and objects moving or falling without anyone touching them. Also in 1967 American researchers Gaither Pratt and William Roll witnessed and recorded 224 accounts of paranormal activity at a warehouse in Miami, Florida. Over and over they watched as books and boxes slid around and bottles and glasses flew, dropped and shattered all by themselves.

"One time I watched Julio place a ceramic alligator on a shelf when a glass four feet behind him fell to the floor and shattered. Both his hands were occupied; in the right he held the alligator, in the left his clipboard. The two other workers in the room were more than 15 feet from the glass. They could not have picked it up previously and then thrown it because we had placed the glass on the shelf ourselves and no one had been near it since then. The glass was among ten targets we had set out that moved when one or both of us had the area under surveillance and when we were the first to enter the area after the incident. The incident was also among seven when Pratt or I had Julio in direct view at the time." -William Roll, "Poltergeists, Electromagnetism, and Consciousness"

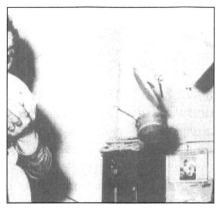

Spiritism, séances and mediums, due to an unfortunate history of hacks, quacks and hoaxes, have long been discounted and dismissed as mere tricks and illusions. Mixed in with the conniving charlatans, however, have been many famous, scientifically verified and documented cases of actual contact with discarnate entities. Mediums such as Eusapia Palladino, Daniel Douglas Home, Gordon Smith and many others have repeatedly produced paranormal phenomena witnessed by teams of scientists and experienced researchers, phenomena including touches from invisible hands, discarnate voices and sounds, apparitions, psychokinesis, levitation, and manifestations.

"There is no question that at the time when spiritism enjoyed its greatest popularity, around the turn of the century, many participants were victims of cunning swindlers ... However, we should not throw the baby out with the bathwater and conclude that this entire area is nothing but fraud. It is difficult to imagine that so many outstanding researchers would have invested so much time and energy in a field with no real phenomena to observe. There exists hardly any other realm where the expert testimony of so many witnesses of the highest caliber has been discounted as stupidity and gullibility and thus written off. We have to realize that among serious researchers were many people with outstanding credentials, such as, the famous physicist Sir William Crookes, the Nobel Prize-winning physician and physiologist Charles Richet, and Sir Oliver Lodge, a Fellow of the Royal Society in England."
-Stanislav Grof, "The Holotropic Mind" (177-8)

University of Arizona psychiatry professor Gary Schwartz has performed laboratory studies of several mediums and recorded the results in his book "The Afterlife Experiment: Breakthrough Scientific Evidence of Life After Death" and over 450 other  scientific papers on the subject. In experiments carefully controlled to eliminate fraud or cheating, several mediums were able to produce over 80 bits of information about deceased relatives such as names, jobs, appearance, personal stories, and the nature of death. Combined the mediums averaged an astonishing accuracy rate of 83%. Gary Schwartz and his team concluded that "the most parsimonious explanation is that the mediums are in direct communication with the deceased."

"Tested in Glasgow by Roy and Robertson, British medium Gordon Smith performed with the greatest accuracy of anyone yet measured. He achieved 98 percent success rate with his information deemed specific and accurate under the tight experimental protocol ... When asked what,

in his view, is his most convincing proof of the continuation of human consciousness beyond the brain, he told of a particular case that he'd been involved with. A woman, Sally, had come to see him in great distress to ask if he could help her find her missing son. Without her providing any other information, Smith was able to contact her son, who told him that his name was Blake and what his mother would find out 'she wouldn't like' – a message that was sadly true. He went on to say that he had been a soldier training in France when, after a night out, he had been accidentally killed. He described to Smith the river where his body now lay. All the personal details were correct. A year later, a human thigh bone was found in the exact place where Blake had told Smith he would be. And when the DNA was tested, it proved to belong to Sally's dead son." -Ervin Laszlo and Jude Currivan, "Cosmos" (151-2)

Reincarnation

One of the cornerstone beliefs of many world religions such as Hinduism, Buddhism, Jainism, Sikhism, Taoism, Shintoism, and Zoroastrianism, is the idea of reincarnation. From the Orphics, Pythagoreans, and Platonists to the Essenes, Pharisees, and Karaites; from Polynesian Kahunas and Brazillian Umbandas to the Jamaican Rastafarians and American Indians; the Gauls, the Druids, the Celts, the Gnostics, and even early Christians all believed in reincarnation. Great minds like Plato, Socrates, Spinoza, Leibnitz, Voltaire, Hume, Schopenhauer, Goethe, Emerson, Whitman, Napoleon, Franklin, Tagore, and Ghandi all believed that our consciousness, our souls, survive bodily death and continue on.

"A theory which has been embraced by so large a part of mankind, of many races and religions, and has commended itself to some of the most profound thinkers of all time, cannot be lightly dismissed." -George Foot Moore, "Metempsychosis"

"The concept of reincarnation is widespread in the world's cultures. Throughout ancient Egyptian, Greek, Judaic, and early Christian traditions; Buddhism; many schools of Hinduism; Japanese Shintoism; and Chinese Taoism, it is less a 'belief' than a 'fact' based on direct

experience and observation." -Ervin Laszlo and Jude Currivan, "Cosmos" (153)

Julius Caesar wrote of the Celts that they "*were fearless warriors because they wish to inculcate this as one of their leading tenets, that souls do not become extinct, but pass after death from one body to another.*" Elderly Eskimos have a tradition of selecting newly married couples to permit them to <u>be</u> (reincarnate into) their children. If they prove good and honorable, the family gives their consent, and the elderly Eskimo commits suicide believing their soul will enter into the family's newborn. The British Museum has receipts and other legal documents showing that it was actually once common practice for the Druids to borrow money and promise to repay in a future life!

Origen, St. Augustine, St. Gregory, St. Francis of Assisi and many other early Christian scholars wrote about souls returning to Earth and reincarnating. For example, Origen wrote that "*it can be shown that an incorporeal and reasonable being has life in itself independently of the body... then it is beyond a doubt bodies are only of secondary importance and arise from time to time to meet the varying conditions of reasonable creatures. Those who require bodies are clothed with them, and contrariwise, when fallen souls have lifted themselves up to better things their bodies are once more annihilated. They are ever vanishing and ever reappearing.*"

Reincarnation was a widespread belief among early Christians, but at the Second Council of Constantinople in 553 AD, Emperor Justinian condemned and outlawed the belief or teaching of reincarnation stating *"If anyone assert the fabulous pre-existence of souls and shall submit to the monstrous doctrine that follows from it, let him be anathema!"* Since then the non-belief in reincarnation has continued to dominate western metaphysical thought to the point that 19th century German philosopher Arthur Schopenhauer once quipped *"were an Asiatic to ask me for a definition of Europe, I should be forced to answer him: It is that part of the world which is haunted by the incredible delusion that man was created out of nothing, and that his present birth is his first entrance into life."*

"Reincarnation is a difficult subject, for so much silliness has been presented about it that many people dismiss it out of hand. Most do not realize that in addition to (and one might even say in spite of) the sensational claims of celebrities and the stories of reincarnated Cleopatras that garner most of the media attention, there is a good deal of serious research being done on reincarnation. In the last several decades a small but growing number of highly credentialed researchers have compiled an impressive body of evidence on the subject." -Michael Talbot, "The Holographic Universe" (213)

There are several doctors, scientists, and researchers who have dedicated their life's work to the mystery of reincarnation. One such person was Dr. Ian Stevenson, professor of psychiatry at the University of Virginia, who spent over 40 years investigating and compiling evidence for reincarnation. He meticulously documented and verified over three thousand cases of children remembering and confirming knowledge from past lives. So many children from around the world are able to remember so much about their previous lives that he repeatedly located former friends, relatives, villages, houses, and possessions based solely on their testimony. For instance one three year-old girl was able to recall so much of her previous life that Dr. Stevenson was able to find her old family and take her to her old home.

"It all started when the family was traveling approximately 100 miles from their home. The girl suddenly pointed and asked the driver of the car in which they were traveling at the time to go down a road to 'my home,' saying they 'could get a better cup of tea there.' Soon afterwards she started to relate numerous details of her past life associated with her previous family living in this home, including her previous name and that she had two sons. The little girl also provided a very wide range of highly accurate information regarding the precise details of the home including its

location relative to other landmarks in the area, and numerous other details regarding the interior, details which she could not possibly have known any other way. The little girl said she had died after experiencing a pain in her throat ... The family confirmed every single detail of what the little girl had previously stated including that she had died very suddenly leaving behind a grieving husband and two young sons. The two families lived one hundred miles apart and had certainly never heard of each other previously." -Adrian Cooper, "Our Ultimate Reality" (180)

When the girl's parents drove through her old town she was able to provide directions all the way. Upon arriving at her old house she immediately recognized her former brother and called him by his pet name. She then proceeded to correctly state the name and relation of each person present including her former husband and sons. As incredible as it sounds, this story is far from unique. There are hundreds of credible past-life researchers and Dr. Stevenson alone has published 6 volumes with over 3000 such cases. He says genuine spontaneous past-life recall is actually so common among children that the number of cases considered worthy of investigation far exceeds his staff's ability to do so.

"As unorthodox as many of Stevenson's conclusions are, his reputation as a careful and thorough investigator has gained him respect in some unlikely quarters. His findings have been published in such distinguished scientific periodicals as the American Journal of Psychiatry, the Journal of Nervous and Mental Disease, and the International Journal of Comparative Sociology. And in a review of one of his works the prestigious Journal of the American Medical Association stated that he has 'painstakingly and unemotionally collected a detailed series of cases in which the evidence for reincarnation is difficult to understand on any other grounds ... He has placed on record a large amount of data that

cannot be ignored. '" -Michael Talbot, "The Holographic Universe" (219)

"Ian Stevenson investigated more than 3,000 cases of past-life memories that arose spontaneously in young children. Taking this approach to minimize the influence of cultural conditioning either to promote or suppress the memories, he worked meticulously to investigate, validate, and record the pertinent memories ... These included precise knowledge of their previous homes, environments, and families, and even extended to birthmarks that corresponded to injuries or fatal wounding in the people whose lives they appear to experience ... memories like those of the children's reveal the details of specific remembered lives that can sometimes be correlated and whose accuracy has often been validated." -Ervin Laszlo and Jude Currivan, "Cosmos" (154)

In another Dr. Stevenson case, a two and a half year-old boy was able to recall very specific memories and details about his "other life." He started telling his parents regularly about how he had been shot and thrown into a river. He said in his other life he was the owner of an electrical appliance shop. He had a wife and two children whom he called by their names and said incessantly how he was homesick and wanted to see his family. The boy's parents didn't take him seriously for some time until one day he packed his clothes and threatened to leave if they refused to take him to his family. Deciding it was time to appease their son's wishes the parents followed his directions and took him to his old village from his previous life. Upon seeing his former wife the boy shouted her name and ran to see her. They talked for hours as the boy recounted several specific memories and events known only by the dumb-founded widow and her deceased husband. He even accurately described the location of some gold he had buried behind their house and changes that had been made to the home since his death. He was also immediately able to pick his former sons out of a playground full of neighborhood children and call them by name.

"Later the boy recalled the full circumstances of his 'death,' how he had been shot in the head while sitting in his car after arriving home from work. The autopsy report, which was filmed, confirmed he had indeed been shot in the head and had died as a result of a bullet wound to the temple. The autopsy showed the exact size and location of the entry wound and also of the exit wound on the opposite side of the man's head. It was later decided  *to shave off some of the boys hair around the region of the fatal wound inflicted in his previous life. The boy had a birthmark at exactly the same location as the bullet entry point of exactly the same size and shape as the bullet that killed him in his previous life. He also had a second birthmark on the opposite side of his head corresponding with the exit point of the same bullet. The case later attracted so much interest that it was presented in court in order to conclusively prove the boy was indeed the reincarnated former husband of the widow. As a result of this case a professor at a major University was quoted as saying that due to the police involvement 'this is one of the best documented cases of reincarnation he had ever seen.'"* -Adrian Cooper, "Our Ultimate Reality" (181-3)

It appears quite common for distinctive features or deformities to carry over from one life to the next. Physical injuries like the boy's bullet wounds tend to carry over as scars or birthmarks. In another case a boy who remembered being murdered by having his throat slit retained a long red scar straight across his new neck. Another boy had a birthmark perfectly resembling a surgical scar with marks in the pattern of a stitch wound. The autopsy pictures of his previous body showed the birthmark in the exact same place/pattern as his previous personality's surgery.

"In fact, Stevenson has gathered hundreds of such cases and is currently compiling a four-volume study of the phenomenon. In some of the cases he has even been able to obtain hospital and/or autopsy reports of the deceased personality and show that such injuries not only occurred, but were in the exact location of the present birthmark or deformity. He feels that such marks not only provide some of the strongest evidence in favor of reincarnation, but also suggest the existence of some kind of intermediate nonphysical body that functions as a carrier of these attributes between one life and the next. He states, 'It seems to me that the imprint of wounds on the previous personality must be carried between lives on some kind of an extended body which in turn acts as a template for the production on a new physical body of birthmarks and deformities that correspond to the wounds on the body of the previous personality.'" -Michael Talbot, "The Holographic Universe" (218-219)

"A dramatic example of reincarnation involving a person who physically died and returned very soon afterwards was in the case of a Turkish

bandit. This involves a boy who claimed he was formerly a Turkish bandit, who when cornered by the authorities shot himself through the lower jaw in order to evade capture. Medical examination of this boy, the reincarnation of the bandit, highlighted a large mark in his jaw where the bullet would have entered in his previous life, and there was also hair missing from the top of his head where the bullet would have emerged. A witness to this incident is still alive today and was able to confirm the precise details as given by the boy as to how he took his own previous life." -Adrian Cooper, "Our Ultimate Reality" (178)

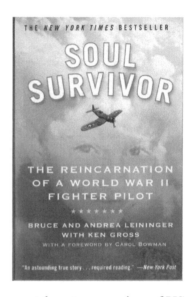

In 2005, FOX News reported on 11 year-old James Leininger's amazing reincarnation story. James was always fascinated by airplanes, drew intricate fighter pilot scenes, and increasingly was struck with nightmares of being stuck in a crashing plane. He told his parents of recurring visions involving his Corsair plane being shot down by the Japanese during WWII. He remembered taking off from a ship called the Natoma and his old name was Jim Houston. The parents tracked down WWII veteran Leo Pint who served on the Natoma and remembered Jim Houston who was indeed shot down by the Japanese in his Corsair plane. Later the boy was taken to a reunion of US Natoma vets and was able to correctly name several of them at first sight. Then he was taken to meet Jim Houston's sister Anne Houston, whom James insisted he always called "Annie" not Anne, and she wasn't his only sister, he had an older sister named Ruth as well. Upon meeting Annie, James talked about many childhood possessions and events that only she and her brother could have known. They have since put the whole story together in an excellent book titled Soul Survivor.

"In Paris at the beginning of the present century lived a certain Mme. Laure Raynaud. From childhood this lady distinctly remembered that she had lived before and was able to give an accurate description of a previous home and the conditions surrounding her death. When Mme. Raynaud was forty-five years of age she traveled for the first time to Italy where she was able to recognize the scenes of her previous life. She was

in Genoa when she described the type of house in which she had lived. With the aid of a friend she located the house and made a statement subject to historical verification. She said that in her previous life she had not been buried in the cemetery, but in a particular church some distance away. Research proved that a young lady answering Mme. Raynaud's description of her previous self had died in the house on October 21, 1809, and had been buried in the church which Mme. Raynaud had indicated." -Manly P. Hall, "Reincarnation: The Cycle of Necessity" (148-9)

"*In Buddhist countries, it is no very unusual thing to have children gravely claiming to have had such-and-such a name, and to have lived in such-and-such a place, in their previous lives; and occasionally these claims are in a sort of fashion substantiated. Such children are in Burma called Winzas, and it is no uncommon thing for a sort of rough test to be carried out by taking a Winza to the scene of his former life, when it is said that he or she can generally identify his former dwelling and friends, and can state facts known only to the dead person and one other living man. These Winzas are so relatively frequent in Burma that their existence is commonly taken for granted; the power of remembering the past life is generally stated to disappear as the child grows up, though we have met adult Winzas who still claimed to remember the past.*" - Manly P. Hall, "Reincarnation: The Cycle of Necessity" (149)

The most amazing well-known and well-documented account of reincarnation in modern times comes from a young Hindu girl, Shanti Devi, who at four years old began frequently referring to incidents and people from her former life. She claimed she was a Choban by caste and lived in Muttra with her husband, a cloth-merchant named Kedar Nath Chaubey.

As she grew older Shanti Devi often spoke of her previous life, family, and experiences. Her recollections were so lucid that she even remembered her old address and could describe her old house in complete detail. At eleven years old she decided to send a letter to her former husband and shocked her family when Kedar Nath Chaubey wrote back stating emphatically that Shanti Devi must be his wife! Based on all the things she wrote which only his deceased partner knew he could not escape the astonishing conclusion.

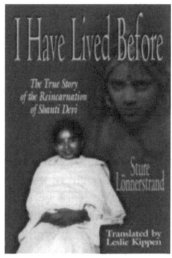

Kedar had already remarried but was so intrigued that he travelled to Delhi to meet Shanti. When he arrived she immediately picked him out of a crowd and they spent the next few days together, Kedar asking several intimate questions, and Shanti consistently giving correct and characteristic answers convincing Kedar that it could only be his dead wife speaking. She perfectly described the town of Muttra, the special temple she always visited, their village, house, and even the location of some money buried under their floor.

Kedar returned to Muttra, and soon after Shanti began growing weary and impatient, insisting she was a grown married woman and belonged with her husband. Eventually, after enduring several tantrums, her reluctant family and a party of fifteen researchers made a trip to Muttra with Shanti. Upon arriving she was completely familiar with the town and directed the driver exactly how to reach her former village and house. On the way she saw a man she recognized as her former father-in-law and called him out by name. Her house had been repainted a different color but she knew every detail about the interior before entering. That evening at dinner she immediately identified her former mother and father out of a group of over 50 people, called them out by name and ran to embrace them.

At the end of her visit a huge open-air meeting was arranged for the public at a local high school. Over ten thousand people gathered, many of whom had personally known Shanti in her previous incarnation. The villagers in attendance were so profoundly interested and impressed that they requested she be left there with them. Shanti herself also pleaded with her parents to let her stay but to no avail. They felt it would be better for her to return to Delhi and brought her home with them kicking and screaming, quite literally. All the way home Shanti argued and insisted she stay in

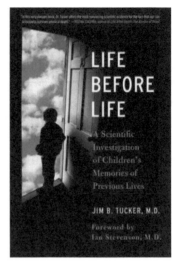

Muttra. Soon after arriving back in Delhi, she became very depressed and reserved, her spirit seemed crushed, and for the rest of her life Shanti Devi never married remaining faithful to her lost love Kedar.

"The facts of her story have been carefully checked by men of the highest character, including Lala Deshbandhu Gupta, managing director of the Daily Tej, the leading newspaper of Delhi; N. R. Sharma, leader of the National Congress Party of India and a close associate of Mahatma Gahndhi; and T. C. Mathur, a leading attorney of Delhi. These men, with many others, have issued a report on their findings in which they conclude that the story of Shanti Devi is not only entirely genuine but one

of the most remarkable records of the remembrance of a previous life ever witnessed and documented." -Manly P. Hall, "Reincarnation: The Cycle of Necessity" (150)

Dr. Joel Whitton, regression hypno-therapist and author of Life Between Life has documented dozens of cases where patients have successfully regressed into a past life or into the between life state. For instance, one of his patients was a Canadian psychologist who possessed a few quirks: He had a lifelong nail-biting problem, irrational fears of air travel and breaking his leg, an obsessive fascination with torture, and as a child he strangely spoke with a British accent for years. While under hypnosis Dr. Whitton regressed him to his previous life and the man began telling what he was experiencing. He was a British WWII pilot on a mission over Germany under heavy fire. A spray of bullets hit his plane and one of them penetrated the fuselage breaking his leg. His plane crash-landed in enemy territory and he was captured then tortured for information by having his nails ripped out. After reliving this experience and coming out of hypnosis, the patient was soon able to recover from his quirks and obsessions.

"Whitton's most remarkable discovery came when he regressed subjects to the interim between lives, a dazzling, light-filled realm in which there was 'no such thing as time or space as we know it.' According to his subjects, part of the purpose of this realm was to allow them to plan their next life, to literally sketch out the important events and circumstances that would befall them in the future. But this process was not simply some fairy-tale exercise in wish fulfillment. Whitton found that when individuals were in the between-life realm, they entered an unusual state of consciousness in which they were acutely self-aware and had a heightened moral and ethical sense. In addition, they no longer possessed the ability to rationalize away any of their faults and misdeeds, and saw themselves with total honesty. To distinguish it from our normal everyday consciousness, Whitton calls this intensely conscientious state of mind, 'metaconsciousness.' Thus when subjects planned their next life, they did so with a sense of moral obligation. They would choose to be reborn with people whom they had wronged in a previous life so they would have the opportunity to make amends for their actions. They planned pleasant encounters with 'soul mates,' individuals with whom

they had built a loving and mutually beneficial relationship over many lifetimes; and they scheduled 'accidental' events to fulfill still other lessons and purposes." -Michael Talbot, "The Holographic Universe"

Many of Whitton's other patients gave incredibly accurate historical details about the times and places in which they had lived, and some even began speaking long lost languages. One man, a 37 year old behavioral scientist, was brought back to a past life as a Viking then began shouting in a language unknown to both Whitton and himself. Linguistic professionals later identified the recording as being Old Norse. Later, upon being regressed to an ancient Persian lifetime, the same man began writing in a language previously unknown to both of them. An expert in Middle-Eastern languages later identified the script as Sassanid Pahlavi, an extinct Mesopotamian language that flourished between 226 – 651AD.

"Some of the most remarkable situations arise when children spontaneously start speaking in a foreign language or 'speaking in tongues' as the situation is often referred to, and which languages they could not possibly have learned from anywhere on Earth during their present life. Sometimes these are very ancient languages and dialects that are now and have long been extinct, and accordingly no longer spoken in the modern world today, only being known to historians. In other cases children can describe their previous homes and lives in very

considerable detail, including the town or area in which they lived in their previous life, their home, family, friends and often much more specific detail." -Adrian Cooper, "Our Ultimate Reality" (177)

Dr. Whitton and other hypnotists have recorded several cases where patient's visions have been subsequently confirmed by further research. Dr. Peter Ramster actually produced a TV documentary in 1983 starring four of his Sydney patients. These four women had never left Australia yet had all given remarkably detailed accounts of events, people and places across the world experienced during past-life regressions. The documentary followed Dr. Ramster and the women to the people, countries, towns, villages, and specific houses they envisioned in their past lives. For instance, one of the women, Gwen McDonald, who was at first a staunch skeptic, recalled during hypnosis a life in Somerset, England. When taken to Somerset for the first time she was miraculously able to correctly identify the location of several villages, roads, landmarks and directed them straight to her old house. She was able to lead the film crew to many destinations far more accurately than their maps. She also knew many local legends and family lines all of which were confirmed by Somerset historians. In fact a group of locals began coming to see her every night to quiz her on local history and there wasn't a single question that Gwen couldn't answer.

"She knew the location of a waterfall and the place where stepping-stones had previously been located; the locals confirmed the stepping-stones had been removed about forty years before. She pointed out an intersection where she claimed there had been five houses; enquires proved this was accurate; the houses had been demolished some thirty years previously. One of the demolished houses had been a 'cider house' as she had claimed. She knew the names of the villages as they had been two hundred years ago even though the names do not

appear on modern maps. People she claimed to have known were proved to have existed, one of whom was listed in the names of the regiment to which she apparently belonged ... She correctly used obscure West Country words that were no longer in use and in fact did not even appear in dictionaries. In Sydney she had described carvings that had been in an obscure old house twenty feet from a stream in the middle of five houses located about one and a half miles from Glastonbury Abbey. She knew the local people called Glastonbury Abbey 'St. Michael's,' a fact only proven by reading an obscure two hundred year old history book not available in Australia. She was able to draw while still in Sydney the interior of her Glastonbury house, which was subsequently proven to be completely correct. She described an inn on the way to her house that was indeed found to exist and was able to lead the team directly to the house, now a chicken shed. After cleaning the floor they discovered the

stone carvings she had referred to in Sydney."-Adrian Cooper, "Our Ultimate Reality" (183-5)

What other explanation can be given for these reincarnation experiences? Can all of these incredible stories be discounted? How can such overwhelming evidence be explained away? With thousands upon thousands of documented and factually verified reincarnation experiences on file it seems that the most obvious and serendipitous explanation is that reincarnation is in fact a reality.

"So convincing is the evidence in favor of past life influences that one can only conclude that those who refuse to consider this to be an area worthy of serious study must be either uninformed or excessively narrow-minded. Over the years my observation of people who have had past life experiences while in non-ordinary states of consciousness has convinced me of the validity of this fascinating area of research ... There are observable facts about reincarnation. We know, for example, that vivid past life experiences occur spontaneously in non-ordinary states of consciousness. These require no programming or previous knowledge about the subject. In many instances, these experiences contain accurate

information about periods before our own that can be objectively verified. Therapeutic work has shown that many emotional disorders have their roots in past life experiences rather than in the present life, and the symptoms resulting from those disorders disappear or are alleviated after the person is allowed to relive the past life experience that underlies it." - Dr. Stanislav Grof, "The Holotropic Mind" (123-9)

In most of Asia reincarnation is a generally accepted fact, and the mechanism that drives it is karma. Gautama Buddha said, "Everything in the Universe is the fruit of a Just Law, the Law of Causality, the Law of Cause and Effect, the Law of Karma." Karma is basically the moral/spiritual equivalent of Newton's physical law of cause and effect: For every action there is an equal and opposite reaction. What goes around comes around, do unto others as you would have done unto you, because either in this life or the next, the equation will remain balanced.

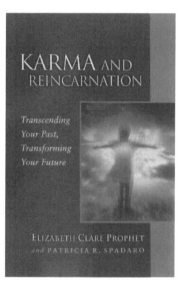

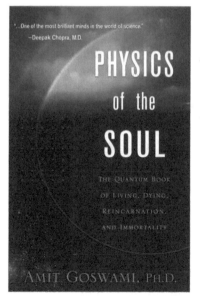

"It is karma which makes reincarnation necessary in order that compensation may justly be administered. Man is eternally suffering and misfortune is a constant goal impelling him forward toward a more perfect state. Karma is the law, and reincarnation is the means by which that law is administered ... Reincarnation and karma are the only explanations for the mystery of life that the reason can embrace. These laws give purpose to action, meaning to existence. These same laws release man from the monotony of the daily routine by giving him perspective and the power to see beyond the horizon of his present life ... Reincarnation and karma also light the dark mystery of ethics and morality. These laws give reason to right action, revealing that every action is intimately related to

the progress of the individual. We no longer do right because of scriptural admonition, but because we have learned the meaning of right and wrong as they react upon us through the law of karma. We grow through every thought and action. We learn not for one life, but for eternity. Each art and science that we master becomes part of the immortal self flowing through the ages." -Manly P. Hall, "Reincarnation: The Cycle of Necessity" (110-114)

In the Hindu epic Ramayana, each pearl on Lord Indra's necklace represents a complete lifetime, one individual incarnation. The string running through each jewel represents the immortal consciousness or soul which reincarnates and experiences several physical lifetimes. The entire necklace, jewels and string, rests upon the neck of God. This metaphor beautifully symbolizes the cyclical journey individual souls undergo away from and back to pure consciousness, enlightenment, God.

"Each individual lifetime can be likened to a facet of a diamond. The full sparkling diamond with all of its many facets represents the entire self, the individual, while each facet of the diamond represents each separate life. A diamond has many facets, the total of which constitutes the whole glittering gem. Each lifetime will add a new facet to the diamond until the whole diamond is ultimately complete in all of its sparkling splendor. Life, individuality, continues then in the inner spheres of life and reality as a complete glistening diamond, becoming ever brighter, more perfected and more beautiful as the ascent back to God progresses." - Adrian Cooper, "Our Ultimate Reality" (166)

"If one person can prove that he has lived before, then man's whole concept of life is changed. He is no longer limited by the narrow confines of a single existence. He need no longer live for the now alone. The realization of the truth of reincarnation bestows upon the human being not only the realization of his immortality but of his kinship with the ages.

He is part of all that has been, is, or ever shall be." -Manly P. Hall, "Reincarnation: The Cycle of Necessity" (153-4)

God, Brahma, Tao, Void, Oneness, Infinite Consciousness

Until now, the prevailing Newtonian mechanistic worldview has dominated Western culture, science and metaphysics for hundreds of years. The idea that we live in an unintelligently designed universe - the idea that out of nowhere, nothing, for no reason spontaneously became everything, has been accepted as scientific gospel. This atheistic, nihilistic, purely materialistic paradigm presented by believers of Big Bang evolution, however, cannot explain the multitude of non-physical, non-local findings in quantum mechanics. They cannot explain how consciousness, intelligence and life supposedly evolved from unconscious, unintelligent, dead matter. They cannot explain why apple seeds grow apple trees and pear seeds grow pear trees, or how arm cells know to be arms and leg cells know to be legs. They cannot explain the holographic universe or morphogenic fields, the placebo effect, psychoneuroimmunology, acupuncture, the aura, chi or remote healing; telepathy, psychokinesis, clairvoyance, precognition and the entirety of psi science; they cannot explain out-of body or near-death experiences, ghosts, entheogens, the soul, the spirit world or reincarnation.

"Although the true nature of the Universe has been known and taught throughout the ages by many and varied sources throughout the world, all of which are highly consistent and in broad agreement, it is also now being substantiated by the work of modern quantum physics, and increasingly by

other branches of the sciences as well. All areas of the sciences will surely soon have to accept the fact that true Universal reality is not and never can be based entirely in the familiar three-dimensional world of physical matter as has been assumed since the days of Isaac Newton, but is rather an infinite, multi-dimensional reality, a Universe of living Consciousness of which everyone and everything without exception is an integral and equal aspect. The true nature of the Universe will certainly challenge the perceptions of most people, if for no other reason that throughout the ages there has been a prevalent misperception of a 'God' who is completely separate from everyone and everything else in existence, and who 'rules' over 'his' three dimensional world of matter from high places." -Adrian Cooper, "Our Ultimate Reality"

The emerging wisdom of spiritual science has rendered the atheist materialist paradigm extinct. Consciousness, life, the beautiful diversity, complexity and interconnectedness of nature and the universe are <u>not</u> the result of some random coincidental physical phenomenon. Remember, the odds against our universe containing the precise physical forces and attributes necessary to sustain life is one octillion to one. In other words, there is only a 1 in 1,000,000,000,000,000,000,000,000,000 chance that the universe was unintelligently designed. So if there is an intelligent designer, a creative force beyond all space, time and

matter, what are the properties of this entity? Theologists and metaphysicians throughout history have agreed that this intelligent creative force must by definition be all-knowing (omniscient), all-powerful (omnipotent), and all-present (omnipresent). Furthermore, by definition if "God," an omniscient, omnipotent, omnipresent being exists, then we all must be a part of it! In my Asbestos Head book I wrote:

"Either God is causal, singular and separate - an outside entity somehow responsible for His own existence, the creation of the universe, and the creation of other beings to recognize Him, or existence is non-causal, plural, parts and whole of all that is with nothing outside Us because We're all infinite self-reflexive pieces of God interacting, changing, acting out eternity."

Many people are happy to accept the notion that God is some external entity like a bearded white man in the clouds who created us and watches over the universe like a cosmic fishbowl. Others are happy to accept that there is no God and the universe, consciousness, life, matter, space and time are all the result of a random spontaneous big bang accident. Personally, neither of these ideas have ever resonated with me, and both are relatively modern. If instead we consult the most ancient culture and the oldest texts in recorded history, the Indian Vedas, a very different story presents itself:

"Here's a parable, an analogy, which comes from India, from the Upanishads, and is thousands of years old. It presents a parabolic answer to the root question of all religion and philosophy (Who am I and what is this?), and does so in a way which everyone can relate to. In the beginning of the world (and though it probably had no ultimate 'beginning' as we think of them, you have to start somewhere), there was only Brahma. Being all there was, and therefore totally known to himself, Brahma soon realized that this totality of awareness would eventually become extremely boring . . . after all, when you know everything there is to know, then there's no surprise, nothing to keep you interested. It's like reading the same book for the seventy-eight millionth time. Anyway, since he was omnipotent (all-powerful), omniscient (all-knowing), and omnipresent (all-everywhere), Brahma decided to create a diversion for himself, a way of introducing the elements of surprise, intrigue and drama into his experience. He thought, 'What would it be like to forget who I really am?' So, he invented the game of cosmic hide-and-seek. According to the rules of this game, Brahma would pretend to break pieces of himself off from the whole so that to all appearances they would seem separate. That's the 'hide' part. Then, as the

apparently separate consciousness at the center of each of those apparently separate pieces, and through their apparently separate and unique perspectives, he would 'seek' to rediscover who he really was, which was, of course, everything. Imagine seeing yourself from an infinite number of different perspectives, each one initially ignorant of its relationship to all the rest. Imagine going to sleep and dreaming a different lifetime each night, each lasting for more or less years, each complete with the full range and variety of emotional life and death details. Imagine having the same dream but playing a different role in it each night, seeing it through different eyes each time. Well, guess who

274

those apparently separate pieces are? Since there is only one I Am in the universe, one consciousness, it's all a game of hide-and-seek, and each one of us is in the same state: I'm IT AND You're IT!" -Roger Stephens, "A Dangerous Book" (22-23)

Brahma, God, Tao, Universal Mind, the One, the Void, the Field, Infinite Consciousness, or whatever you want to call it, by definition is everything, exists everywhere, and is completely known to itself. Try to picture, if that was your reality, what would you do with your existence? What can you do with your existence as an omnipotent, omniscient, omnipresence with nothing unknown or outside yourself? There really is only one possibility. You play make-believe. Hide and seek.

Since you are the One objective infinite consciousness, to hide from yourself you must first divide your sense of self into several subjective finite packets of consciousness. At and as the root of each of these subjective packets of consciousness will be the feeling of "I am" and "I am not" – the feeling of existing as an individual entity separated from the totality. With that, the hiding part is complete.

The next step is creating a sensory rich, holographic, and ultimately illusory material world and physical bodies where these subjective awarenesses can interact, play and experience. To best accommodate this, since God is a singularity, the material world must be a world of duality, a world of polar opposites, where each soul, each individuated facet of God may experience the heights, depths, and breadth of possibility, so there must exist both good and evil, male and female, positive and negative, pleasure and pain, birth and death, inhale and exhale, black and white, dark and light, day and night, sun and moon, yin and yang, intelligence and ignorance and so on and so forth.

The one golden rule and driving force of God's universal hide and seek game is called karma, or cause and effect, what goes around comes around, do unto others as you would have done unto yourself, because fundamentally there is no "you" or "others," there is only God, the one true Self. Your physical body, your name, your entire human identity and the feeling of being an individual entity separated from the totality is a secondary and ultimately illusory experience of the One true being. Your feeling of being Tom, Dick or Harry is a purposely induced state of amnesia so that the creator may experience His creation. Each subjective packet of consciousness, each soul, ultimately <u>is</u> and wishes to reunite with the One, Tao, God, Brahma. But life as Brahma, to be honest, gets boring and sometimes Brahma would rather play hide and seek. God wants to experience through you what it is like to be you, a fractal fragment of Himself. Thus begins lifetimes of cyclical hiding and seeking, karmic creation and destruction, moving away from and back towards God, your true Self.

"In the Eastern view, then, the division of nature into separate objects is not fundamental and any such objects have a fluid and ever-changing character. The Eastern world view is therefore

276

intrinsically dynamic and contains time and change as essential features. The cosmos is seen as one inseparable reality - for ever in motion, alive, organic; spiritual and material at the same time. Since motion and change are essential properties of things, the forces causing the motion are not outside the objects, as in the classical Greek view, but are an intrinsic property of matter. Correspondingly, the Eastern image of the Divine is not that of a ruler who directs the world from above, but of a principle that controls everything from within: He who, dwelling in all things, Yet is other than all things, Whom all things do not know, Whose body all things are, Who controls all things from within - He is your Soul, the Inner Controller, The Immortal." -Fritjof Capra, "The Tao of Physics" (24-5)

"*Think of the difference between a droplet of water and the ocean; the droplet symbolizes the sense of division, of being an individual 'me', unconnected to anything else. This is like identifying with being 'Bill Bloggs' or 'Ethel Jones'. But, put that droplet back in the ocean, and where does the ocean end and the droplet begin? There is no beginning and no end, no Alpha and Omega, because all is One. At that level there is no 'we' - only an Infinite 'I'. Part of that ocean may be calm and peaceful and another may be angry and rough, but it is still the same ocean, the same Oneness. We are always the ocean, always Infinite Awareness, and we cannot literally become disconnected from that. However, when we forget who we are, we can be confused into a sense of division, of being the droplet, and we perceive reality through the tiny lens that this creates in our minds ... We are the ocean, Infinite Awareness, but we believe we are just a little powerless, insignificant droplet. We identify with division and 'parts', not unity.*" –David Icke, "The David Icke Guide to the Global Conspiracy" (3)

Another way to understand this concept is through dreams. In dreams you create entire worlds, environments, situations, and even other people.

You interact and converse, create conflict and resolutions, get emotional and involved, but suddenly when you wake up from the dream you realize that all those environments, situations, and other people were really all you! They only seemed like separate individuals because of the level of consciousness you were operating on at the time. It is the same in this world, where you think you are a separate person, but in fact when you die, a piece of God wakes up to realize He was only dreaming.

"To many, the statement 'I am God' rings of blasphemy. God, according to conventional religion, is the supreme deity, the almighty eternal omniscient creator. How can any lowly human being claim that he or she is God? Yet when mystics say 'I am God,' or words to that effect, they are not talking of an individual person. Their inner explorations have revealed the true nature of the self, and it is this that they identify with God. They are claiming that the essence of self, the sense of 'I am' without

any personal attributes, is God. The contemporary scholar and mystic Thomas Merton put it very clearly: If I penetrate to the depths of my own existence and my own present reality, the indefinable am that is myself in its deepest roots, then through this deep center I pass into the infinite I am which is the very Name of the Almighty. 'I am' is one of the Hebrew names of God, Yahweh. Derived from the Hebrew YHWH, the unspeakable name of God, it is often translated as 'I AM THAT I AM.' Similar claims appear in Eastern traditions. The great Indian sage Sri

Ramana Maharshi said: 'I am' is the name of God... God is none other than the Self. In the twelfth century, Ibn-Al-Arabi, one of the most revered Sufi mystics, wrote: If thou knowest thine own self, thou knowest God. Shankara, the eight-century Indian saint, whose insights revitalized Hindu teachings, said of his own enlightenment: I am Brahman... I dwell within all beings as the soul, the pure consciousness, the ground of all phenomena... In the days of my ignorance, I used to think of these as being separate from myself. Now I know that I am All." -Peter Russell, "From Science to God"

Since people always misinterpret the phrase "I am God," I prefer to explain it as "I am, is God." The self-awareness and continuity of being expressed by the words "I am," our inner witness and intuition, is our direct channel to God. It is undeniable that if God is omnipresent, then He must exist in you, He must be you, and everyone and everything else in existence as well. We are all playing an equal part as lost ripples in God's infinite ocean of consciousness.

"There is a Hindu myth that human consciousness began as a ripple that decided to leave the ocean of 'consciousness as such, timeless, spaceless, infinite and eternal.' Awakening to itself, it forgot that it was a part of this infinite ocean, and felt isolated and separated. Adam and Eve's expulsion from the Garden of Eden may also be a version of this myth, an ancient memory of how human consciousness, somewhere in its unfathomable past, left its home in the implicate and forgot that it was a part of the cosmic wholeness of all things. In this view the earth is a kind of playground in which one is free to experience all the pleasures of the flesh provided one realizes that one is a holographic projection of a higher-order." -Michael Talbot, "The Holographic Universe" (300)

In the Judaic Kabbalistic belief this concept is present as the entirety of creation is seen as "an illusory projection of the transcendental aspects of God." In Christianity it is said the Father and Son are one, thy Father art in heaven (the non-physical) but the Son lives in the flesh (the physical). The Father is Brahman, the ultimate objective implicate reality, and the Son is Atman, a fractal fragment of the One sent to experience and enjoy the Father's creation. The Mother Mary is nature, or Mahamaya, the sustainer of the material world. She is the illusion maker, the agent of change, keeping all things from atoms to galaxies in constant motion and flux between polarities. It is her dynamic endless dance of forms which keeps us from realizing that there is ultimately no such thing as separateness. The Upanishads state that *"one should know that nature is an illusion (maya), and that Brahman is the illusion maker. This whole world is pervaded with beings that are parts of him."*

"The basic recurring theme in Hindu mythology is the creation of the world by the self-sacrifice of God - 'sacrifice' in the original sense of 'making sacred'- whereby God becomes the world which, in the end, becomes again God. This creative activity of the Divine is called Ma, the play of God, and the world is seen as the stage of the divine play. As long as we confuse the myriad forms of the divine with reality, without perceiving the unity of Brahman underlying all these forms, we are under the spell of maya. Maya, therefore, does not mean that the world is an illusion, as is often wrongly stated. The illusion merely lies in our point of view, if we think that the shapes and structures, things and events, around us are realities of nature, instead of realizing that they are concepts of our measuring and categorizing minds. Maya is the illusion of taking these concepts for reality, of confusing the map with the territory. In the Hindu view of nature, then, all forms are relative, fluid and ever-changing maya, conjured up by the great magician of the divine play." -Fritjof Capra, "The Tao of Physics" (87-8)

In the Vedanta our individual souls, our separate subjective packets of "I am" consciousness are called "atman" and the One unified objective infinite wellspring of consciousness from which everyone's atman arises is "Brahman." Atman is our divided, dualistic self and Brahman is our whole true Self, but fundamentally it is taught that Atman is Brahman and Brahman is Atman. Your true Self beyond this earthly identity is not divided and dualistic, your true Self is not separate and subjective, your true Self is not Jack, Jill, Joe, Jen, Jim, John, James or Jason, your true Self is the same as my true Self as everyone's true Self is God.

"This ultimate reality is called 'Brahman' and is exactly the same as 'The One', 'The All', Spirit, 'everything that is', and in the West might be regarded as the true definition of 'God'. Brahman, Universal Consciousness, considered to be the ultimate reality, is infinite, exists beyond the five physical senses and is incomprehensible. Most ancient wisdoms of the world teach that human beings are 'God' in the microcosm, immortal Spirits 'made' in the 'true image of God'. Hinduism teaches the same principle in the form of 'Atman' which is equivalent to the human Soul. The Hindu culture teaches Atman and Brahman, the individual reality and the ultimate reality are one." -Adrian Cooper, "Our Ultimate Reality" (26-7)

"The Hindus call the implicate level of reality Brahman. Brahman is formless but is the birthplace of all forms in visible reality, which appear out of it and then enfold back into it in endless flux. Like Bohm, who says that the implicate order can just as easily be called spirit, the Hindus sometimes personify this level of reality and say that it is composed of pure consciousness. Thus, consciousness is not only a subtler form of matter, but it is more fundamental than matter; and in the Hindu cosmogony it is matter that has emerged from consciousness, and not the other way around." -Michael Talbot, "The Holographic Universe" (288)

Finally, quantum physicists like David Bohm and consciousness researchers like Peter Russell have now proven what the world's most ancient spiritual teachings have long espoused for thousands of years - the faculty of consciousness is primary to the creation of the material world. A conscious observer must first exist to collapse the wave function allowing particles to manifest into the explicate reality. This means that before the creation of the material world there must have existed a self-aware conscious observer (God) and every physical manifestation is actually the result of His conscious creation.

"The basic elements of the world view which has been developed in all these traditions are the same. These elements also seem to be the fundamental features of the world view emerging from modern physics. The most important characteristic of the Eastern world view - one could almost say the essence of it - is the awareness of the unity and mutual interrelation of all things and events, the experience of all phenomena in the world as manifestations of a basic oneness. All things are seen as interdependent and inseparable parts of this cosmic whole; as different manifestations of the same ultimate reality. The Eastern traditions constantly refer to this ultimate, indivisible reality which manifests itself in all things, and of which all things are parts. It is called Brahman in Hinduism, Dharmakaya in Buddhism, Tao in Taoism. Because it transcends all concepts and categories, Buddhists also call it Tathata, or Suchness: What is meant by the soul as suchness, is the oneness of the totality of all things, the great all-including whole. In ordinary life, we are not aware of this unity of all things, but divide the world into separate objects and events. This division is, of course, useful and necessary to cope with our everyday environment, but it is not a fundamental feature of reality. It is an abstraction devised by our discriminating and categorizing intellect. To believe that our abstract concepts of separate 'things' and 'events' are realities of nature is an illusion. Hindus and Buddhists tell us that this illusion is based on avidya, or ignorance, produced by a mind under the spell of maya. The principal aim of the Eastern mystical traditions is therefore to readjust the mind by centering

and quietening it through meditation. The Sanskrit term for meditation Samadhi - means literally 'mental equilibrium'. It refers to the balanced and tranquil state of mind in which the basic unity of the universe is experienced: Entering into the samadhi of purity, one obtains all-penetrating insight that enables one to become conscious of the absolute oneness of the universe." -Fritjof Capra, "The Tao of Physics" (130-1)

Made in United States
Troutdale, OR
09/25/2024

23105554R00159